THE SCIENTIFIC BASIS OF PSYCHIATRY

General Editor
Professor Michael Shepherd
Editorial Board
Professor H. Häfner
Professor P. McHugh
Professor N. Sartorius

The achievements of modern medicine have been largely derived from the understanding of biological structure and function which has accrued from advances in a number of basic sciences. On the foundations of such well-established fields as anatomy, physiology, pathology, bacteriology, pharmacology, genetics and immunology it has been possible to construct a clinical science directed towards the causation and rational treatment of many physical diseases. The slower development of psychological medicine can be attributed partly to historical factors bearing on its development and status. In addition, however, progress has been retarded by the innate complexity of a subject which one of its most distinguished representatives has defined as 'the study of abnormal behaviour from the medical standpoint'. The study of human behaviour goes beyond structure and function to incorporate the psychological and social sciences, and so calls for a wider range of scientific inquiry than is required for most other branches of medicine. The purpose of this series of monographs is to provide individual accounts of those disciplines which constitute the scientific basis of psychiatry.

Each volume is written by a practising scientist whose work is related to psychiatric practice and theory so that his/her review of a particular subject reflects a personal contribution and outlook. Together they are intended to provide a conspectus on the problems and challenges posed by a major and growing branch of medicine.

Artificial intelligence

and psychiatry

D.J.HAND

Institute of Psychiatry, University of London

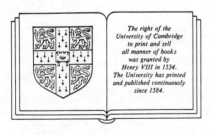

The right of the
University of Cambridge
to print and sell
all manner of books
was granted by
Henry VIII in 1534.
The University has printed
and published continuously
since 1584.

CAMBRIDGE UNIVERSITY PRESS

Cambridge

London   New York   New Rochelle

Melbourne   Sydney

Published by the Press Syndicate of the University of Cambridge
The Pitt Building, Trumpington Street, Cambridge CB2 1RP
32 East 57th Street, New York, NY 10022, USA
10 Stamford Road, Oakleigh, Melbourne 3166, Australia

© Cambridge University Press 1985

First published 1985

Printed in Great Britain at the University Press, Cambridge

Library of Congress catalogue card number: 84-22950

British Library Cataloguing in Publication Data
Hand, D. J.
Artificial intelligence and psychiatry. –
(The Scientific basis of psychiatry)
1. Artificial intelligence   2. Psychiatry
I. Title   II. Series
001.53′5′024616   Q334
ISBN 0 521 25871 5

PN

To Rachel

CONTENTS

PREFACE

There are now available several good books on artificial intelligence, so it is only natural to enquire what is unusual about this one. What does it deal with that the others handle inadequately or not at all? The fundamental difference is, of course, summed up in the title. This book is addressed to a particular intellectual community upon whom the advent of artificial intelligence can be expected to have an especially significant effect. The aims of this book are to outline artificial intelligence methods in a way which will be intelligible to psychiatrists (and others) with no knowledge of computers. Other books either require such knowledge, or they only deal with certain aspects of artificial intelligence, or they discuss the subject at a high level which does not convey a taste of the practical issues. Thus this book seeks both to present an introductory overview of the state of the art, showing how the field achieves what it achieves, and to relate artificial intelligence work to the wider context of psychiatry. In aiming at these objectives I have made a conscious effort to highlight major projects and publications, quoting important sources where appropriate.

However, it should be recognised that space constraints meant that the first of these aims could not be completely attained – too much detail was undesirable and choices about what to include and what to leave out had to be made. (For example I felt that, for psychiatrists in general, the important artificial intelligence work on vision was of peripheral interest, and so omitted it.) As a general rule I have concentrated on what is well known and incorporated into the overall knowledge base of artificial intelligence, rather than presenting too much very recent material whose worth has yet to be established. In a fast growing field this means I may have underrepresented the most recent and most advanced systems.

Regarding the second of my aims – relating artificial intelligence to psychiatry in general – again I have not delved too deeply into the philosophical and ethical issues, and yet clearly these are of growing importance. My hope is that this book will make more people aware of these issues and perhaps provide them with a basis for understanding them at an informed level. I do outline some of the issues but leave their resolution to the future and to those more able than myself.

It is perhaps necessary to say something about the use of the masculine pronoun (he, his, . . .) in this book. My intention is that it covers both genders, as has been traditionally the case in the past. I acknowledge that there may be unfortunate subconscious mental orientations set up by its use but am still searching for something better. The use of the plural or phrases such as 'he or she' seems clumsy and contrived and interferes with the flow of the text. The use of the feminine pronoun (as in Boden, 1977) jars one's concentration as one reads. Perhaps I should remark that this general issue is sufficiently to the fore in my own mind that now even reading the masculine pronoun causes me a slight hiatus when I read it intended in the general human sense!

Now I come to the pleasurable task of thanking those who contributed support while I was preparing this book. Of these the one who deserves most thanks is my wife, Catherine, for appreciating my aims and objectives in writing it, and for putting up with the occasional deluge of logorrhoea as I enthused about how well it was going (and also for putting up with the more common periods when progress seemed painfully slow). I must also thank my daughter Rachel, to whom this book is dedicated, for providing me with a living example of natural intelligence developing in parallel with the book. (And compared to whom the artificial intelligence community has a long way to go!) Most important, also, is Christine Dunne, who provided a rewarding and stimulating environment for Rachel with what seemed to me to be superhuman patience – and kept her out of my study while Daddy was working.

I also express my appreciation to Professor Michael Shepherd for being sufficiently far-sighted to recognise the potential importance of artificial intelligence to psychiatry and for suggesting I write this book in the first place.

Mrs Bertha Lakey deserves especial thanks for transforming my longhand scribble into typewritten text under severe time pressure while I was recovering from post-natal exhaustion on completing the book.

Thanks are also due to the many authors and publishers who gave permission for text and figures to be reproduced here.

D. J. Hand

London University Institute of Psychiatry
1984

1

Introduction

The last few years have witnessed a dramatic increase in the availability of computers. This is a direct result of a decrease in the price of computer hardware – the actual physical components comprising the computer. This availability is illustrated by the fact that many readers of this book (or, perhaps, their children) will have a small machine at home. 'Small', of course, is a relative term: in terms of a decade or so ago these 'small' personal computers are extremely powerful machines. And today's large machines are vastly more powerful than those of not long ago.

This availability and power has had its impact on life through many routes and, in view of the continuing rapid development of these machines, we can expect this impact to continue and grow even larger. A prime example of an exciting new development which was totally impracticable before the computer and which is just beginning to affect our lives is *artificial intelligence*.

Most people will have heard the phrase 'artificial intelligence' (perhaps from newspapers, television, radio, or cinema) but few have any real conception of what it is, what it aims to accomplish, or how it attempts to achieve its objectives. Even fewer have any idea of how this new technology will affect our lives over the next few decades.

A sensible place to begin any book is with a definition of its subject matter. For books on artificial intelligence this is notoriously difficult. One might justifiably presume that such a definition would have as a prerequisite a definition of the word 'intelligence', and we all know the problems that causes. We shall, therefore, assume we all know what human intelligence is and begin by looking at others' attempts at defining artificial intelligence.

(i) By 'artificial intelligence' I therefore mean the use of computer programs and programming techniques to cast light on the principles of intelligence in general and human thought in particular. (Boden, 1977.)

(ii) The development of a systematic theory of intellectual processes, wherever they may be found. (Michie, 1974.)

(iii) Boden (1977) also remarks that some researchers regard 'intelligibility' as being an essential characterising feature of intelligence. Thus, to qualify, a system must be comprehensible – and perhaps even able to explain its actions. We shall see examples of this below.

(iv) Artificial intelligence is the study of ideas which enable computers to do the things that make people seem intelligent. (Winston, 1977.)

(v) Artificial intelligence (AI) is the part of computer science concerned with designing intelligent computer systems, that is, systems that exhibit the characteristics we associate with intelligence in human behaviour . . . (Barr & Feigenbaum, 1983.)

These definitions are sufficiently woolly or circular that the basic difficulty must be apparent. Below we consider some of the common objections to and misconceptions of the notion of artificial intelligence. One, however, is worth introducing at this early stage since it leads to a neat operational definition (though, naturally, one not without its weaknesses). This objection begins with a sceptic's statement that 'I would consider a machine intelligent if it could do X', where X has been various things (beat him at chess, converse with him, pass an intelligence test, and so on). The next step is to present him with a computer program which can do X: to which he responds: 'Ah! Well, if a machine can do X then X cannot require intelligence after all.'

This, of course, is unbeatable.

An example of this seems to be provided by Dreyfus (1981) when he says (on p. 179) in the light of programs for interpreting mass spectrograms and carrying out medical diagnosis which perform as well as human experts: 'In principle, interpreting mass spectrograms or batteries of specific symptoms has as little to do with the general intelligence of physicists and physicians as disentangling vertices in projections of polyhedra does with vision. The real, theoretical problems of AI lie elsewhere.'

Psychoanalysis has been criticised as falling into the same trap as our figurative sceptic above: the underlying ground changes so that psychoanalysis can never be refuted and nothing the computer does requires intelligence. However, whereas in the case of a scientist faced with psychoanalysis it might be a source of irritation and frustration, such is not the case when confronted with the artificial intelligence sceptic. On the contrary, such a person simply sets new targets which, history suggests, eventually succumb, so that the sceptic is continually being forced backwards. (And perhaps, in the end, will exhaust the list of things he can propose for the role of X.)

Anyway, however one regards this absurd (but painfully true) intellectual dance, it has led to the definition (due to Marvin Minsky, 1968): Artificial intelligence is the science of making machines do things that would require intelligence if done by men.

One thing that may be apparent from the above attempts to define the field is that artificial intelligence can be viewed from two different perspectives. It can be seen as an attempt to model the way the human mind works – that is, to explore human mental processes by simulation. Or it can be seen as an attempt to build a system which behaves intelligently, regardless of the mechanism by which it does this. These might be termed, respectively, the *process* and *function* objectives: the first is concerned with emulating the processes within an intelligent human brain, and the second with duplicating the functions of that brain. There is something here of the division into science (process) and technology (function). A useful analogy to this situation is that of flying. A study of flying animals (cf. studying natural brains) can lead to ideas about how one might build a flying machine (use wings). But such is not completely necessary (one could use rockets instead). We shall see examples of the process/function distinction below, notably in Chapter 5 on diagnosis.

Turning now to objections to and misconceptions of artificial intelligence, we find a number of these occurring repeatedly:

(i) Gödel's proof. In 1931 Kurt Gödel proved a remarkable theorem which states, informally, that any (sufficiently powerful) consistent axiomatic system includes a proposition which can neither be proved nor disproved, and yet which can be seen to be true by humans. Sceptics take this to demonstrate the superiority of the human brain since it appears to be an example of something the latter can do which machines cannot. (See also Lucas, 1961.) However, there are at least two major objections to this. The first is that Gödel's proof applies to *closed* systems – systems with fixed axioms and inference rules. Although our artificial intelligence programs are programs, this does not imply that they are fixed. The environment with which they interact does not merely provide an infinite variety of data, but can in many cases also alter the basic axioms and inference rules, adding new ones and modifying old ones. Lenat's AM (1976; see below) can grow in this way. The second objection is what we later term a 'level' mistake. Basically, the natural world is a fuzzy affair: something composed of ambiguities and loose approximate definitions (a six foot man being tall or short according to whether he is a jockey or a basketball player). An artificial intelligence program which works on this reality is not directly mapping the rigid on/off binary digits within the computer onto the world. It is working at a higher level, mapping constructs which may be able to convey the same ambiguities and approximations. The implication is that it may make the same kinds of mistakes as a human but that it might also be able to make the same kinds of ill-defined leaps. Of this sort of thing, Lucas (1961) says:

> Although it sounds implausible, it might turn out that above a certain level of complexity, a machine ceased to be predictable, even in principle, and started doing things on its own account, or, to use a very revealing phrase, it might begin to have a mind of its own. It would begin to have a mind of its own when it was no longer entirely predictable and entirely docile, but was capable of doing things which we recognised as intelligent, and not just mistakes or random shots, but which we had not programmed into it. But then it would cease to be a machine within the meaning of the act.

(ii) A second objection might be regarded as an evolutionary one. This says that the way we think is crucially dependent on the way we are. Our bodies have to survive in a certain environment and are subject to a tremendous variety of desires and influences. Any program or robot would be so different – its objectives and motives would be so alien – that we would never really understand each other. Weizenbaum (1976), for example, says:

'What could be more obvious than the fact that, whatever intelligence a computer can muster, however it may be acquired, it must always and necessarily be absolutely alien to any and all authentic human concerns?' (We shall see more of Weizenbaum below. He represents an extreme in his views – he goes on to say: 'The very asking of the question "What does a judge (or a psychiatrist) know that we cannot tell a computer?" is a monstrous obscenity. That it has to be put into print at all, even for the purposes of exposing its morbidity, is a sign of the madness of our times.'.)

To continue the argument: the claim is that any computer program must, by its very nature, be so alien that it could not possibly be considered (recognised?) to be intelligent.

However, alienness is a matter of degree. An ant's objectives and motives are so alien to me that it is indeed impossible for us to really understand each other. In my terms an ant is certainly not very intelligent. But there are also humans (especially those from very different cultures) whose objectives and motives are difficult for me to comprehend. And yet I accept them as intelligent. A similar point applies to the blind, deaf, and disabled. They inhabit different 'worlds' from mine in that their perceptions of the world and their ability to affect things within it differ from mine. And yet they are intelligent. At present, admittedly, the kind of worlds that artificial intelligence programs exist in (moving toy blocks around, answering questions about databases, playing games, etc.) may have more in common with the ant's world than with ours, but this is changing. Our ultimate aim is not to build systems which will function in alien universes, with their own physical laws, but to build systems for our physical universe or our intellectual universes – with our physical laws or circumscribed by our definitions. Within those universes both we and the program are subjected to the same (physical or intellectual) forces. Moreover – by virtue of our design objectives – the system's motives will be similar to our own (as they are already: story understanding, chess playing, etc.). Thus although the program's behaviour may differ in certain subtle ways from that of humans (as humans differ from each other) and although the internal mechanisms may be different, the behaviour will not be so alien as to be completely incomprehensible.

(iii) A common objection is that 'a computer can only do what it is told'. The misconception underlying this statement is discussed after we have introduced the concept of 'levels' below. Here it suffices simply to point out that it has already been disproved – in self-improving programs and systems which learn from their environment, for example. There now exist many programs which, on occasion, produce a result unexpected by even their creators.

(iv) There are, of course, those whose objection is refreshingly simple: it is impossible to create an artificial intelligence. To such people McCorduck (1979) says: 'Those who said a thing (in artificial intelligence) could never be done were later replaced by those who had to concede that it could, but then said that it ought not to be.'

'Ought not' is an interesting suggestion – the social responsibility of science. McCorduck is presumably thinking of people like Weizenbaum (1976). This present book is practically rather than philosophically oriented and does not address these issues. My hope is that this book will serve to inform psychiatrists of the aims and capabilities of artificial intelligence work and that, thus equipped, concerned psychiatrists will be able to join the philosophical debate. Such readers should also see Weizenbaum (1976), Sloman (1978), McCorduck (1979), and McDermott (1981).

(v) Earlier, we introduced the imaginative approach to proving that artificial intelligence was impossible by arbitrarily changing the collection of tasks which required intelligence. A similar approach, which may not prove artificial intelligence to be impossible but certainly makes it more difficult to establish indisputably, has been termed the *superhuman human fallacy*. This is to require that a program be able to play chess like a grandmaster and solve differential equations like a mathematician and write sonnets like Shakespeare and music like Beethoven and so on before accepting that it is truly intelligent. Brought into the open like this, clearly no more need be said about this objection. The trick, however, is to recognise when sceptics are adopting this strategy.

(vi) Another common suggestion is that creativity and originality are solely human attributes. Unfortunately this is not true – we have already referred to Lenat's AM (1976) which identifies new and potentially interesting concepts in number theory (and which discovered the concept of prime numbers for itself).

So much for definitions and misconceptions. Now that we have a better idea of the range of possibilities, we must naturally ask: of what relevance is artificial intelligence to psychiatry? How can artificial intelligence help? That others think it is of some relevance is demonstrated rather convincingly by Sloman's statement (1978):

'Within a few years philosophers, psychologists, educationalists, psychiatrists, and others will be professionally incompetent if they are not well-informed about these developments.'

The answer to these questions has two aspects, deriving directly from the two motivations for artificial intelligence described earlier. One lies in the tools that artificial intelligence provides for describing psychological and psychiatric theories, and the other lies in its effect on diagnosis and treatment. Let us take these in that order.

Typically psychiatric and psychological theories are framed in natural language – they are described in normal everyday words. But this is known to be inadequate. The classic examples of effective sciences (meaning that their resultant technologies have a high probability of success) are physics and chemistry – leading to various types of engineering. And one of the reasons for their success is their strong base in formal languages – in mathematics. Here it is important to understand that it is not the mathematics *per se* which guarantees success. Rather it is the fact that a clear mapping has been established between the physical and chemical concepts and the symbols of the formal mathematical languages, coupled with the clarity and precision of the basic physical and chemical concepts. Psychology and psychiatry have attempted to follow the same route but with a notable lack of success. What is needed is a different sort of mathematical language, one that is more suited to describing psychological concepts; one that is more natural for the requisite mapping from the real world. Many people believe that artificial intelligence provides just this formal language. I summarised this in Hand (1981*c*):

> It is all very well formulating psychological and psychiatric theories
> verbally but, when using natural language (even technical jargon),
> it is difficult to recognise when a theory is complete; oversights are

all too easily made, gaps too readily left. This is a point which is generally recognised to be true and it is for precisely this reason that the behavioural sciences attempt to follow the natural sciences in using 'classical' mathematics as a more rigorous descriptive language. However, it is an unfortunate fact that, with a few notable exceptions, there has been a marked lack of success in this application. It is my belief that a different approach – a different mathematics – is needed, and that AI provides just this approach. Others have expressed the same opinion:

The very eloquence that natural language permits sometimes illuminates our words and seems (falsely, to be sure) to illuminate our undeserving logic just as brightly. An interpreter of programming language texts, a computer, is immune to the seductive influence of mere eloquence. (Weizenbaum, 1976.)

A large range of questions about the activity and organisation of human memory can be posed with greater clarity than before by way of hypotheses drawn from a programming context. Consequently, an increasing number of workers in cognitive psychology express their theories with computational models in mind. (Boden, 1977.) (Examples of such computational model-builders are Norman & Rumelhart (1975), Johnson-Laird (1983), and Newell & Simon (1972).)

Artificial intelligence, whatever its merits or defects as a technological aspiration, can provide us with ways of thinking about the human mind which are of great potential value in the formulation of cognitive theories . . . the process of constructing a fully explicit theory, in the form of an effective procedure, is itself illuminating; it invariably draws attention to important questions of detail which might otherwise have been overlooked. (Longuet-Higgins, 1981.)

The attempt to characterise exactly models of an empirical theory almost inevitably yields a more precise and clearer understanding of the exact character of a theory. The emptiness and shallowness of many classical theories in the social sciences is well brought out by the attempt to formulate in any exact fashion what constitutes a model of a theory. The kind of theory which mainly consists of insightful remarks and heuristic slogans will not be amenable to this treatment. The effort to make it exact will at the same time reveal the weakness of the theory. (Suppes, 1961.)

Computer models differ from mental models in important ways. The computer models are stated explicitly. The 'mathematical notation' that is used for describing the model is unambiguous. It is a language that is clearer and more precise than the spoken languages like English or French. Computer model language is a simpler language. Its advantage is in the clarity of meaning and the simplicity of the language syntax. The language of a computer model can be understood by almost anyone, regardless of educational background. Furthermore, any concept and relationship that can be clearly stated in ordinary language can be translated into computer model language. (Forrester, 1970.)

It is worth remarking that some people see these advantages of computer models as not being restricted to the 'soft' sciences:

I believe that not only psychology and social sciences but also biology and even chemistry and physics can be transformed by attempting to view complex processes as computational processes, including rich information flow between subprocesses and the construction and manipulation of symbolic structures within processes. This should supersede older paradigms, such as the paradigm which represents processes in terms of equations or correlations between numerical variables. (Sloman, 1978.)

In fairness, it should be acknowledged that not all of the advantages lie with the computer:

Computer models have, as we have seen, some advantages over theories stated in natural language. But the latter have the advantage that patching is hard to conceal. If a theory written in natural language is, in fact, a set of patches and patches on patches, its lack of structure will be evident in its very composition. Although a computer program similarly constructed may reveal its impoverished structure to a trained reader, this kind of fault cannot be so easily seen in the program's performance. A program's performance, therefore, does not alone constitute an adequate validation of it as a theory. (Weizenbaum, 1976.)

The quotation from Hand (1981c) above described artificial intelligence as a different kind of mathematics with which to describe psychological theories. Others have also been moved to remark on the novelty of the artificial intelligence approach, describing it in various ways according to their predisposition and backgrounds. Thus Zenon Pylyshyn has described it as 'a technical language with which to discipline one's imagination' and Longuet-Higgins (1981) suggests that it may be 'a new theoretical psychology'. Boden (1977) says that artificial intelligence may be taken as a case study of 'a different sort of science' because of its basically non-reductionist approach – discussed below. However, one might also adopt such a description because of the emphasis within artificial intelligence on writing its 'theories' as programs. This is in contrast to the classical hard sciences, which require a theory to be something which can be written as a parsimonious set of fundamental axioms. Thus artificial intelligence is a language for providing *algorithmic* as opposed to *dialectic* descriptions. Its theories are models which can actually be run and tested using a computer. It does not attempt to prove by logical deduction the existence of mental features. There is a direct parallel to algorithmic and dialectic mathematics:

> *Dialectic mathematics* is a rigorously logical science, where statements are either true or false, and where objects with specified properties either do or do not exist. *Algorithmic mathematics* is a tool for solving problems. Here we are concerned not only with the existence of a mathematical object, but also with the credentials of its existence. *Dialectic* mathematics is an intellectual game played according to rules about which there is a high degree of consensus. The rules of the game of *algorithmic* mathematics may vary according to the urgency of the problem on hand. We never could have put a man on the moon if we had insisted that the trajectories should be computed with dialectic rigor. The rules may also vary according to the computing equipment available. *Dialectic* mathematics invites contemplation. *Algorithmic* mathematics invites action. *Dialectic* mathematics generates insight. *Algorithmic* mathematics generates results. (Henrici, 1972.)

As far as artificial intelligence goes, it is to be hoped that the algorithmic approach, by comparison of its results with the real world, will also generate insight.

Mentioning *results* in this way brings us back to the *functional* role of artificial intelligence and hence to the second way in which it can be valuable to psychiatry – through its application in diagnosis and therapy. This is discussed at length in Chapter 5. The point of the functional approach is that it is not necessary for a machine to arrive at a diagnosis in the same way that a human does – so modelling process may not be necessary or even the best approach. Some workers suspect that it will prove to be the most effective (human cognitive processes having been refined by millennia of evolutionary steps) but it is worth remembering that humans make mistakes, and in diagnosis and therapy our aim is to *get it right*, not duplicate human errors.

Colby (1967) feels quite strongly about the relevance of computers and (by implication of the nature of his work) artificial intelligence to psychiatry:

> If it [a computer] can be used to further our understanding and treatment of mental suffering then there can be no question of its value. If it can be used as a psychotherapeutic instrument for thousands of patients in understaffed hospitals, we have no choice

but to use it because the healing professions are unable to supply sufficient manpower to meet this great social need . . . It is dehumanising to herd thousands of patients into mental hospitals where they will never see a doctor . . . If a computer can provide therapeutic conversation, then there can be no hesitation in exploring these potentials. It may give us a chance to rehumanise people now being dehumanised by our . . . psychiatric systems.

At this juncture it is convenient to note some general points about artificial intelligence. The first is that artificial intelligence is not computer science. It is, in fact, a fundamentally interdisciplinary subject (as must surely be becoming apparent by now), combining ideas from computer science with ideas from psychology, linguistics, mathematics, and even philosophy.

The second point is that although we use the terms 'program', 'machine', 'computer', and sometimes 'system' to describe artificial intelligence creations, we are really always talking about *programs*. The computers themselves are simply substrata on which the structures described by the programs are etched. (As an aside, we should also remark that, where computers are involved, progam is the more correct spelling. See, for example, the 1982 supplement to the *Oxford English dictionary*, Volume O to Scz.)

A third point relates to the impact that artificial intelligence work has had on the overall way that mental functions are now perceived. Things like walking, seeing, and so on are carried out without conscious effort and hence were originally thought to be things which could be achieved easily in a machine, leaving researchers to concentrate on higher mental functions such as problem solving. However, it turned out that in computational terms the former were the more difficult problems, requiring vast computational resources. We return to this topic after discussing the concept of 'levels'.

To introduce this we can quote Boden (1977), who said: 'Computers do not crunch numbers; they manipulate symbols.'

To many laymen computers are simply vast calculating machines. Admittedly they may be able to perform millions of operations (additions, multiplications, etc.) per second, but in principle they are thought of as being no more than a large pocket calculator which can follow the instructions on a previously written list (that is, a program).

This is a misconception. Referring to Boden's symbols, these *may* be numbers, but they need not be. They could be letters, complete words, geometric shapes, or (as we shall see later in this book) extremely complicated structures.

The way a computer represents and manipulates such symbols is by defining them and the operations upon them in terms of simpler *lower level* symbols.

At the lowest level we have the *binary digit* or *bit*. This is simply an electronic switch, which can be in one of two states. The switch is useful, even at this lowest level, since the states can stand for two mutually exclusive possibilities. They might represent yes or no, black or white, on or off, success or failure, and so on. (They can even represent the numbers zero and one!)

The next level up arises when we group the bits together and consider several of them at a time. If we take them in groups of eight each then such a group has 256 possible combinations of on/off amongst its eight components. Thus groups of eight can represent 256 distinct symbols. This is sufficient to represent all the letters of the alphabet, upper and lower case, plus the Greek alphabet, and many other symbols besides. Or they could represent 256 different geometric shapes. Or 256 physiological states. And so on. When using combinations of bits in this way we define a mapping from each combination to the thing it is to represent – to the real world.

The next step is to take groups of these higher level symbols. If the symbols represent letters then the higher level ones could be words; if the symbols represented shapes then the higher level ones might be objects in a picture.

Continuing the process to yet another level yields groups of words – perhaps phrases or sentences – and configurations of objects – perhaps whole pictures.

This process can have any number of levels and can continue to an arbitrarily high level. Somewhere towards the top we have very abstract conceptual structures. Translating these directly into the very lowest level of bits (if we represent the bits as 0's and 1's) would produce lengthy strings of 0's and 1's which would be incredibly difficult to grasp and interpret. Imagine Shakespeare's *Twelfth Night* reduced to this very low level and ask how clear would be (i) the division into Acts and Scenes, (ii) subtle word play, (iii) the humour. Such considerations are only properly made at the higher levels of words, sentences, and above. Imagine trying to explain the principles of psychoanalysis or transactional analysis when the most complex single utterance one can make is *bip* or *bleep* (representing the two states of a bit). Some kind of chunking into higher levels is imperative.

Sloman (1978) describes level confusion this way:

> I want to undermine a common misconception about computers, namely that however complex the programs that run in them they are always essentially unintelligent, uncreative mechanisms,

blindly following simple rules one at a time. Such a description may well be true of the underlying electronic components, just as it may well be true to say that a human brain is always an essentially unintelligent uncreative bundle of nerve-cells (or an assemblage of atoms) blindly reacting to one another in accordance with chemical and physical laws of nature. But just as the latter description may omit some important features of what a brain can do, so also the former description omits important 'high-level' features of complex computer programs. What is true of a computer need not be true of a program, just as what is true of a brain need not be true of a mind. In both cases the whole is far more than the sum of its parts.

The remark 'a computer only does what it is told' is right at some levels but wrong at others. At the bit and combination of bits levels it is correct. Given two patterns of bits and told to compare them, the computer does just that, indicating whether the patterns are the same or not. But at higher levels it is not correct. In comparing two patterns of complex symbols an exact match may not be necessary. Moreover, at higher levels complex symbols within the computer may be interacting with a very complex and confusing environment. The program facing this environment may be very complex. And it is naive to suppose that the programmer is aware of all possible states that the program, with its multitude of high level symbols, can take in response to an intrinsically unknowable environment. (A recent development in modern physics is relevant here. Until recently it was thought, quantum mechanical considerations aside, that given enough initial information about any system, it would be possible to predict that system's state at any arbitrary time in the future. However, it has now been recognised that 'enough information' is never possible. Infinitesimal deviations in the initial conditions amplify through time (like a dust mote starting an avalanche) and lead to completely different later states. Only if the initial conditions can be specified *exactly* – which is meaningless in the real physical world – can later states be predicted precisely.)

Sometimes this belief that a computer program can only do what it is told is expressed as 'a program can go no further than its creator' or 'can do nothing its creator cannot'. This, however, is simply false – for example, computer programs have beaten their creators at chess. The observation should also be made that most large artificial intelligence programs involve teams of programmers rather than a single person. Thus there is no one person who understands all that the program does. The system can certainly do things any particular creator cannot predict.

We referred above to the unexpected discovery that operations that humans apparently carry out with negligible effort in fact require extensive computational resources, while others which we find 'difficult' (geometric analogy intelligence tests, for example) can be programmed relatively easily into a computer. The resolution of this puzzle lies in level confusion.

Humans see geometric analogy intelligence tests as difficult because they involve low level symbol manipulation (a few shapes: triangles, squares, and so on; Chapter 2 describes a computer program which can do such tests) and humans are forced to define these low level symbols in terms of the high level symbols humans use to interact with the everyday world. These high level symbols can handle ambiguity, woolliness, abstraction, and so on, and the high level manipulation process can recognise multiple interpretations. A triangle, in a human's high level symbols, is not just a particular shape, but has all sorts of other connotations – which, in the case of low level IQ tests, must be disregarded. If the problem happens to be cast in low level symbols the human cannot tackle the problem directly using corresponding low level symbols but must perforce use high level symbols, with all their additional complications and interrelationships.

Early artificial intelligence programs shortcut the process by tackling many problems, which to humans were hard, directly in terms of low level symbols. For such problems this, of course, is an ideal approach. Unfortunately, however, difficulties will arise when one tackles problems which require the subtleties of high level symbols. (Early artificial intelligence work was associated with optimistic claims that in 'a decade or so' all the problems would have been solved. This mistaken optimism was a direct result of the fortuitous match between low level computer symbols and the types of problems being tackled. It disappeared when problems which required high level symbol manipulation were studied.)

Minsky (1981) has described the sort of problems that have arisen from confusion between levels. (Here he is using the actual word 'level' in a different way from us. However, his distinction between 'logical' and 'suggestive but defective' thinking is one of level in our sense.):

> I cannot state strongly enough my conviction that the preoccupation with Consistency, so suitable for Mathematical Logic, has been incredibly destructive to those working on models of mind. At the popular level it has produced a weird conception of the potential capabilities of machines in general. At the 'logical' level it has blocked efforts to represent ordinary knowledge, by presenting an unreachable image of a corpus of context-free 'truths' that can stand almost by themselves. And at the intellect-modelling level it has blocked the fundamental realisation that *thinking begins first with suggestive but defective plans and images that are slowly (if ever) refined and replaced by better ones.*

Lehnert (1978) describes the change in artificial intelligence research which we remarked on above, consequent on the implicit recognition of level differences:

> Many people who are acquainted with the field of artificial intelligence are amused by the general direction of inquiry the field has taken. In its early years artificial intelligence was dominated by an interest in behaviours that were ostensibly intelligent: theorem proving, chess playing, and general problem solving were strong areas of research activity. These tasks are no longer in the mainstream of artificial intelligence. Research is currently dominated by such 'fundamentalist' problems as visual scene analysis and natural-language processing. Research in artificial intelligence seems to have regressed from activities that are impressively 'adult' to those that are mastered by 3-year-olds.

It is also worth noting that it is only at the higher levels that mistakes become possible. At lower levels the relatively simple symbol structures and the limited rules for manipulating them leave no scope for ambiguity or error (short of hardware failure or an incorrect symbol being input, of course). The higher levels thus allow us to model the basic irrationality of humans. In view of this it is accurate but ironic to observe that, when used in the process mould of simulating humans, *intelligence* may be something of a misnomer!

The controversy between the reductionist and what (following Boden, 1977) we shall term the humanist approach to psychology is too well known to need expounding here. The former emphasises observable and measurable phenomena, and often uses statistical techniques, while the latter stresses the underlying subjective psychological constructs, things that by their very nature cannot be quantified. We now examine the position, relative to the reductionist and humanist approaches, of artificial intelligence methods.

A newcomer's immediate suspicion, arising from recognition of the computational foundation of artificial intelligence, will most probably be that artificial intelligence is fundamentally reductionist. After all, reductionist statistical approaches also rely heavily on computers. Of course, this extension is a fallacy: the use of a common tool does not imply identity of aims. Any more than the fact that engineers and poets both use pens implies that their approaches or philosophies are identical.

The situation is doubtless aggravated by terms such as 'artificial intelligence' and 'machine intelligence'. The first because of the overtones of the word 'artificial' (false, plastic, unnatural, ersatz, etc.). The second because of Victorian implications of the word 'machine': great black clunking steel monsters, intrinsically large, clumsy, and dirty. This does not convey in any way the extraordinary internal complexity or the extraordinary potential for complex interactions with the external environment of a modern computer – also called a 'machine'. (Recall the passage from Lucas (1961) quoted above, ending: 'But then it would cease to be a machine within the meaning of the act.' This resembles the verbal footwork outlined at the beginning of the chapter involving changing requirements for something to be deemed intelligent. Only now it applies to something to be called a machine.) Computers are machines, but machines which manipulate information – symbols, not mechanical energy.

Weizenbaum (1976) attributes a lot to this unfortunate word and its associations:

'[The layman's] misconception of what computers are, of what they do, and of how they do what they do is attributable to the pervasiveness of the mechanistic metaphor and the depth to which it has penetrated the unconscious (*sic*) of our entire culture.'

Boden (1977) says:

The new concept of 'machine' provided by artificial intelligence is so much more powerful than familiar concepts of mechanism that the old metaphysical puzzle of how mind and body can possibly be related is largely resolved.

Of course, the fundamental problem with humanist psychology is one of validation. Since it talks in terms of subjective reality how can one explore the truth of what it says? It is the contention of myself and others that one way in which we can attempt to validate humanistic psychology is through using the tools of artificial intelligence – and thus that artificial intelligence has closer affinities to the humanist approach than to the reductionist approach. Artificial intelligence does not provide all the answers (as we shall see in Chapter 6) but it goes along the path. As we have seen, one way in which it does this is by shifting emphasis to procedural approaches. An artificial intelligence theory is *implemented*; it is not simply described as a possible way things could go, but is built as a 'working model' which can then be compared with the human reality. Artificial intelligence acknowledges some irreducible high-level psychological content to human mentation, accepting such things as thoughts, subjective processes, and emotions as being central to the functioning of the human brain. Hence the claim that it does not adopt a simplistic reductionist approach. It does not reject these internal phenomena in favour of neurophysiological mechanisms or stimulus/response patterns. Boden (1977) points out the implications of this observation:

Contrary to what most people assume, this field of research has a potential for counteracting the dehumanising influence of natural science, for suggesting solutions to many traditional problems in the philosophy of mind, and for illuminating the hidden complexities of human thinking and personal psychology. The common view that machine research must tend to display us humiliatingly to ourselves as 'mere clockwork' is false.

And later:

Artificial intelligence, in short, cannot only acknowledge but can even elucidate the essentially subjective mental realities so stressed by human psychologists.

Finally on this topic, we have McCorduck's (1979) eloquent avowal of the fundamentally humanist nature of artificial intelligence:

Here I address my fellow humanists more than anyone else, because so many of them are convinced that science is somehow alien to the humanities. I want them to see that it is not. I want them to see a science whose genesis was in the literary texts they cherish. I want them to see a science whose thinkers are humans, with human motives and goals.

One thing which the reader will notice as he works through this book is that many of the programs written to test various psychological theories or to demonstrate intelligent behaviour are limited to tightly constrained domains. The programs are often able to recognise and manipulate concepts only within a very small universe. The reason for this is perhaps obvious – it is one of practicability. We remark elsewhere on one characteristic which distinguishes between psychological research and artificial intelligence research, namely that the former has a tendency to try to perfect each building block (hoping to fit them together later) while the latter goes for a global whole (worrying about details later). And yet restrictions of some kind need to be imposed: one cannot leap in and build a machine of human intelligence in one go without a gradual process of accumulating knowledge about the way it should work. Artificial intelligence imposes its constraints in a way orthogonal to that of psychology. Instead of looking at tiny parts of behaviour it looks at global patterns, but applied in small domains. Thus Winograd's program (Winograd, 1976) works in a universe of geometric blocks; the diagnosis programs of Chapter 5 do not cover the range of all possible diseases; and language processing programs are not initially supplied with vast vocabularies. Actually, this need for working within a manageably sized domain is one of the motivating influences behind the artificial intelligence work which has been carried out on games. Many of the fundamental advances of artificial intelligence have been developed in the games arena. As Clarke (1977) says:

> Many of us would maintain that chess, with its simple
> representation yet deep structure and richly developed culture,
> may even be the best system in which to study these problems [that
> is artificial intelligence] in their purest and most readily quantifiable
> form.

This probably represents a rather old-fashioned view, with more workers now being interested in problems which do not have such simple representations, but such interests have certainly promoted major advances in the past.

By analogy with molecular biology, Winston (1977) describes such small domains as being the *E. coli* of artificial intelligence research.

As we draw towards the end of this introductory chapter, it is appropriate to say a few words about alternative approaches to artificial intelligence. By far the most dominant route is that described in this text. It might be termed the 'design' approach. The basic principle is to try to build a program (functional or process) which can carry out the required task using theoretical ideas about how the task can be done. For example, in Chapter 3 we outline natural language understanding systems based on various kinds of grammar. These grammars present the theoretical ideas and the programs implement them – perhaps revealing weaknesses in the ideas in the process. Other parts of the book give other such examples, and indeed all the examples in the book are based on this kind of approach.

This much may be obvious, but one thing which will probably not be obvious is the extent to which the theories and programs described here depend on the architecture of the computer. The current generation of computers (as well as earlier ones) are serial machines: they only do one thing at a time. The programs and models described in this book have been designed bearing this in mind (coupled, perhaps, with the fact that parallel – non-serial – systems, systems which carry out several operations simultaneously, are much harder to think about). The concept of parallel processing, constrained by being simulated on serial machines, is beginning to be made use of (as in Winograd's (1976) heterarchical community of interacting programs and as in the rules of production systems described in Chapters 2 and 5; see also Fahlman, 1982), but this parallelism in no way approaches the fundamentally parallel nature of the human brain.

One alternative to this serial design approach is through simulating parallel networks of neurons. Investigations along such lines have been carried out (in many cases motivated by neurophysiologists) right from the earliest days of artificial intelligence and they continue into the present (see, for example, Palm, 1982). Such systems achieve very simple behaviour with striking elegance, though as yet their behaviour on more complex tasks does not compare with that of the serial design approach. (It was an introduction to the notions behind perceptrons (Minsky & Papert, 1972) which originally attracted the author into the fields of artificial intelligence and pattern recognition: the fact that a *randomly-wired* mechanism could be trained to recognise patterns and behave in an apparently rational manner.)

A second alternative approach is to simulate the process which gave rise to the human brain itself, namely evolution (Fogel, Owens & Walsh, 1966). In terms of results this seems to have been less successful than the neural network ideas. The author's own experience has been that the most striking, but hardly surprising, fact is the large number of generations needed. (An informal article describing some of my own work is given in Hand, 1979.) The basic reason for the large number of generations seems to be the technical one that there are so many possible random changes that could occur in each generation that only a very small proportion yield substantial benefit. The process is thus usually painfully slow. Despite these problems, I find this an exciting area – perhaps again because of the way structure emerges from randomness.

The remainder of the book is organised as follows. Chapter 2 discusses what is perhaps the single most important issue: how to represent concepts, ideas, emotions, thought, and so on inside a computer. There are many ways in which this can be done and some are better than others. This chapter contains brief descriptions of the most powerful representations.

Chapter 3 switches from general issues to a particular one which many regard as central to the notion of intelligence and which is certainly very important as far as the relation between artificial intelligence and psychiatry goes. This is machine understanding of natural language. Again the major developments are discussed, showing how each lent a contribution to the state of current programs. Several important examples are discussed in detail.

Chapter 4 is a short one dealing with two very important topics. The first is *search*, a general notion that crops up all over the place in artificial intelligence work. Different approaches to search are summarised. The second topic is *proof*, something which is of much wider applicability than this rather dry name might seem to imply. A particular example – resolution refutation proof – is given, a proof method which works in the general representational domain of predicate calculus.

Chapter 5 returns to particular issues, namely to psychiatric diagnosis. The possibility of machines which can make more accurate diagnostic classifications, and which can recommend therapeutic regimes with a greater degree of success than humans, is a very exciting one. It is also a prospect fraught with ethical and acceptability problems. Both technical issues and these more delicate moral issues are discussed.

Apart from diagnosis, artificial intelligence promises to be particularly valuable to psychiatry in several other domains. Chapter 6 discusses two of these, an interconnected pair. One is teaching – how modern developments of early teaching machines provide a very powerful educational tool. The other is simulation, a central part of modern instructional programs and which, in its own right, can be used to explore the validity of psychological and psychiatric theories. One of the most controversial of all artifical intelligence programs in psychiatry falls into this category of simulations. This is PARRY, a simulated paranoid. The second part of Chapter 6 discusses it in detail.

Chapter 7 is a short concluding note.

Anyone inspired by this book will want to take things further. The text is liberally sprinkled with references, notably to the major works and formative publications which can be followed up to provide a very solid grounding in artificial intelligence. Other general works, each with their own orientation, have been written.

Boden (1977) has written a book in which psychiatrists might be particularly interested. It differs from this book in that it does not discuss diagnosis and does not deal with the technical issues in as much detail. One would therefore find it difficult to write one's own artificial intelligence programs after reading only Boden (1977). On the other hand it does give an excellent discussion of the implications that artificial intelligence work has for psychology, sociology, philosophy, and society in general.

Whereas what follows in this book is practically oriented – an introduction to artificial intelligence for psychiatrists who wish to find out how artificial intelligence accomplishes what it does, if not to actually do artificial intelligence work themselves – Sloman (1978) presents a philosophical discussion on artificial intelligence and the theory of mind. It is recommended for readers interested in that aspect of the subject.

A broadly philosophical discussion from quite the opposite viewpoint, squarely confronting the ethical issues, is given in Weizenbaum (1976), referred to earlier in this chapter.

McCorduck (1979) presents an extremely readable history of the subject, written in terms of the people rather than the technology. It is thoroughly recommended as a companion volume to this one.

Turning to the technical side of things, there are several excellent books. Winston (1977) presents a general overview, with a detailed discussion of the programming language, LISP. Nilsson (1982) concentrates on the mechanics of artificial intelligence rather than applications, presenting things from a production system perspective and superbly demonstrating the power of this representation. Barr & Feigenbaum (1983) also give a general survey. The latter does not go into very great detail but has very impressive breadth (it consists of three volumes) and is an ideal sourcebook. Szolovits (1982*a*) concentrates on diagnosis and presents a technical discussion of several projects. It is essential reading for anyone interested in the application of artificial intelligence techniques to medical diagnosis.

Finally, a number of collections of important papers from the artificial intelligence field have been published, combining both early and recent ones. Recommended books along these lines are Feigenbaum & Feldman (1981) and Haugeland (1981).

2

Knowledge representation

2.1 Introduction

McCarthy & Hayes (1969) began their important paper relating artificial intelligence to certain philosophical problems with the paragraph:

'A computer program capable of acting intelligently in the world must have a general representation of the world in terms of which its inputs are interpreted. Designing such a program requires commitments about what knowledge is and how it is obtained. Thus, some of the major traditional problems of philosophy arise in artificial intelligence.'

Knowledge representation addresses just these problems of what knowledge is and how it is best described in the computer. Of knowledge representation, Barr & Feigenbaum (1983, vol. I, p. 144) say: 'Our understanding of these matters is still incomplete; knowledge representation is the most active area of AI research at the present time.'

A representation of something, then, is a model or description. By studying and manipulating the representation we can deduce properties of the original object and determine how it would behave. For any particular object there is an arbitrary number of possible representations. However, some representations are particularly *powerful*, meaning that they can describe a large range of types of objects, that the descriptions are very accurate in that they describe all the important features of the objects, and that they are easy to manipulate. Moreover, in assessing the worth of a particular representation we must bear in mind the purpose for which it is to be used.

To introduce the ideas let us take a simple example. Suppose we have arrived at the railway station in a strange town and we wish to travel to the town hall.

One possible representation would be an aerial photograph. By studying this we could work out which roads to walk along to get from the station to the town hall. It might not be easy – roads are not always very clear in aerial photographs, and unless one happened to know what the town hall looked like from above it might be difficult to identify.

Another possible representation would be a map. Here the roads would be clearly marked and named, which would make it easier to match the representation to reality (i.e. to check one actually was where one thought one was). Moreover the town hall might well be labelled as such on the map.

Each of these representations contains information not held in the other. The photograph, for example, would enable one to count the number of houses, while the map may not be sufficiently detailed for this. Conversely the map may indicate routes of any underground trains which run in the town.

A third possible representation which could be used for tackling the problem of how to get from the station to the town hall consists of an index of addresses of the major public buildings, coupled with a list of all road junctions and intersections in the town. One could plan one's journey by noting that the station is in street A which intersects B which joins C which . . . which joins Z, in which is situated the town hall. This is clearly not as convenient as a map for humans to use, but it would work.

These three representations have different strengths and weaknesses. It seems fairly clear which would be the most suited for tackling the route-finding problem, but there are other problems for which the order of preference differs (as an exercise, the reader might like to try to think of some). The relative suitability for a problem defines the power of a particular representation for that problem. The map is clearly quite power-ful for finding routes, and it can also be used for many other purposes. (If it were not such a powerful representation it would presumably have been rejected in favour of some alternative by now.)

In this text we are, of course, particularly concerned with representations suitable for encoding into a computer. A map could be digitised and stored in a computer's memory as a picture, but the result would not be very easy for the computer to manipulate. As it happens, something more like the index of addresses and list of intersections might be more suitable (as we shall see below). Using such a representation a computer could quickly produce a good route from the station to the town hall.

It should be noted at this point that all computer representations de-scribing an object and used to solve problems in a specific domain are equivalent in some sense. By virtue of the fact that they can all solve problems in the same domain, anything that any one can do so can any other. This might seem to make the question of which representation to use rather uninteresting. But, as the route example above demonstrates, some representations are more powerful than others in that they make it easier to solve some problems. Of two representations for tackling a problem, we would prefer one which took five seconds to one which took 5000 years.

To illustrate further, consider the following puzzle found in many brain teaser books. Take an ordinary eight by eight chessboard and mutilate it by removing two diagonally opposite corner squares. This leaves 62 squares. Now, given a set of 31 dominoes, each rectangles of size two squares, can these dominoes be placed so as to cover the mutilated chessboard completely?

This problem might be approached in a number of ways. One might base one's representation on geometric configurations of dominoes and search for a configuration which covered the board. Some systematic approach would have to be adopted to ensure that all possible configurations were explored (one would not want to miss the vital one!). It seems likely that even for a computer this would take some time.

An alternative approach concentrates on representing the colours of the squares. Each domino must, by the very nature of a chessboard, cover one black and one white square. Thus, however they are arranged, the 31 dominoes will cover 31 black and 31 white squares. But opposite corners of a chessboard have the same colour. The 62 squares of the mutilated board thus do not divide equally into 31 black and 31 white. So the dominoes cannot cover them.

This example is an extreme one, deliberately chosen to illustrate the power of a good representation, and there will be other situations for which an explicit examination of all configurations is the only approach guaranteed to find a solution (tangram puzzles, for example?). There are, of course, other problems relating to chessboards, such as chess itself, for the description of which far more information is needed.

As a final simple example, we ask the reader to multiply two thousand nine hundred and forty two by thirty eight, first using Roman numerals (i.e. MMCMXLII times XXXVIII) and second using Arabic numerals (i.e. 2942 times 38). Even bearing in mind the reader's greater familiarity with Arabic numerals he will probably agree that the latter is a more convenient representation. A computer carrying out the same operation would probably use neither representation, instead adopting binary arithmetic (i.e. 101101111110 times 100110).

Good representations are easier to find for some problem domains than for others. The small examples above all have fairly straightforward and easily identified good representations. For natural language processing, however, it is by no means obvious what is a good representation, and many different approaches have been adopted, with varying degrees of success (see Chapter 3).

To some extent whether or not a good representation is easy to find depends upon the degree of *structure* in the problem domain. *Well-structured problems* can be fairly directly expressed in formal notation and tackled using formal procedures; *ill-structured* problems are altogether more loosely defined, with more ambiguity and woolliness. The distinction is discussed more fully in Chapter 5, where we consider how well structured is the problem of psychiatric diagnosis.

When considering which representation to adopt it is vital to identify those aspects of the problem domain which are relevant. This may be so obvious that it does not need saying, but the obvious is not always easy. Raphael (1976) gives a nice example. The problem is to compute the length of time it would take for a cannonball dropped from the top of the Tower of Pisa to hit the ground. Clearly, building a miniature model will not work, no matter how accurate the detail or the material of its construction. Some fundamental aspect of the problem has been omitted from the model.

The same applies generally in science, of course. Perhaps the mark of genius is the ability to recognise the relevant aspects of a problem. How, for example, did Newton recognise that the substance of which the moon was composed was irrelevant to its orbital mechanics?

Choosing a representation to suit a problem is one way to approach things. We can also approach from the other side and ask: for a given representation, what kind of reasoning is easy? McCarthy & Hayes (1969, p. 466) distinguish sharply between choosing a representation and working within it:

> According to this definition, intelligence has two parts, which we shall call the epistemological and the heuristic. The epistemological part is the representation of the world in such a form that the solution of problems follows from the facts expressed in the representation. The heuristic part is the mechanism that on the basis of the information solves the problem and decides what to do.

(We shall find that this distinction crops up again later in the book.) If we wish to tackle many different kinds of problem, the reasoning approach might be the most appropriate direction.

Sometimes it might be sensible to use multiple representations running in parallel. In chess programs, for example, different descriptions of the state of play may be suited for different kinds of searches – for examining different kinds of strategies. Thus, at the cost of requiring larger computer memory, it might be worthwhile storing more than one description so that faster searches can be carried out.

It will be clear from the above that representations must be able to describe not only objects (chess positions, words, feelings, mental states, etc.) but also properties of objects, relationships between objects, and processes operating on objects. The examples above are quite straightforward and in some cases are sufficiently well-structured to permit an immediate translation into a formal representation which renders the domain trivial (the mutilated chessboard, for example). Other domains, for example natural language processing (Chapter 3) or modelling human emotions (Chapter 6), do not permit such obvious mappings. Instead we have to adopt a general representation, one which is sufficiently powerful for our purposes. The remaining sections of this chapter discuss some important powerful general representations which have been implemented in computers and which are widely used in artificial intelligence work.

This section concludes with a discussion of an early artificial intelligence program (over twenty years old at the time of writing) for tackling geometric analogy intelligence tests (Evans, 1968). This illustrates several things. First, although it is a particular representation for the domain, it contains within it many of the ideas fundamental to more general representations: ideas such as transformations, matching, and relationships. Second, it illustrates how relatively simple programs can do fairly complicated things. This is interesting because, as we noted before, artificial intelligence work has shown that it is often the things humans can do easily (such as walking or recognising objects in scenes) which require phenomenal amounts of computation, while the things humans regard as difficult (IQ tests, calculating, and so on) are often easy in computer terms.

An example of the type of test tackled by the program is given in Fig. 2.1. The objective is to select a diagram from the set labelled 1 to 5 such that the relationship between C and the chosen diagram is the same as the relationship between A and B. Clearly the fundamental problem is to represent the difference between A and B and to compare this representation with representations of each of the differences between C and 1 to 5. The pair C–1, C–2, . . ., C–5 which most closely matches A–B will be chosen. This could be attempted in a number of ways. The approach Evans used is as follows. Each A–B pair is described by a three component representation:

(i) A description of A, using ABOVE, LEFT, and INSIDE to describe the relative positions of its shapes.

(ii) A similar description of B.

(iii) A description explaining how each of the shapes change (removed, rotated, shrunk, etc.) in moving from A to B.

Similar representations describe each pair C–1, . . ., C–5. In principle it is then just a matter of comparing these with the A–B description. In some cases one of the C–1, . . ., C–5 transformation descriptions will match the A–B description perfectly. In other cases there will be no perfect match, so some measure of similarity must be adopted. (This concept of 'similarity' is one of the powerful general ideas mentioned above – see also Chapter 5.) A basic approach is to add up the number of agreements between the two pair transformation descriptions, choosing that of C–1, . . ., C–5 which has the greatest number of agreements with A–B. This can be extended by *weighting* the component agreements using numbers so that more important agreements have larger weights. This is exactly the same principle as is used in some of the pattern recognition procedures described in § 5.6.

As described so far, the program is simple enough. However, some situations call for an extension which illustrates a more general point. The description above nowhere indicates *which* shapes are to be matched with which. Fig. 2.2 illustrates the sort of problems that can arise. Humans map the square in A to the square in B and thus recognise that the dot has gone. Applying a similar transformation to C yields choice 2. But a system which does not recognise that the object in B is a square might map A's dot to B's square and regard the transformation as having deleted A's square. Applying this to C yields choice 1. To avoid such a situation some extra descriptive

Fig. 2.1. An example of geometric analogy intelligence test problem. (From Evans, 1968, Case 5. Reprinted by permission of Educational Testing Service, the copyright owner.)

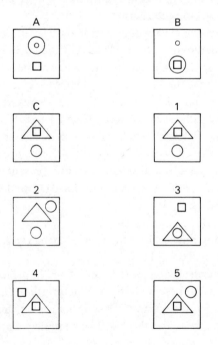

information is needed in the program's representation. Evans allowed for shape matches by using larger weights for agreement between matching shapes than between non-matching shapes. However, this illustrates the question of the depth of description. A decision has to be made regarding how much information is relevant to the comparison. In this program the programmer made that decision. It is perhaps worth remarking that humans at first rapidly improve on such tests as they learn what kinds of information are relevant.

Although working on intelligence tests it would clearly be fatuous to claim that this program was intelligent. It does, however, demonstrate a number of important points:

(i) Problems that humans regard as difficult (or, at least, as requiring intelligence) may be rather straightforward.

(ii) A good representation makes a problem amenable to solution.

(iii) There are levels of description.

(iv) It uses embryo concepts which have been applied in many such more sophisticated artificial intelligence programs.

Fig. 2.2. A more subtle geometric analogy intelligence test problem. (From Evans, 1968, Case 15. Reprinted by permission of Education Testing Service, the copyright owner.)

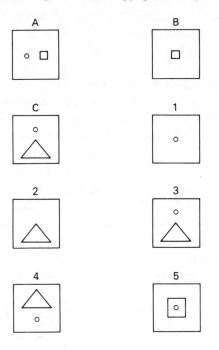

2.2   Logic

Logic is defined (amongst other definitions) by *Chambers Twentieth Century dictionary* as 'the science and art of reasoning correctly', so perhaps it is not surprising that there has been a great deal of interest in producing intelligent programs through automating logic. It may have been partly because of an idealised image of man as a rational creature or partly because automating logic was seen as a limited and relatively amenable problem that there was much early artificial intelligence work in this area. However, as elsewhere in life, things were not as straightforward as they seemed. Difficulties were encountered in applying, to the fuzziness of the real world, systems which were really suited to clearly defined and artificially precise problems. Nonetheless, as we mention briefly at the end of this section, logic programming is currently undergoing something of a renaissance.

Perhaps the difficulty of applying early logical systems to real life domains is a contributory factor to the uneven history of artificial intelligence research. Initial claims of great things just around the corner – perhaps based on the deceptive ease with which logic can be automated – were found to be impossible to follow up. The result was that interest in artificial intelligence waned. Now, with new approaches to logic programming, as well as new representations such as production systems (see below) which seem well suited to the real world, interest has been rekindled.

Deductive systems, such as those based on logic, attempt to establish paths connecting facts known to be true to those it is wished to establish. To do this we need to represent two types of object:

(i) Facts themselves

(ii) Rules of inference.

The simplest system which is yet sufficiently powerful to contain these two necessary components is *propositional calculus*. The facts of propositional calculus consist of sentences or statements which may be true or false as well as sets of such statements connected together. Examples of such statements are 'the sky is green', 'the Earth is round', 'the tree is tall'. Of these the first is false, the second is true, and the third may be true or false. But all three of them are well-structured – they may thus be legitimately combined into logical formulae and manipulated by the inference rules of logic. In contrast 'yellow bananas' is not well-structured. It asserts nothing and is neither true nor false.

In the three legitimate examples above their acceptability was determined by a syntactic examination – an examination of their ,structure. Their meaning was irrelevant.

The examples above are particularly simple. More complex and interesting examples can be obtained by combining simple statements. 'The sky is green *or* the sky is blue'; 'John hit Mary *and* the ball rolled down the road'. Similarly, statements can be *negated*: 'the sky is *not* green'; 'John did *not* hit Mary'.

Statements (or *propositions*) are combined in this way through the use of *logical connectives*. They are represented symbolically in order to help to clarify the deductive processes, to make each step precise, and to eliminate the confusion and ambiguity which unavoidably creeps into natural language discourse. Their usual symbolic representations are:

Or	$\vee$
And	$\wedge$
Not	$\sim$

Thus, if we let the symbol p stand for 'the sky is green' and q stand for 'the sky is blue' we can represent 'the sky is green or the sky is blue' by $p \vee q$. The symbols p and q serve in the same role as letters for variables in school algebra.

There are two other common logical connectives. One is 'implies', written $\Rightarrow$. For example, 'the man is reading the book *implies* that the book is open'. This is also often read as 'if . . . then . . .', as in '*if* the man is reading the book *then* the book is open'. The other is 'equivalence', as in 'John hit Mary' is equivalent to 'John did not not hit Mary'. Equivalence is written $\equiv$. In fact, as we ask the reader to demonstrate below, neither $\Rightarrow$ nor $\equiv$ is needed since they can be expressed in terms of $\sim$, $\wedge$, and $\vee$. We merely introduce them to make expressions easier to read.

The properties of these five logical connectives can be summarised in a 'truth table'. This is simply a table indicating the truth or falsity (the 'truth value') resulting when two propositions are combined using one of the connectives. If p and q represent any propositions, which may be true (T) or false (F), then the five connectives give truth values

p	q	$p \vee q$	$p \wedge q$	$\sim p$	$p \Rightarrow q$	$p \equiv q$
T	T	T	T	F	T	T
T	F	T	F	F	F	F
F	T	T	F	T	T	F
F	F	F	F	T	T	T

These patterns conform to the everyday usage of 'and', 'or', and so on, but even at this very basic level we see examples of how the formalisation is clarifying the concepts involved. For example, the common usage of 'or' is ambiguous. If one said 'John is certain to be eating an apple or reading a book' one might mean that John is doing one or the other but definitely not both, or one might mean that he is doing one or the other or perhaps both. The first is called the *exclusive or* and the second the *inclusive or*. Since our aim is precision we must adopt one or the other (but not both!) and our truth table shows that we have adopted the inclusive or.

Of course, sometimes we might want to make use of the exclusive or: 'either p or q but not both'. How, then, can we represent it using our five connectives? A moment's thought shows that the truth table for the exclusive or must be

p	q	p (exclusive) or q
T	T	F
T	F	T
F	T	T
F	F	F

Studying the truth table of our five connectives shows that one easy way to represent it would be $\sim (p \equiv q)$. This makes everyday sense: 'either p or q but not both are true' is the same as saying 'true when p and q have different truth values'.

We should discuss the notion of implication since this can be confusing – again primarily because of an ambiguity in natural language. Implication might be associated with causality: 'If I fall off a cliff then I will be killed'. But it can also mean the simultaneous truth of two statements: 'If I am sitting on a chair then the chair must be beneath me'. It is this second usage that we are adopting here. Its sense can be seen by relating the example to the truth table for $p \Rightarrow q$ above. If both 'I am sitting on a chair' and 'the chair is beneath me' are true, then this suggests the implication is true (it cannot be false). If the first is true but the second is false, then certainly the implication is false. If the first is false, then it does not matter what the second is since it can neither establish nor disprove the implication. By convention we then take the implication to be true.

We have remarked that the acceptability of a sequence of words as a proposition is syntactically determined. The structure tells us if the sequence is a well-formed formula. The structure is quite separate from the truth or falsity of the statement. The latter is determined semantically – by relating the proposition to the real world.

However, some statements are unusual in that they have predetermined truth values no matter what interpretation is put on their constituent symbols. For example, '$p \lor \sim p$'. If p represents 'the sky is blue' then we have 'the sky is blue or the sky is not blue' – clearly true. Equally, if p represents 'the sky is purple' we have 'the sky is purple or the sky is not purple'. Again clearly true. Such statements, which are always either true or false no matter what the interpretation of their symbols, are called *tautologies*.

So much for the objects upon which logic works – the propositions. Now we must consider the *rules of inference*. These allow us to examine whether some proposition (called a *theorem*) is guaranteed to be true whenever certain other propositions (called *premises*) are true.

A simple example is called *modus ponens*. This has two premises:

(i) If p is true then q is true

(ii) p is true

And the theorem is:

q is true.

We can represent it symbolically as $(p \land (p \Rightarrow q)) \Rightarrow q$.

A second simple example of an inference rule is called *modus tollens*. In symbols $(\sim q \land (p \Rightarrow q)) \Rightarrow \sim p$. In words

(i) If q is false

and (ii) if p is true then q is true

then (theorem) p is false.

One method for establishing the validity of a rule of inference is by using truth tables. The table below gives an illustration for *modus ponens*. We begin by listing all possible true/false combinations of the basic propositions. In general, if there are n propositions there will be 2^n rows in the table. In our case, with two basic propositions (p and q) there are four such rows. We then evaluate the premises and theorem for each row and check to see that the theorem is true whenever the premises are true. Thus

p	q		(i) $p \Rightarrow q$	(ii) p	q
T	T		T	T	T*
T	F		F	T	F
F	T		T	F	T
F	F		T	F	F

Only for the row marked with an asterisk are both premises p and $p \Rightarrow q$ true so we need only check the theorem for this row. This is seen to be true, so the theorem is established.

At this point the reader might like to find expressions involving only $\sim$, $\land$, and $\lor$ which are equivalent to $\Rightarrow$ and $\equiv$. Answers, the validity of which can be checked using the truth table method of proof (or any other method), are given below.

The truth table method of proving theorems is straightforward but slow if there are many basic propositions forming a complex interrelationship and hardly in the spirit of artificial intelligence.

A first step toward a more elegant proof method was provided by Wang in the 1960s. His method involves systematically reformulating the statement of the inference to be made until a proof is established. The reformulation is carried out by applying a number of rules and is guaranteed to find a proof if one is possible.

A more interesting method of proof is that of *propositional resolution*. However, we shall not describe it here because it is a special case of *resolution proof*, a proof procedure for work in *predicate calculus*, which itself includes propositional calculus as a subdomain. Instead we shall move on to predicate calculus and, in a later chapter, return to the more general resolution proof procedure.

Answers to the exercises above, namely to find equivalent expressions to $\Rightarrow$ and $\equiv$, are, respectively, $\sim p \vee q$ and $(p \wedge q) \vee (\sim p \wedge \sim q)$. These are, of course, not the only possible answers.

It will not have escaped the reader's notice that propositional calculus is somewhat limited for describing mental states or modelling either minds or the world in general. We need not only to be able to ascertain the truth or falsity of statements, but also to be able to describe objects and the relationships between them. Predicate calculus does just this.

The basic units of predicate calculus are not statements but are individual objects. Thus John, psychiatrists, a bus, yellow bananas, and open books are legitimate objects for manipulation by the predicate calculus.

Predicate calculus retains the logical connectives of propositional calculus but adds the notion of *predicates*. A predicate is a property of an object. It takes the value 'true' if the object has the property, and 'false' otherwise. Examples of predicates would be *is-a-psychiatrist*, *has-schizophrenia*, *is-John's-sister*, *is-yellow*, and *hit-Mary*.

We can write a predicate applied to a particular object in the form *predicate(object)*. Thus *is-a-psychiatrist(the Prime Minister)*, *hit-Mary(John)*, and so on. Often, as with the propositional calculus, we shall simplify things by adopting single symbols to represent predicates. U might represent *is-the-uncle-of* and so on.

Predicates can involve relationships. For example, we might have a general predicate *is-the-father-of* as in *is-the-father-of(John, Mary)*. Or *dislikes*, as in *dislikes(Harry, George)*.

Another property of predicate calculus not possessed by propositional calculus is the notion of a *quantifier*. There are two quantifiers: the *universal quantifier* and the *existential quantifier*.

The first is written $\forall$ and is read *all* or *for-all*. Thus if *psychiatrist* and *medically-qualified* are predicates we have

$$\forall X, psychiatrist(X) \Rightarrow medically\text{-}qualified(X)$$

meaning that all X's which are psychiatrists are medically qualified.

The existential quantifier is written $\exists$ and is read as *there exists* or *there is*.

So

$$\exists X, psychiatrist(X) \Rightarrow MD(X)$$

means there is some X who is a psychiatrist who has an MD.

An example of a rule of inference which makes use of quantifiers is *universal specialisation*. This simply says

$$\forall X, F(X) \Rightarrow F(A)$$

where F represents any syntactically correct expression with a variable term X and where A is a constant symbol. For example, by using this rule we can infer from

$$\forall X, is\text{-}a\text{-}father(X) \Rightarrow has\text{-}a\text{-}child(X)$$

that

$$is\text{-}a\text{-}father(John) \Rightarrow has\text{-}a\text{-}child(John)$$

where the universal specialisation rule of inference has allowed us to replace the variable X by the particular item 'John'.

Another addition often used with the predicate calculus is an extension of the predicate idea. This is the idea of *function* or *operator*. Instead of simply giving a value of true or false, a function can take other values. An example would be a function *mother-of*. Then *mother-of(John)* would be John's mother. *Mother-of(Mary)* would be Mary's mother. *Mother-of(Mother-of(John))* would be John's maternal grandmother. And so on. Another example is the function *disease*, with *disease(John)* being the illness from which John is suffering.

Functions, like predicates, can act on multiple objects (we say they can have multiple *arguments*). For example, the function *plus*, as in *plus*(3,4) which gives the sum of its arguments.

In predicate calculus the basic elements are predicates applied to arguments. Thus *is-a-psychiatrist(Mother(Mary))*. Such basic elements are termed *atomic formulae*. Atomic formulae and the combinations of them obtained by using the logical connectives of propositional calculus are the *well-formed formulae* of predicate calculus (in logic texts this is often abbreviated to w.f.f.). This just means that they are structured correctly. When prefixed by the quantifiers $\forall$ or $\exists$, they become *sentences*. For example,

$$\forall X, is\text{-}a\text{-}psychiatrist(Mother(X))$$

means that for any person X, X's mother is a psychiatrist (which is well formed, though false since there are mothers who are not psychiatrists).

$$\exists X, is\text{-}a\text{-}psychiatrist(Mother(X))$$

means that there is some X (there exists an X) whose mother is a psychiatrist.

With x and y being integers, if *greater-than*(x,y) is a predicate taking the value true when x is greater than y, and if *plus-one*(x) is a function taking the value $(x+1)$, then

$$\forall y, \exists x, \textit{greater-than}(x,\textit{plus-one}(y))$$

means that for every integer y there is some integer x which is bigger than $y + 1$.

Predicate calculus is an extremely powerful representation, and one which can be used to describe almost any concept. It also has the merit of being sufficiently well formalised to permit deductive processes about the domain it is describing. As with any formal system, such deductions are termed *theorem proving*. The mathematical sound of this should not conceal the fact that the subjects of the descriptions need not themselves be mathematical, but could be the physical world, mental constructs, or indeed anything else. Rather than diverting from our present subject of discussion, namely representation, we shall leave the outline of theorem proving in predicate calculus to Chapter 4.

Although predicate calculus can be used to represent almost anything, as one might expect there are situations for which it is not an ideal representation. Some concepts are in fact extremely difficult to represent using this language and can only be modelled in inelegant and clumsy ways – ways which would lead to extremely long deductive processes, sometimes impracticably long. Because of this, other logical systems have been explored.

The form of predicate calculus outlined above is a *first order logic*. This means that the quantifiers $\forall$ and $\exists$ work on the elements in the formulae, but not on the predicates. Thus we can talk of 'the mothers of all men' or 'all numbers greater than 3', but we cannot talk of the set of 'all possible predicates applied to John'. In the former case the universal quantifier applies to 'men' and in the latter case to predicates. *Higher order logics* permit this. Thus

$$\forall P, P(\textit{John}).$$

Clearly this is a valuable and powerful extension. Unfortunately it carries with it the disadvantage that general proof procedures are more difficult to find than in first order predicate calculus.

A second extension which has gained popularity in recent years is the concept of fuzzy logic. Fuzzy logic replaces the hard true/false categorisation, which might be represented by the integers 1 and 0, by the range of numbers from 1 to 0, where a situation's value represents its *degree of truth*. A typical example of ordinary logic would be the predicate *tall*, where $tall(X)$ has the value 1 (true) if person X is tall, and 0 (false) if he is not tall. In fuzzy logic $tall(X)$ could take any value from 0 to 1, the taller the person the closer the value being to 1. The point is that a team of basketball players might regard a six foot man as short, but for a jockey 5'8" might be tall. 'Tall' clearly has degrees of truth.

It is important to distinguish between on the one hand fuzzy logic, and on the other hand probability applied to classical logic. In classical logic every proposition is either true or false and will have a certain probability of being one or the other. The proposition 'it is raining' is either true or false and before I look out of the window I can calculate my measure of belief (my probability estimate) in the proposition. But some people might regard a fine drizzle as not rain at all. In this case a more accurate representation might be via fuzzy logic – to say that the truth value of 'it is raining' is not 1 but 0.9, for example. In fuzzy logic all propositions are both true and false: what matters is the strength of truth. In classical logic this strength is simply either 1 or 0.

Early examples of systems which used logic as a representation are QA3 (Green, 1969) and STRIPS (Fikes, Hart & Nilsson, 1972). The first of these was a question-answering system that could solve simple problems in arbitrary domains. It used the resolution proof method for deduction but found this inefficient for even a moderate number of facts. STRIPS (Stanford Research Institute Problem Solver) worked out how a robot should rearrange objects in a room in order to achieve a desired configuration. This really involves two subprocesses – finding out if a particular fact is true for a particular configuration, and working out how to get from one configuration to another. The first of these subprocesses was tackled by resolution proof.

A more recent example of a system using logic is FOL (Filman & Weyhrauch, 1976), which checks first order logic proofs.

Prolog (Clocksin & Mellish, 1981) is a very important recent development along the path to logic programming. In logic programming one does not *tell* the computer what to do, as is the case with other programming languages. Instead one *asks* the computer to make deductions. In theory this should make programs easier to understand because all the nitpicking detail of *how* to do things is left out and what is to be done is presented instead.

2.3 Semantic networks

As with other high level representations, such as production systems, semantic networks have been applied in a wide range of areas and studied for many different purposes. The latter range from human psychological modelling at one extreme to, at the other extreme, the performance oriented black-box approach aimed at getting correct results by whichever method is most efficient. Because of this range of purposes and the diversity of application areas we are faced with the common problem of trying to summarise systems exhibiting a multitude of different features.

In such circumstances all one can attempt to do is to identify shared features and thus note the major characterising features of semantic networks.

We might begin by noting the role that semantic networks have played in artificial intelligence work. In the 1970s such structures were a very widely used knowledge representation. Emphasis nowadays seems to have shifted to production system concepts (§ 2.5) but semantic networks are still very important. This is partly because the different representations are not mutually exclusive – use of one does not preclude the simultaneous use of another. For example, one might find the rules of a production system having, as antecedents, fragments from a semantic network. When the network contains parts which match the fragments then the rule operates – perhaps modifying the network in some way.

Semantic networks represent knowledge by graph structures (see also § 2.6), structures consisting of *nodes* with *links* connecting them. Loosely, the nodes represent objects, situations, actions, or ideas and the links represent the relationships between them. Following on from this, each link will have a direction. For example, in the fragment in Fig. 2.3 *John* and *Man* are nodes linked by the directed relationship *is-a*. Note that *is-a* can be inverted, so that this graph fragment also contains the knowledge that the concept *Man* – and the attributes which apply to individuals within *Man* – includes *John*.

Most nodes will be linked to many other nodes, each link defining different aspects of the node in question and doing so by specifying the relationships with other concepts.

Perhaps we should point out at this stage that it is a common practice to attach labels to the nodes and links. Such a practice is not without risks. When studying labelled semantic networks there will be a natural tendency to impute a depth of meaning to each node beyond that derived via the linkages, and instead derived from one's own understanding of the label. It is for precisely this reason that computer programs are so powerful for evaluating theories in cognitive psychology. A computer program cannot impute more by virtue of a label. Its knowledge is solely derived from the link structure and related nodes.

Fig. 2.3. A fragment of a semantic network showing two nodes and a single relationship between them.

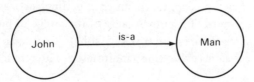

Before developing the idea in more depth, it might be a good idea to glance at a simple example. Fig. 2.4 shows a set fragment describing John and Mary and their occupations. In this figure the *is-a* kind of link plays a major part and has an obvious meaning.

By working through the network simple deductions can be made. For example, we can see that Mary works as a psychiatrist and that psychiatrists are medical doctors and hence that Mary is a doctor. Or we can deduce (a relief for Mary) that John is human.

We should note that in general not all relationships are binary. For example 'John gave Mary a present' is a three way relationship. However, although we do not show it here, it is possible to convert all relationships into a set of binary ones.

This simplistic approach to representing structure in semantic networks can have problems. For example,

(i) Proliferation of links. If we wished to add to Fig. 2.4 the information that John had been a doctor before he became interested in computers then we would need both an *occupation-is* and an *occupation-was* link. Unless some steps are taken, an arbitrary and, indeed, arbitrarily large, set of links (and presumably nodes) will arise.

(ii) Following on from (i), suppose we were asked whether Mary *works-as* a psychiatrist. If a net fragment linking Mary and psychiatrist using a link labelled *works-as* is established then no match will be found in Fig. 2.4. The system would be unable to answer the question. Something fundamental seems to be lacking.

(iii) As presented above, there is a lack of distinction between individuals and classes. Fig. 2.5a shows a link conveying the information that members of the class of psychiatrists belong to the British Psychoanalytic Association. It also shows the previous link indicating that Mary is a psychiatrist. But

Fig. 2.4. A fragment of a semantic network.

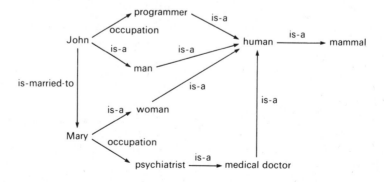

what if Mary is not a psychoanalyst? Our network fragment seems to let us deduce that she is! Similarly, it is true that mathematicians study abstract concepts – hence the second link in Fig. 2.5b. It is also true that Intellectual Property Law is an abstract concept. However, I have yet to meet a mathematician who studies Intellectual Property Law. Again, some subtlety seems to be missing.

When one looks closely at the problems arising in such simplistic representations one sees that they arise in part from the high level concepts involved in the links and nodes. The ideas need to be broken down into smaller elements. One common approach is to transform the more complicated relationships into nodes. Thus instead of Fig. 2.6a we have 2.6b.

This aim of making the system easier to use and less context dependent also leads to the idea of *semantic primitives*. A semantic primitive is a basic element, one so basic that it does not have a definition within the program (for a general survey see Winograd, 1978). These are the atoms from which the conceptual molecules are constructed. Wilks (1977) notes that there is no unique correct set of semantic primitives, but, on the contrary, that many different sets may be adequate. It is the adequacy of performance which provides the acid test. He also argues that semantic primitives effectively provide an elementary natural language – with all the shortcomings and ambiguities inherent in those.

(To anyone with even a passing knowledge of computers, the influence of the computer – or at least the analogy of the computer – will be obvious. With the levels of human language, from semantic primitives up, we can match assembler and source code.)

Wilks (1977) identifies five properties as desirable for a set of semantic primitives:

(i) *Finitude*. The number of primitives should be finite and should be

Fig. 2.5. Problems with the simplistic approach.

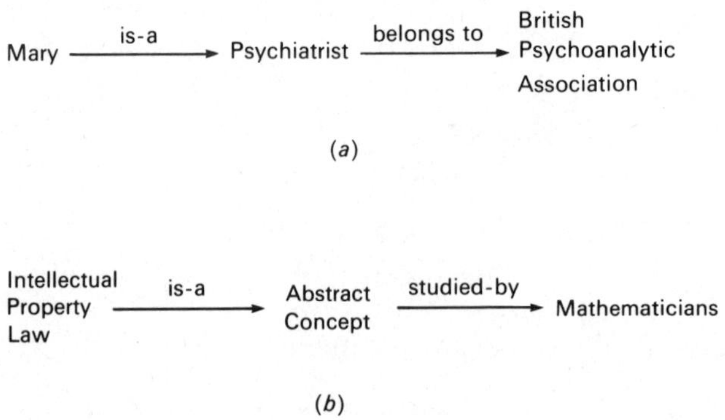

Mary ───is-a──→ Psychiatrist ───belongs to──→ British Psychoanalytic Association

(a)

Intellectual Property Law ───is-a──→ Abstract Concept ───studied-by──→ Mathematicians

(b)

smaller than the number of words whose meanings the representation scheme is to encode.

(ii) *Comprehensiveness*. The set should be adequate to express and distinguish among the senses of the word set whose meanings it is to encode.

(iii) *Independence*. No primitive should be definable in terms of other primitives.

(iv) *Noncircularity*. No two primitives should be definable in terms of each other.

(v) *Primitiveness*. No subset of the primitives should be replaceable by a smaller set.

Wilk's original interest was machine translation. Rumelhart & Norman (1975) are primarily interested in cognitive modelling. The contrast between Wilks's properties above and the six of Rumelhart & Norman below is therefore particularly interesting. The last one, especially, is relevant to artificial intelligence as cognitive modelling, rather than to artificial intelligence for producing intelligent systems irrespective of process. Rumelhart & Norman's six properties are:

(i) *Completeness*. The set of semantic primitives must be capable of representing any information we might want to store.

(ii) *Invariance under paraphrase*. The semantic representations should be invariant under paraphrases of the same information.

(iii) *Preservation of overlap in meaning*. If two concepts share elements then the representations in terms of semantic primitives should share elements.

(iv) *Continuity*. Small changes in meaning should cause only small changes in representation.

(v) *Extensibility*. It should always be possible to link new information onto previously constructed semantic structures.

(vi) *Psychological validity*. The representations should be consistent with what is otherwise known about the human information-processing system.

As examples of sets of semantic primitives, we have Wilks's list and Schank's list (see, for example, Schank, 1972 and Schank & Colby, 1973).

Fig. 2.6. Transforming complicated relationships into nodes.

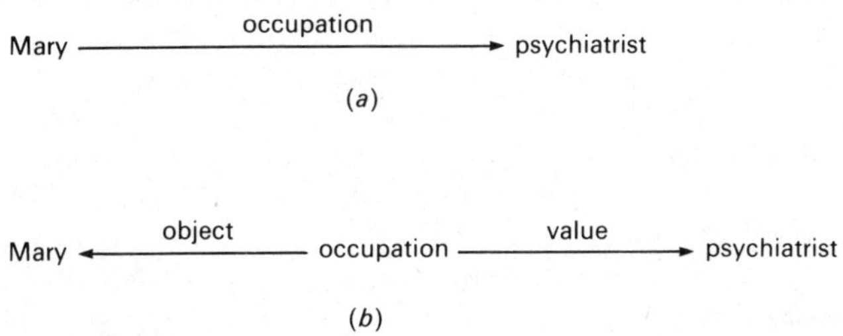

(a)

(b)

Wilks: Preference Semantics has around 80 primitives divided into five classes. We give examples

  (i) *Entities*
    MAN a human
    ACT acts
    BEAST animals

  (ii) *Actions*
    FORCE to compel
    PICK to choose
    CAUSE to cause to happen

  (iii) *Qualifiers*
    GOOD morally acceptable
    THRU an aperture
    MUCH much

  (iv) *Cases*
    TO direction toward something
    LOCA location
    IN containment

  (v) *Type*
    HOW type of action
    KIND being a quality

Schank: Conceptual Dependency has been used as the basis for programs for translation, paraphrase, deduction about texts, and question answering. One set of primitive acts which have proven effective for handling general world knowledge is

   (i) ATRANS – the transfer of ownership or control.
  (ii) PTRANS – the transfer of physical location.
 (iii) PROPEL – the application of a physical force.
 (iv) MTRANS – the transfer of information.
  (v) MBUILD – construct new information from old.
 (vi) INGEST – take something into an animal or human.
(vii) EXPEL – move something out of an animal or human.
(viii) MOVE – movement of (part of) an animate object.
 (ix) SPEAK – a vocal act.
  (x) ATTEND – focus a sense organ on a stimulus.
 (xi) GRASP – physically grasp an object.

Fig. 2.7. A single node representing the verb 'hit' leads to confusion between two actions. (Adapted from *Explorations in cognition*, ed. by D. A. Norman & D. E. Rumelhart. W. H. Freeman & Co. Copyright © 1975.)

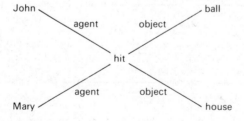

We illustrate the sort of net that arises when one uses more primitive concepts by extracting an example from Rumelhart & Norman (1975). They distinguish between *primary* and *secondary* nodes. Primary nodes refer directly to natural language concepts and in a sense stand for the abstract idea that they are to represent. In contrast, secondary nodes represent the concepts as used in particular cases. Thus the secondary nodes are always examples of, or types of, primary nodes.

The necessity for secondary nodes is conveyed by attempting to represent the two sentences

> John hits the ball
>
> Mary hits the house.

As shown in Fig. 2.7, if a single node represents 'hit' the result is confusion.

The solution using secondary nodes is illustrated in Fig. 2.8. In John's case, what he did is a concept of type 'hit', and the same for Mary, but now there is no confusion. Secondary nodes will, in fact, also be required for the concepts 'house' and 'ball' etc. (so that several houses and balls can be distinguished).

Another point relates to the labelling of nodes, as we remarked above. Rumelhart & Norman describe things very well:

> Nodes are abstract entities; they are where the set of relations that comprise a concept come together. The natural language name for a node is itself a form of information, and it too must be given some representation. This information is contained in a *vocabulary*. When the concept represented by a node has a name in natural language, then that fact is represented by a relation that points from the node to the location in the vocabulary that contains the appropriate words.

Fig. 2.8. Resolution of ambiguity by introducing secondary nodes. (Adapted from *Explorations in cognition*, ed. by D. A. Norman & D. E. Rumelhart. W. H. Freeman & Co. Copyright © 1975.)

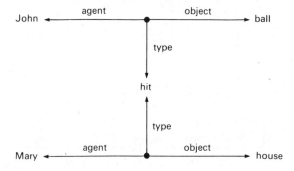

To illustrate the use of secondary nodes for all concepts and the use of links to a vocabulary, we continue the example of Rumelhart & Norman. Adding the information

John hit a house (different from the one hit by Mary)

The ball hit by John hit the same house that Mary hit,

we get the network fragment shown in Fig. 2.9.

Brachman (1977, 1978) has also presented a way of sharpening the semantic net concept. His KLONE (Knowledge Language One) system also distinguishes between descriptions of the characteristics of a class and descriptions of individual concepts which fall within the class (cf. Rumelhart & Norman's primary and secondary nodes above). He calls these, respectively, the *intension* and *extension* of the class. For example, the intensional description of a man will give the attributes something must have in order to be a man (two arms, two legs, a head, breathes, etc.) and also the relationships between the items (the arms join the torso at the shoulders, etc.). In contrast, the extension of the concept 'man' contains the set of individual men, and each of these has his own associated description.

The value of this description can be seen from the following points: the intension gives a range of values for each attribute (a man's eye colour can be brown, blue, and so on) while a particular extensional description contains a particular value (this man's eyes are blue); some attributes of the

Fig. 2.9. An example of a semantic network fragment. (Adapted from *Explorations in cognition*, ed. by D. A. Norman & D. E. Rumelhart. W. H. Freeman & Co. Copyright © 1975.)

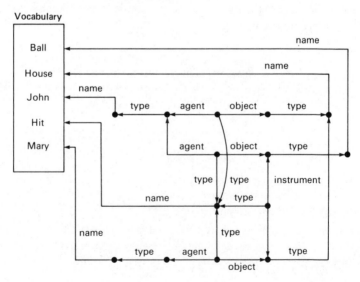

intensional description are optional (a man who has lost a leg is still a man), but they are not optional in the extension (a particular man either has or has not got both legs).

A large amount of the work on semantic networks has been oriented to language and language processing systems (see Chapter 3). However, semantic networks are primarily a system for representing knowledge, and examples not concerned with language manipulation have been built, for example the systems described in Duda, Hart, Nilsson & Sutherland (1978), Quillian (1968) and Anderson & Bower (1973). The first is concerned with evaluating the mineral potential of geological sites and the latter two with psychological models of associative memory. Of course, in view of the central role of language it is hardly surprising that structures for representing language have a lot in common with more general knowledge structures. In this vein perhaps we should also mention the close relationship between semantic nets and frames (§ 2.4). Frames can be regarded as chunks of semantic networks which pull together all the information relating to a particular situation or event.

Finally, just to demonstrate the point made at the beginning of this section, namely that semantic networks come in many shapes and forms, McDonald & Hayes-Roth (1978) should be mentioned. This describes a semantic network for language processing and is interesting because it does not rely on semantic primitives. Instead it is based on two hypotheses: '(1) That syntactic structures embody semantic knowledge that is sufficient for many understanding tasks and (2) that the actual words occurring in text are a more desirable basis for representing meaning than predefined abstract semantic primitives.'

2.4   Frames and scripts

There are many difficulties associated with handling any large body of knowledge:

(i) How should it be grouped or chunked so that it can be efficiently searched and manipulated?

(ii) How can a possibly confusing abundance of incoming data best be coordinated?

(iii) What kind of knowledge structures lead to easy interpretation of incoming data and how can these data be set in a context?

(iv) What sort of knowledge structures permit new information to be efficiently related to previous experience?

(v) Above all, what sort of structures permit all of the above and yet do not unduly restrict the range of actions which can be carried out on the knowledge?

Marvin Minsky described one general approach which can be applied in a wide range of domains, ranging from visual perception, through natural language processing to problem solving. (This section relies heavily on Minsky's work. His 'A framework for representing knowledge' was originally published as Memo 306 of the AI laboratory at MIT. Excerpts have been reprinted in a number of places, and an abridged version appears in Haugeland (1981). It is from this that the quotations below are taken.) He begins with a criticism of other knowledge representation schemes:

> It seems to me that the ingredients of most theories both in
> Artificial Intelligence and in Psychology have been on the whole too
> minute, local and unstructured to account – either practically or
> phenomenologically – for the effectiveness of common sense
> thought. The 'chunks' of reasoning, language, memory, and
> perception ought to be larger and more structured; their factual
> and procedural contents must be more intimately connected in
> order to explain the apparent power and spread of mental activities.

In an attempt to find a representation which had these properties Minsky introduced the concept of the *frame*. (Of course, no idea springs from virgin ground. Similar ideas to frames had been expressed, with different emphasis and in different contexts, in the past. Minsky refers to the writings of the psychologist F. C. Bartlett and the philosopher T. S. Kuhn. In psychological work frames are often called 'schemata'.) A frame is a knowledge structure describing a family of objects, situations, or events. It provides a framework relating the different features of the object in question to each other. In Minsky's words:

> We can think of a frame as a network of nodes and relations. The
> top levels of a frame are fixed, and represent things that are always
> true about the supposed situation. The lower levels have many
> *terminals* – slots that must be filled by specific instances or data.
> Each terminal can specify conditions its assignments must meet.
> (The assignments themselves are usually smaller subframes.)
> Simple conditions are specified by *markers* that might require a
> terminal assignment to be a person, an object of sufficient value, or
> a pointer to a subframe of a certain type. More complex conditions
> can specify relations among the things assigned to several
> terminals.

To take a simple example, we might have a frame standing for a house. This house frame will have various slots, as indicated below:

House FRAME
Type: Terrace, semi-detached, detached.
Number of rooms: an integer (default = 6).

Date-built:
Style:
Exterior finish: (default = brick).
Kitchen:

    .
    .
    .
    .

The slots might have default values, as demonstrated above. This implies that the default value will be assumed unless there is evidence to the contrary. But different systems make different use of defaults – a default might be some kind of average value and not necessarily one which represents any real house. In some cases slot fillers might have measures of confidence attached to them.

Slots can be still more complicated – they might, for example, have procedures associated with them. Thus if a value for 'style' is given, then the procedure associated with this slot could check that there is such a style and perhaps even evaluate the other information given about the house in the light of its claimed architectural style. Some systems have procedures which are activated automatically whenever a certain combination of information occurs (such procedures are called *demons*) and some have procedures which only run if they are explicitly activated (called *servants*).

As an example of a demon being used in a frame context Minsky describes the work of Charniak (1972). Charniak's work was on how children understand simple stories. For example:

'Jane was invited to Jack's Birthday Party. She wondered if he would like a kite. She went to her room and shook her piggy bank. It made no sound.'

A demon could respond to the phrase 'Birthday Party' and activate associated concepts such as 'present', in turn leading to 'money' and so making the inferential connections between the kite and the piggy bank – connections which are not explicit.

Although we have indicated possible slot fillers by single words and numbers above, these are just labels. In fact the slot fillers will more usually be pointers to other frames. Thus in the house example above the kitchen slot will have a pointer to a 'kitchen' frame, with slots of its own describing its characteristics. This, then, is one way in which a complete knowledge structure is built up out of individual frames: they exist in a network of subframes acting as slot fillers to other frames, which in their turn act as slot fillers, etc.

There is also another kind of relationship connecting frames. This is the *specialisation* or *property inheritance hierarchy*. It is analogous to the *is-a* relationship described in § 2.3. A house is a type of dwelling, so we will have another 'dwelling' frame which describes a more general concept than house. Fig. 2.10 illustrates this. In this figure we have illustrated two alternative fillers for the 'purpose-built?' slot of flat. This representation has one frame for purpose-built flats and one for conversions. Note that the *is-a* type of link allows slots to be filled by inheritance without having to discover the fillers anew and without having to copy them explicitly. If the dwelling frame has a known *date-built* then this data also applies to the house frame.

The description above might seem to imply a static structure. However, we must use it in a dynamic way to represent knowledge growing, changing and being manipulated. This has two aspects: first, how is the static frame

Fig. 2.10. The property inheritance hierarchy and frames as slot fillers.

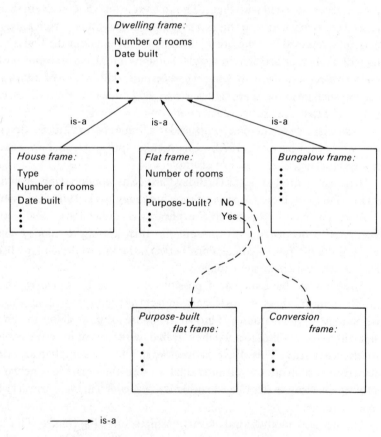

structure used, and secondly, how is it modified? Minsky, in fact, separates these issues into five components:

EXPECTATION: How to select an initial frame to meet some given conditions.

ELABORATION: How to select and assign subframes to represent additional details.

ALTERATION: How to find a frame to replace one that does not fit well enough.

NOVELTY: What to do if no acceptable frame can be found. Can we modify an old frame or must we build a new one?

LEARNING: What frames should be stored, or modified, as a result of the experience?

Noting that 'Thinking always begins with suggestive but imperfect plans and images; these are progressively replaced by better – but usually still imperfect – ideas', Minsky describes how frame systems are used:

> The effects of important actions are mirrored by *transformations* between the frames of a system. These are used to make certain kinds of calculations economical, to represent changes of emphasis and attention, and to account for the effectiveness of imagery . . .
> For nonvisual kinds of frames, the differences between the frames of a system can represent actions, cause–effect relations, or changes in conceptual viewpoint. *Different frames of a system share the same terminals*; this is the critical point that makes it possible to coordinate information gathered from different viewpoints.

A simple example of such a transformation would be the switch from one frame to another associated with the word 'sell'. The action 'John sold the book to Mary' is mirrored by a shift from a frame in which John fills the 'owner' slot to one in which Mary fills this slot.

Frames must be matched to a situation in order that the information within them can be applied. That is, so that their default values can provide *expectations* about what one might expect to find in a situation, so that the relationships of the situation (object, etc.) to other situations can be clarified, and so that changing situations can be identified. Matching will be controlled by information within the frame and by the system's goals. It is very interesting to see what Frederick Hayes-Roth (1978) has to say on the problems of matching:

> A few years ago, the foremost problem of knowledge system design was how knowledge should be represented. While knowledge representations are continually improving, many good frameworks have already been developed. Since pattern-directed function invocation is obviously desirable for many applications of these

knowledge systems, attention has recently focussed upon good
methods to invoke appropriate knowledge units . . . the most
difficult problem arising in very large and flexible knowledge
systems is to determine, as quickly as possible, the *most useful*
knowledge for the task at hand. Because many diverse elements of
knowledge may be weakly contributory to an overall solution, new
ways of organising computation must be developed to prevent
intractable, combinatorial searches. In the future a major shift in
attention can be anticipated toward the deceptively easily stated
but fundamental question: How should partial and best matches be
computed?

Of course, in contrast to this, as well as deciding when a frame matches
and so should be instantiated (made the focus of attention), it is also
necessary to decide when a frame ceases to match, that is, ceases to be
relevant. In this case the frame must be deactivated and attention focussed
on some other.

Turning from the question of how to manipulate knowledge using an
existing frame structure to the question of how to modify the structure, we
are confronted with a much more challenging problem. A typical situation
necessitating modification is when there is no adequately matching frame.
Sometimes modification can be avoided by reference back up the property
inheritance tree to a more general frame which can handle the situation, but
in other cases new frames must be synthesised. One process through which
new frames might be created is by means of analogy to existing frames. This
can provide the basis for creative thought. Boden (1977, p. 325) gives the
example of Harvey coming to an understanding of blood flow by means of
an analogy with hydraulics systems.

A notion very similar to that of the frame is the concept of a *script* (Schank
& Abelson, 1977). Scripts are prototypical knowledge structures for
describing sequences of events – for example, dining at a restaurant
(involving arriving, finding a table, ordering, eating, getting the bill,
paying, and so on). As with a frame, a script will have slots filled with default
events which normally occur and which can be replaced by other 'values' if
the need arises. We give an example of a story-understanding program
based around scripts below.

The frame structure concept is clearly an extremely powerful idea. To
what extent it describes human cognition is not yet clear (Barbara Hayes-
Roth, 1978, for example, describes a study which seems to show it is not an
adequate explanation). In any case, it is apparent that it is not just a simple
hypothesis or model, but is really a whole complex of interlocking ideas.
Winston (1977) calls it an armamentorium.

Frame systems have been built to explore many different aspects of cognition. Examples include the work of Bobrow *et al.* (1977) on natural language understanding using frames, Novak (1977) on solving elementary problems, Lenat's (1976) work on finding interesting results in mathematics, Goldstein & Roberts's (1982) work on scheduling, Sridharan & Schmidt's (1978) work on interpreting others' actions, and, for a well known example on scripts, Schank & Abelson (1977). An examination of these will soon convince the reader of the truth of the observation above that the frame concept is not just a simple, clearly defined and unique theory. Let us consider some examples in more detail.

Goldstein & Roberts (1982) describe a frame-based system, NUDGE, which takes as input informal management scheduling requests, possibly incomplete, inconsistent, or only qualitative, and yields a schedule showing possible conflicts along with a list of strategies for resolving those conflicts. A program, BARGAIN, implementing traditional decision analysis techniques then takes NUDGE's output and resolves the conflicts. A system such as this would be of immense value in a hospital or medical practice, where complex scheduling of highly skilled professionals is necessary.

NUDGE has been written in the frame representation language FRL-0, which Goldstein & Roberts 'view as an experimental medium to study the utility of a few specific capabilities and their interactions'. They stress that it is not as comprehensive as, for example, KRL (Bobrow & Winograd, 1976).

To illustrate the structure of NUDGE, let us work through an example (see Goldstein & Roberts, 1982). Suppose NUDGE is asked to:

'Schedule a meeting with Bruce for Tuesday'.

This is informal, omitting such things as the place of the meeting, what time is preferred, the length of the meeting, whether there are preconditions (such as that Bruce should prepare a report to bring along), and what to do if Bruce is unavailable.

NUDGE has a hierarchical frame structure of around 100 frames, describing people, plans, demands on time and space, and so on. Aspects of a particular request cause particular frames to be instantiated, and this set of frames forms a *frame gestalt*, a data structure containing the information in the request. Default values, constraints, and procedures in the frame *gestalt* provide any missing data in the request. We shall look at this process in more detail below, but first let us continue with the example. In this case, using default values in the frames describing the preferences and other properties of the persons for whom the meeting is to be arranged, NUDGE expands the request to:

'Schedule a meeting with Bruce and you at 3 in the afternoon next

Tuesday, one week from tomorrow, lasting one hour, in your office to discuss the "Personal Assistant" project.'

The instantiated frames, the frame *gestalt*, which led to this expansion also provide a list of possible conflicts and suggest strategies for resolving them. Control then passes to BARGAIN which uses conventional techniques to select the optimal strategy and relay to the user:

'Your preferred time for meeting with Bruce on Tuesday is already filled by meeting with Mark. However, Mark's purpose is to discuss language research and Candy is available. Shall I reschedule Mark to see her instead?'

The simple approach to the difficulty would have been to find an alternative time for the meeting at which both the instigator of the request and Bruce were free. This might have meant choosing some day other than Tuesday, or some time other than 3 p.m., which is the known preference. These conflicts are avoided by taking a broader perspective – namely, by NUDGE knowing (by default) that the primary aim of the meeting with Mark is to discuss a particular topic which could equally well be handled by someone else. NUDGE is able to include this in its list of possible conflict resolution strategies for BARGAIN to consider.

Continuing the example, in reply to the question, the user says 'yes' and NUDGE responds:

'The meeting with Bruce is scheduled. Should Bruce prepare a written 'Personal Assistant' report?'

And so on.

The partially instantiated frames triggered by the informal request form the input to the *gestalt* formation process. A frame for the proposed meeting is activated and contains whatever can be extracted from the request. For example (the example frames below are adapted from Goldstein & Roberts, 1982):

MEETING37   FRAME
A-kind-of   PA-Meeting (Source: pragmatics S1)
Who   Ira   (Source: pragmatics S1)
                     Bruce   (Source: semantics S1)

. . .

S1 refers to the initial request, and Ira is the known name of the instigator of the request. *A-kind-of* indicates that *MEETING37* is a kind of *PA-Meeting* (this is a link in the property inheritance structure), that is, a meeting to discuss the 'Personal Assistant' project. This is known by default, on the basis of the common interests of Bruce and Ira. If no such defaults existed then a more general meeting frame (labelled simply *MEETING*) would have been used in place of *PA-Meeting*. *Who* has two values, Ira, and Bruce; this means that Ira and Bruce are the two participants for the meeting, Ira since he made the request, and Bruce because he was explicitly named in S1. Frames for *MEETING37*, Ira, and Bruce are linked by virtue of their slot/slot filler relationships above, as well as other relationships.

FRL-O uses six techniques to form the *gestalt* from the initial request:

(i) *Comments*: As the *MEETING37* frame above illustrates, comments (right hand side) record the source of the value in each slot. Using this information NUDGE can resolve any inconsistencies arising from different frames during *gestalt* formation. BARGAIN can also use this information to assess the reliability of various constraints.

(ii) *Abstraction*: This is the property inheritance feature. If we know something about meetings in general then we know it applies to the special case of *PA-Meetings*, unless we have information to the contrary.

(iii) *Defaults*: As we have remarked above, these provide powerful information on what the system should expect and what answers are typical. In NUDGE, the defaults of superior frames apply unless more reliable information usurps them.

(iv) *Constraints*: These can be applied to a slot to indicate requirements or preferences. For example in

> MEETING FRAME
> A-kind of   Activity
> Who   (Require)   A person with role 'chairman'
> When   (Preference)   Duration less than one hour
> . . .

The (Require) facet of the slot *Who* insists that a chairman must be present at each meeting.

(v) *Indirection*: This is information which appears in the *gestalt* if two frames are activated – information which is not relevant to either alone (or in conjunction with other frames), but only when they are instantiated together.

(vi) *Procedures*: FRL-O supports procedural attachment to slots. As an example of a demon, when the time of *MEETING37* is arranged, a procedure enters its name in a calendar for easy reference.

There is, of course, much more to FRL-O than the above might suggest. Interested readers are referred to Goldstein & Roberts (1982). This paper is particularly valuable because it does not simply stress the merits of FRL-O, but is honest about the weaknesses. They caution researchers about over-rapid introduction of complex techniques, and say: 'We plan to introduce additional techniques only as the simple generalised property list (i.e. frame) scheme of FRL-O proves inadequate.'

Goldstein & Roberts contrast frame structure approaches with the use of semantic primitives (§ 2.3). They illustrate the strength of the former (for certain kinds of situation) by noting that in the above dialogue the original request could have been instantiated as a *MEETING* frame and when, later, information permitting it to be recognised as a *PA-Meeting* occurred, the only necessary adjustment would be to redirect a pointer.

For our second example we turn to AM, a system described by Lenat (1976), which explores a particular domain within mathematics and attempts to find interesting new theorems. Note that this is not a theorem proving or deductive system (see Chapter 4). It confronts the task which many believe to lie at the root of human intelligence – not the (mechanistic) application of inference rules to prove a conjecture, but the very genesis of that conjecture itself. (One definition of human genius has it that genius is the ability to recognise new and important questions.) The system is excellently summarised by Lenat & Harris (1978).

Each mathematical concept that AM possesses is represented by a frame. Fig. 2.11 (adapted from Lenat & Harris, 1978) illustrates the prime number frame.

As usual the frames have many kinds of interrelationship and one standard kind is the specialisation and generalisation link – the property inheritance hierarchy. In the frame in Fig. 2.11 these links are stated explicitly in the *GENERALISATION* and *SPECIALISATION* slots.

Fig. 2.11. The prime number frame in AM. (From Lenat & Harris, 1978.)

NAME: Prime Numbers
DEFINITIONS:
 ORIGIN: Number-of-divisors-of $(x) = 2$
 PREDICATE-CALCULUS: Prime (x) iff (For-all z)
        $(z/x$ implies $z = 1$ XOR $z = x)$
 ITERATIVE: (for $x > 1$): For $i = 1$ from 2 to $x - 1$, not $(i \mid x)$
EXAMPLES: 2, 3, 5, 7, 11, 13, 17
 BOUNDARY: 2, 3
 BOUNDARY-FAILURES: 0, 1
 FAILURES: 12
GENERALISATIONS: Numbers, numbers with an even number of divisors.
        Numbers with a prime number of divisors.
SPECIALISATIONS: Odd primes, prime pairs, prime Uniquely-addables.
CONJECS: Unique factorisation, Goldbach's conjecture, Extrema of
        Divisors-of
ANALOGIES: Maximally-divisible numbers are converse extremes of
        Divisors-of
INTEREST: Conjec's tying Primes to Times, to Divisors-of, to closely
        related operations
WORTH: 800

AM begins with a set of partially completed frames and seeks to complete them and define new frames by applying heuristic rules (see § 2.5). There are 250 of the latter (see below), each being attached to the most general (highest in the property inheritance structure) concept to which they can be applied. By virtue of the specialisation links, each rule then applies to concepts lower in the structure.

AM maintains a list of tasks that it might try, these tasks being placed in a priority order. Examples of such tasks are: 'Fill-in examples of Primes', 'Fill-in new Algorithms for Set-union', and 'Generalise the concept of Prime'. AM's basic procedure is to select the top task from the list and try to accomplish it. To attempt the latter it collects all the rules which might accomplish the task and executes them. This can have three effects:

(i) Slots might be filled in. For example, some examples of primes may be created.

(ii) New concepts (frames) might be created.

(iii) New tasks might be added to the task list.

Lenat & Harris (1978) give examples of rules which might have each of these three effects. Respectively,

(i) R1: If examples of X are desired, where X is a kind of Y (for some more general concept Y), then check the examples of Y; some of them may be examples of X as well.

(ii) R2: If some (but not most) examples of X are also examples of Y (for some concept Y), then create a new concept defined as the intersection of those two concepts (X and Y).

(iii) R3: If very few examples of X are found, then add the following job to the agenda: 'Generalise the concept X.'

When AM proposes a new task, as in R3, it attaches a list of its reasons for suggesting the task. Thus a task suggested by several different rules may be worth investigating for several different reasons and so may be moved up the priority queue. The priority is also influenced by a task's relationship with the last task executed. By favouring tasks with close relations a focus of attention is maintained.

Lenat & Harris (1978, p. 30) give a description of AM at work:

> For example, at one point AM had some notions of sets, set-operations, numbers, and simple arithmetic. One heuristic rule it knew said '*If f is an interesting relation, Then look at its inverse*'. This rule fired after AM had studied 'multiplication' for a while. The r.h.s. of the rule then directed AM to define and study the relation 'divisors-of' (e.g. divisors-of (12) = {1, 2, 3, 4, 6, 12}). Another heuristic rule that later fired said '*If f is a relation from A into B, then it's worth examining those members of A which map into extremal*

members of B.' In this case, *f* was matched to 'divisors-of', *A* was 'numbers', *B* was 'sets of numbers', and an extremal member of *B* might be, e.g., a very *small* set of numbers. Thus this heuristic-rule caused AM to define the set of numbers with no divisors, the set of numbers with only 1 divisor, with only 2 divisors, etc. One of these sets (the last mentioned) turned out subsequently to be quite important; these numbers are of course the primes.

For our third example we turn to SAM (Schank *et al.*, 1975; Schank & Abelson, 1977), which stands for Script Applier Mechanism. SAM parses sentences into semantic primitives using the conceptual dependency representation (§ 2.3) and interprets sequences of events by means of frame-like structures called scripts built out of the primitive elements. After SAM has matched a story to suitable script(s) it can produce a summary or answer questions about it. (And note that, as a consequence of being built using the semantic primitive notion, it can produce summaries in foreign languages.)

SAM has three components:

(i) A parser component, which transforms each input sentence into its basic representation in the semantic primitives of conceptual dependency.

(ii) A memory component which ties the sentences together, sorting out the references of pronouns and updating data structures.

(iii) A third component which matches sentences from component (i) against scripts. A successful match yields a set of expectations about future sentences. This component also fills in any implications which were implicit but not explicitly stated in the story.

SAM has a companion program, PAM (Wilensky, 1978), which examines stories for goals that the characters wish to achieve and then attempts to find *plans* that will match the efforts to achieve those goals. Plans are appropriate for application when a script, highly specialised by definition, cannot be found to match.

Lehnert (1978) gives several examples of SAM at work.

2.5   Production systems

Newell & Simon (1972), in their classic work on human problem solving, neatly encapsulate the early development of production systems:

> The production system was one of those happy events, though in minor key, that historians of science often talk about: a rather well-prepared formalism, sitting in wait for a scientific mission. Production systems have a long and diverse history. Their use in symbolic logic starts with Post (1943), from whom the name is taken. They also show up as Markov algorithms (1954). Their use in linguistics, where they are also called rewrite rules, dates from

Chomsky (1957). As with so many other notions in computer science, they really entered into wide currency when they became operationalised in programming languages.

From their rather abstract origin they have developed in two directions, directions which typify artificial intelligence research as a whole. On the one hand they have been used to implement models of how humans think. (Newell & Simon, 1972, pp. 803–4: 'We confess to a strong premonition that the actual organisation of human programs closely resembles the production system organisation.'.) And on the other hand they have been used to build systems which apparently demonstrate intelligence (with no regard for whether or not they may be emulating humans). The first use provides an example of how the computer-oriented approach implicit in artificial intelligence work has had a major impact on psychology. As we discussed in Chapter 1, through writing programs to evaluate the theories the latter can be made much more precise and solid.

If one agrees with Newell & Simon above, then the suggestion from Davis & King (1977, p. 307) is interesting:

This has led to speculation that the interest in production systems on the part of those building high performance knowledge-based systems is more than a coincidence. It is suggested that this is a result of current research (re)discovering what has been learned by naturally intelligent systems through evolution–that structuring knowledge in a production system format is an effective approach to the organisation, retrieval and use of very large amounts of knowledge.

The success of some production rule based AI systems does give weight to this argument, and the production system methodology is clearly powerful. But whether this is a result of its equivalence to human cognitive processes, and whether this implies artificially intelligent systems ought to be similarly structured, are, we feel, still open questions.

Production systems for psychological modelling, while having the same underlying structure as applications systems, can be very different from them. The latter are generally larger and might be extremely complex (see Chapter 5), with much redundancy, while with the former there is an effort to achieve simplicity. For example, a typical approach to using production systems for psychological models is to study the way humans behave, perhaps by examining transcripts of them thinking aloud as they tackle a problem, and then attempting to find the smallest set of production rules (see below) which will duplicate the behaviour.

We should at least note here the somewhat paradoxical point (discussed in more detail in Chapter 5) that systems aimed at modelling humans are successful only if they also make the same kinds of mistakes and suffer from the same kinds of illusions as humans. Production systems used as the basic representation in an applications system, however, would ideally lead to no errors at all.

Looked at from the outside (as a black-box), production systems seem to present an extremely complex set of paths through a decision network, so complex in fact that it may not be feasible to write it down explicitly. The system thus gives the impression of being able to respond in a very flexible manner to a tremendous range of input data. Indeed, the paths taken through the decision network may not have been explicitly foreseen by the system designers. In contrast, conventional programs have a relatively simple control structure; that is, the branch nodes at which decisions are made regarding what to do next form a tree or graph which is not very complicated. This means that conventional programs can only respond to a relatively small set of input data formats. This fundamental flexibility of production systems has led to programs based on them being called *data-driven* or *pattern-directed*.

So much for production systems from the outside. Now what about the inside?

A production system has three basic components:

(i) A *database* (*blackboard, context, short term memory*, . . .) containing features describing the object (person, disease, concept, etc.) currently being examined.

(ii) A *knowledge-base* (*rule base*) containing a set of *rules*. The structure of these, which lie at the core of the production system concept, is explained immediately below.

(iii) An *interpreter* (*executive, control system*, . . .), a mechanism that compares items in the database with rules in the knowledge base and carries out alterations in the database according to the rules.

Rules in productions systems typically take the form

IF (conditions) THEN (assertions)

or   IF (antecedent) THEN (consequent)

or   IF (condition)   THEN (action)

The interpreter compares the left hand side conditions against the items in the database. When the conditions are satisfied – that is, when the database contains elements which match the left hand side of a rule – then the rule is said to *fire*, and its right hand side action is carried out. A typical action is to insert something into the database. For example the rule

IF A and B and C THEN D

adds D to the database whenever it finds A, B, and C in it. And the rule

IF measurement scale is ordinal THEN nonparametric tests
inserts 'nonparametric tests' in the database whenever it finds it is dealing with data measured on only an ordinal scale.

The left hand side conditions can be simple as in the above examples, or they can be very complex structures, perhaps even involving some kind of calculation or symbol manipulation to be applied to the elements of the database rather than a simple matching. Similarly, the right hand side consequents can be correspondingly as simple or complex. They might assert some formula in propositional or predicate calculus, add some structural description to the database, add a simple fact to the database, or modify some structure in the database.

The basic role of component (iii), the interpreter, is to implement a *recognise–act* cycle. Thus, to take the simple ideal case, the interpreter can take each of the rules one by one and compare their left hand sides with the database. When a match is found the rule fires, perhaps modifying the database, and the cycle starts again at the beginning of the rule list. (In practice, as we shall see, in applications-oriented production systems, this simple ideal has to be modified.)

As with all high level representations, production systems come in many shapes and forms. One useful distinction is between *pure* production systems and *performance* production systems. Pure production systems are simple in that their control structure is a straightforward recognise–act cycle applied to a uniform list of rules. The rules are not grouped into subclasses and there is no complicated *conflict resolution* strategy for choosing from a set of rules all of which have antecedents satisfied by the data base. The first of these eligible ones in the list is simply taken. Pure production systems find their most common use in psychological models.

In contrast, performance production systems can be extremely complicated. The rules may be grouped into subclasses, and sophisticated conflict resolution strategies may be implemented to choose one from the set of eligible rules. The adjective 'performance' is derived from the use of such production systems as the representation in programs aimed at performing some useful task (commonly presumed to require intelligence) and thus is close to our use of the term 'applications-oriented'. A typical example is their use as the fundamental representation in expert systems (Chapter 5).

A second useful categorisation concerns how the rules are applied. One approach is the *forward-planning* or *antecedent-driven* system. Here the left hand sides of the rules are compared with the database and the matching rule induces some modification of the database. The rules thus recognise patterns in the data and fire as soon as they do so. A *post hoc* description of the deductive process through which the system has gone would show a structure beginning with the initial database and culminating, after a series of rule applications, in a database containing the element it was originally wished to establish.

In contrast, in *backward-driven, goal-driven, consequent-driven*, or *expectation-driven* systems, the process starts with the goal element it is wished to establish. The rule base is then searched (in a simple system, sequentially through a list) to find a rule whose right hand side establishes this goal. The left hand side of this rule then provides a set of *subgoals*. If these subgoals can be established then, by application of the chosen rule, the right hand side objective will follow. Some of the subgoals may already be known – they may already exist in the database. Others may not. In this case searches are made to find other rules which have these latter subgoals as their consequents. Ultimately (if all goes well) the system arrives at a state when all the subgoals are already in the database – and the original goal then follows.

It has been claimed (see Chapter 5) that backward-chaining systems more closely resemble the way humans process information, although not every author agrees (Fox, Barber & Bardhan, 1980), and in any case – as we discuss in Chapter 5 – comparison with human processes may or may not be a useful criterion by which to judge expected performance of rule based systems. It is certainly true that backward-chaining systems focus attention and, because they usually have a simpler conflict resolution strategy (described below), it is easier to add new rules to a goal-driven system. In any case, in modern performance systems it is by no means unusual to find *both* forward- and backward-chaining being applied.

At this point it will probably be useful to look at an example. The following simple example of a backward-chaining system is taken from Waterman & Hayes-Roth (1978*b*, p. 10). Referring to Fig. 2.12:

> The letters represent data base elements and are considered true if in the data base. In this simple system, the action of firing a rule inserts the right-hand side letter into the data base.

Fig. 2.12. An example of a simple database and rule base for a production system. (From Waterman & Hayes-Roth, 1978*b*.)

DATA BASE:	*B C*	
RULES:	1. IF *B* and *D* and *E*	THEN *F*
	2. IF *D* and *G*	THEN *A*
	3. IF *C* and *F*	THEN *A*
	4. IF *C*	THEN *D*
	5. IF *D*	THEN *E*
	6. IF *A*	THEN *H*

Assume the given premise is that '*H* is true'. Since *H* is not in the data base it must be deduced by backward chaining through the rules. The system first chooses rule 6 and attempts to show that *A* is true, since *A* implies *H*. Unfortunately *A* is not in the data base and must itself be deduced. This can be attempted through either rule 2 or 3. Assume the system first tries rule 2. It must now show that both *D* and *G* are true. *D* is easy; it can be inferred from rule 4. *G* is another matter; nothing can be inferred about *G* since no rules contain G on the right-hand sides. The system now backs up and tries to infer *A* through rule 3. This time it succeeds since *C* is true and *F* can be inferred by showing that *B*, *D*, and *E* are true. A causal chain has now been produced that proves the given premise '*H* is true'.

Earlier, we defined the term 'conflict resolution' to mean the process of selecting one rule from the set of rules which had antecedents matching the database (or, in a *goal-driven* system, the set of rules which had consequents matching the current subgoal). In general, the problem is more pressing for left hand side driven systems. McDermott & Forgy (1978) discuss and give a comparative assessment of several conflict resolution strategies applied in left hand side driven systems. Since this is a useful assessment we shall summarise it here.

McDermott & Forgy identify two properties of production systems to consider when selecting a conflict resolution strategy:

(i) *Sensitivity*: a production system that is responsive to the demands of its environment is said to be *sensitive*.

(ii) *Stability*: a production system that maintains continuity in its behaviour displays a *stability*.

To some extent these properties are complementary, a sensitive system will adjust to a slight change in input data. On the other hand, a system which leaps around pursuing completely different goals as it responds to the environment would be difficult for the user to follow.

McDermott & Forgy describe five classes of conflict resolution strategies:

(a) *Production order*. Using a pre-established priority order. This is perhaps the earliest idea. It is the simplest and is found in pure production systems.

(b) *Special case*. If two rules match but one is a special case of the other (it has extra matching conditions) then this special case is chosen. And if some other rule is neither a special case nor a general case matches, then this rule takes overall priority.

(c) *Recency*. Selection strategies based on the ages of the matching elements – that is, how long since the data matching the rules was deduced or discovered.

(d) *Distinctiveness*. Use the distinctiveness of currently matching rules from earlier rules which have fired to create an order.

(e) *Arbitrary decision*. For example, randomly select a rule.

These authors discuss how these different strategies support their criteria of sensitivity and stability, and demonstrate that no single method is completely adequate, so that combinations must be adopted.

As an example of a conflict resolution strategy in a forward (left hand side) driven system we describe the approach used by Rychener & Newell (1978). This is an extremely clear description of an implemented conflict resolution strategy. Their project is designed ultimately to yield 'a large, generally intelligent system by gradual instruction, starting from a small initial system'. This initial system is an 'abstract job shop (AJS). The job shop has as its objective to produce objects with specific desired properties from raw materials according to some schedule. The shop contains stacks of raw material and partial products, machines that must be started with explicit commands, and means for transporting objects from one place to another within the shop'.

For conflict resolution they apply the following rules in order:

(i) Refraction: a production is not fired twice on the same data (instantiation of a pattern) unless some part of that data has been reinserted into working memory since the previous firing. This prevents most infinite loops and other useless repetitions.

(ii) Lexicographic recency: the production using the most recently inserted elements of working memory is preferred. 'Most recent' is determined lexicographically, i.e., if there is a tie on the most recent element used, the next most recent elements are compared, and so on; use of any element is considered more recent than using none, e.g. (AX) is ordered before (A). Recency level discriminates at the level of individual actions within productions, rather than taking all the actions performed by a production to be of equal recency. This rule serves to focus the attention of the system very strongly on more recent events, allowing current goals to go to completion before losing control.

(iii) Special case: a production is preferred that has more conditions, including negative conditions that do not match to specific memory elements. Most of the meaning of having one production be a special case of another is captured by rule (ii), since a special case that uses more data than a general one is lexicographically more recent. Preferring special cases to general ones follows the expectation that a specific method is more appropriate to a situation than a more general one. Also, this is consonant with a strategy of augmentation by providing more discriminative rules.

(iv) Production recency: the more recently created production is performed. This allows identically conditioned rules (with perhaps contradictory actions) to be distinguished and assumes that a more recent introduction is more correct.

(v) Arbitrary: a selection is made among multiple matches to the same production using the same data.

As a matter of practice, conflict resolution rarely requires more than the first two rules.

The conflict resolution strategy can be implemented in the interpreter (i.e. the interpreter can decide which rule to examine first) but there is a much more exciting idea. This is the notion of the *meta-rule*. A meta-rule is a rule, just like any other, but it contains information about what rules to try next. Thus, if a particular situation arises in the database a meta-rule may fire and its consequents will lead the system to try a particular subclass of rules next. One merit of meta-rules is that the conflict resolution strategy becomes explicit, rather than being a part of the interpreter and therefore hidden in a programming language which may be opaque to the user. A second property is that the conflict resolution strategy can vary between different parts of the system. Thus, for example, in a goal-driven system each subgoal can have its own conflict resolution strategy.

Although we cannot delve too deeply into the taxonomy of production systems and the differences between various architectures which pass under that name, there are two important types which should be mentioned. First, there are *commutative* production systems. Nilsson (1982) defines these as production systems having the following properties with respect to a database D:

(1) Each member of the set of rules applicable to D is also applicable to any database produced by applying an applicable rule to D.

(2) If the goal condition is satisfied by D, then it is also satisfied by any database produced by applying any applicable rule to D.

(3) The database that results by applying to D any sequence composed of rules that are applicable to D is invariant under permutations of the sequence.

With a commutative system an *irrevocable* control process can be used – that is, one which does not permit backtracking. This limitation is of no consequence because if there is some sequence of rules which can achieve the desired goal, then whatever the sequence used no rule ever yields a database from which the goal state cannot be reached. In some ways this makes things much simpler.

A second important group of production systems is *decomposable* systems. In such a system the database can be split into independent components – independent in the sense that they can be processed separately. Nilsson (1982, p. 37) gives a metaphor:

> We might imagine that such a global database is a 'molecule' consisting of individual 'atoms' bound together in some way. If the applicability conditions of the rules involve tests on individual atoms only, and if the effects of the rules are to substitute a qualifying atom by some new molecule (that, in turn, is composed of atoms), then we might as well split the molecule into its atomic components and work on each part separately and independently. Each rule application affects only that component of the global database used to establish the precondition of the rule. Since some of the rules are being applied essentially in parallel, their order is unimportant.

This is a convenient point to mention a debate which has become known as the 'procedural–declarative controversy'. It might seem obvious that some knowledge is best encoded in the form of procedures – ways to do things – while other knowledge is best encoded as declarations – statements about things. Sometimes, however, there is no apparent best choice and people's opinions differ. This has led to a controversy which has had a formative influence on the development of artificial intelligence. On the one hand we had 'declarativists' extolling the virtues of large collections of static knowledge being processed by relatively simple programs. And on the other we had 'proceduralists' enthusing about the merits of focussing attention on the reasoning processes. It seems, in fact, that a pragmatic approach is best – whether knowledge should be encoded as declarations or procedures depends on what one intends to do with it. Certainly, the controversy faded out rather than reaching any conclusion. (I cannot help being reminded here of a remark made by the eminent psychologist Paul Meehl, who said of theories in psychology (Meehl, 1978, p. 807):

> Most of them suffer the fate that General MacArthur ascribed to old generals – they never die, they just slowly fade away. In the developed sciences, theories tend either to become widely accepted and built into the larger edifice of well-tested human knowledge or else they suffer destruction in the face of recalcitrant facts and are abandoned, perhaps regretfully as a 'nice try'. But in fields like personology and social psychology, this seems not to happen. There is a period of enthusiasm about a new theory, a period of attempted application to several fact domains, a period of disillusionment as the negative data come in, a growing bafflement

about inconsistent and unreplicable empirical results, multiple resort to *ad hoc* excuses, and then finally people just sort of lose interest in the thing and pursue other endeavours.)

As is evident from Nilsson (1982), production system architectures have been used in many different ways. One use in particular is worth singling out because of the impact it is having on the world. This is their use as the basic representation in expert systems (medical examples are given in Chapter 5). When used in expert systems, the basic deductive mechanisms outlined above are extended through the use of 'certainty factors' attached to elements of the database and the rules. These give measures of confidence so that the system can be used for 'inexact reasoning' – an important feature in a real world full of doubt and shades of grey. Chapter 5 discusses these.

We might summarise the properties of production systems and say that the production system concept is a powerful knowledge representation because:

(1) The knowledge is stored in a modular way – permitting easy modification and incremental growth. Rules can be added, modified, or deleted without having to worry about whether some other part of the program must also be changed (as would be the case with a conventional program).

(2) The knowledge representation is *uniform*. This means that other workers can examine and understand the system. In contrast, programs embodying complex interlocking and interrelated structures (such as semantic nets) can be difficult to disentangle.

(3) Production systems have a broad field of attention – any changes in the database can affect the outcome (not so in conventional programs, where the system typically looks at only one or two control items at any point in the flow of control).

(4) Any rule can fire at any time. All rules are eligible to fire should their criterion data items occur.

(5) Production systems react quickly to small changes.

Of course, no knowledge representation is perfect for all applications. Disadvantages of production systems are:

(1) The opacity of their control structure. It is not easy to determine the route through the rules and database elements that the system will choose to examine. Of course since the system is designed to be flexible and to interact with potentially complex environments it would be unrealistic to expect the set of routes it can follow to be simple. One cannot have things both ways. As we suggest below, production systems are suitable for domains in which the knowledge can be specified but for which its use cannot be given.

(2) Searching large rule bases can be a problem and work on ways to make this more efficient is continuing.

Production systems are well suited to domains which can be in many distinct states, which permit a control structure not needing multiple interlocking processes, and which are not sufficiently well formalised for a rigorous mathematical model to be applied. In the latter case a conventional program based on the model would be more efficient.

The last few years have witnessed an avalanche of interest in production systems. This has been stimulated mainly by the practical value of expert systems, which are characteristically based on a production system architecture. The production system idea is undoubtedly powerful, but a cautionary note should be inserted here. It is not the answer to every question; there is a danger of overemphasising the merits of such representations to the detriment of other powerful representations. The time may well come when we need well-developed formalisms in these other areas and we must not be misled by the overenthusiasms of current fashions.

Some examples of programs based on the production system representation are a system which played poker and modified and extended its rule base as it became more experienced (Waterman, 1970); a system for modelling within-group interactions (Friend, 1973); one to model children's seriation behaviour (Young, 1973); the well known work on human problem solving described by Newell & Simon (1972); work on modelling human visualisation processes (Moran, 1974); speech understanding systems (F. Hayes-Roth & Mostow, 1975); and a system for automatic synthesis of computer programs (Barstow, 1977*a*, *b*). Examples of expert systems using production systems are given in Chapter 5.

Fig. 2.13. Levels for knowledge representation.

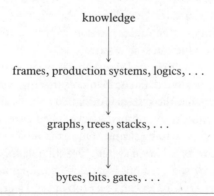

2.6   Levels of representation

Consider Fig. 2.13. This shows the various levels at which one might choose to discuss knowledge representation (see also Chapter 1). At the top we have the *high level* representations discussed in the preceding sections. These are closely related to the structure of the knowledge being studied and address questions which at times verge on the philosophical. As we proceed down the diagram we find more detailed descriptions, descriptions of how the high order structures might actually be put into a computer. Finally, at the bottom, we have a very *low level* representation, describing what is in the computer's memory in very basic elements such as bits and electronic logic gates. Clearly, any description of an interconnecting collection of frames made in the terms of this lowest level representation would be incredibly complex – so complex that it would be of no value in shedding light on the higher level structure. (Note that this diagram illustrates where artificial intelligence and computer science meet – at the 'graphs, trees, stacks, . . .' level.)

However, since all high level representations must be implemented in terms of some lower level representation, it is worth our while to consider them briefly. We shall not sink to the level of the bit, but only to the 'graphs, trees, stacks, . . .' level.

Many representations at this level can be regarded as being a collection of items (sometimes called *records*) each composed of one or more *fields*. Each field can hold either a *symbol* (or several symbols) or a pointer to another record.

A simple example is the *singly-linked list* shown in Fig. 2.14. Each rectangle represents a record, and within each record some field (perhaps the last one) contains a pointer to the next record. The last record has a pointer field containing some symbol showing that it is the last one (and, so, does not point onwards). Starting at the beginning (record A) one can search through the list in order until one reaches the end (record E) extremely efficiently by following the pointers. However, a limitation of this sort of list is that one can only go backwards at great computational expense. To get from B to C one has only to examine the pointer field in B. But to get from C to B one has to examine all records to find that which points to C.

This problem can be overcome by using *doubly-linked* lists (or *two-way*

Fig. 2.14. A singly-linked list.

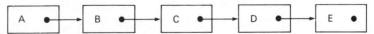

Fig. 2.15. A doubly-linked list.

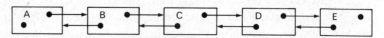

Fig. 2.16. A stack (*a*) having an element added (*b*) and two elements removed (*c*).

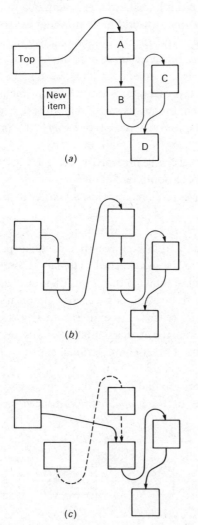

linked lists) as in Fig. 2.15. Now each record contains two pointer fields, one pointing to the preceding list element and the other to the succeeding list element. This leads to greater search efficiency at the cost of more storage requirements.

A second way to overcome the limitation of singly-linked lists is to use a *circular* list. This is a singly-linked list in which the last record contains a pointer leading to the first record.

An important extension of the list concept is the notion of a *stack*. A stack is a linked list which can have records added to or deleted from one end (called the *top*). Fig. 2.16 shows a new element being added and then two elements being removed from a stack. Note that the deletion is accomplished by moving the pointers – that is, by changing the value of the pointer indicating the top of the stack. No actual erasing of data is required. The dotted lines in Fig. 2.16*c* still exist, but they cannot be accessed since TOP points to B. This idea of moving pointers is a very powerful one.

When a new item is added, a stack is said to be *pushed down*. When one is removed the stack *pops up*. The phrase 'last in, first out' is often used to describe this behaviour.

In some cases the pointers in lists can be done away with. This is the case for lists of fixed size and lists that can grow (but not shrink) which have records of a uniform size. In such a case the data items can simply be placed in consecutive blocks in the computer's memory. If the records have different sizes then the same approach can be used provided information about the sizes is stored (for example, in a directory at the start of the list). This sort of structure is called a *table* – but one must not be misled into supposing that this means it can only contain numerical information. As elsewhere, any sort of symbols can be stored.

Another important extension is the *graph*. A graph is a collection of *nodes* (or *vertices*), these being the records, joined together by *edges* (or *links*), these being pointers between records. Fig. 2.17 illustrates one. A semantic network is an example of a graph. If the edges have a direction the graph is

Fig. 2.17. A directed graph.

called a *digraph* and the edges have arrows indicating their direction. Graphs may or may not contain *circuits*, sequences of nodes and edges forming closed loops. Graphs which do not contain any circuits are called *trees*; these are very important structures as we shall see in later chapters. Fig. 2.18 shows a tree graph: node A is called the *root* node (and note that in this drawing, which is typical of the way graphs are portrayed, the root node is at the top of the diagram).

Working down a tree from some node we come to its *daughter* (or *child*) nodes. G, H, and I are the daughter nodes of F. Working up a tree we come to *parent* nodes. C is the parent of F. If there is a path down a tree from a node X to a node Y we say that X is an *ancestor* of Y and Y is a *descendant* of X. A binary tree is a special kind of tree in which each node has at most two offspring.

So much for low level representations. Returning to high level representations, the descriptions that have been given throughout this chapter are rather idealised. In all but the simplest psychological theory-testing models one finds that the implementations are considerably more complex than might have been suggested above. Frequently, multiple representations are used, perhaps because this enables the best of both worlds to be gained, or perhaps because two representations work together (for example, a semantic network being the database of a production system). In choosing a representation one must think about the nature of the knowledge to be modelled and the types of manipulation it is to undergo. On the subject of choice of representation, Szolovits (1982*b*, p. 10) says: 'During the past ten years, the notion has gained acceptance that reasoning becomes simpler if *the structure*

Fig. 2.18. A tree graph.

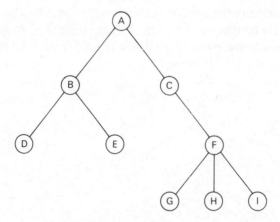

of the representation reflects the structure of the reality being reasoned about. Much current research focuses on the design of new knowledge representation languages which permit this principle to be applied'.

Up until recently LISP (Winston & Horn, 1981; Siklossy, 1976) has been the most popular artificial intelligence language. More recently, Prolog (Clocksin & Mellish, 1981) has attracted considerable interest. With different aims in mind, and to make particular domains easy to describe and particular types of knowledge easy to manipulate, several other languages have been developed. Examples are KRL (Bobrow & Winograd, 1976), OWL (Szolovits, Hawkinson & Martin, 1977), PLANNER (Hewitt, 1972), CONNIVER (Sussman & McDermott, 1972), QA4 (Rulifson, Derkson & Waldinger, 1972) and POPLER (Davies, 1972).

To conclude this chapter it seems fitting to say a word about the relative merits of a large knowledge base with simple reasoning mechanisms on the one hand, and sophisticated reasoning mechanisms on the other. Based on their experience, Goldstein & Roberts (1982, p. 257) say:

'The performance of NUDGE confirms that for well-defined, formal situations, the traditional power-based approach is appropriate. But for the problem of defining these formal situations when given only informal specifications, a knowledge-based approach is necessary'.

Currently the knowledge-based approach seems to be the more popular and I would suggest that this is at least partly due to the adoption of the production system architecture in expert systems encouraging people to tackle ill-structured domains. Chapter 5 contains a lengthy discussion of the impact of the degree of structure in psychiatric theory on the selection of a representation.

2.7 Further reading

Bobrow & Collins (1975) contains an interesting collection of papers referring to issues of representation, while Amarel (1968) gives an illustration of a series of representations, of increasing power, being applied to the missionaries and cannibals river-crossing puzzle.

As far as logic goes, there are, of course, a great many texts available. Pospesel (1976) is a good and in places amusing one, with a large number of examples of analysing English sentences using predicate calculus. Nilsson (1982) has a very clear chapter on the predicate calculus and Clocksin & Mellish (1981) provide an eminently readable introduction to the language Prolog.

On semantic networks, apart from the references cited in § 2.3, other important early work and general descriptions are given in Raphael (1968),

Simmons & Slocum (1972), Simmons (1973), Woods (1975), Hendrix (1976) and Findler (1979).

For work on frames the seminal work is, of course, Minsky (1981). Scripts are described in Schank & Abelson (1977).

Production systems have experienced a tremendous boost in popularity recently. Nilsson (1982) is an excellent volume, providing a general introduction to artificial intelligence using production systems as the basic representation. Davis & King (1977) is to be recommended as a shorter tutorial paper providing an overview. A set of extremely stimulating papers describing work in progress and covering production systems from all angles is Waterman & Hayes-Roth (1978*a*).

As far as the procedural/declarative controversy goes, a discussion is given in Winograd (1975), and Winston (1977) has an entertaining and informative dialogue between a declarativist and a proceduralist.

Recommended books dealing with lower level representations are Beidler (1982) and Knuth (1973).

3

Machine understanding of natural language

3.1 Introduction

Natural languages are simply those used for everyday life by humans. English, Chinese, Urdu, and so on are natural languages. They grow rather than being developed or designed and as a consequence have the characteristic that superimposed on top of their regularities they have a high degree of irregularity and complexity. It is this which makes developing programs for natural language understanding such a challenging and interesting task.

In contrast to natural languages we have *artificial languages*. These are systems deliberately built by humans for communication – usually but not always for communication within a restricted domain about a limited topic. Examples of artificial languages are musical notation, programming languages, and mathematics. The latter is in fact a whole set of languages used for discussing abstract concepts. The advantages of using artificial languages, as we have remarked elsewhere, include their precision (they lack the ambiguity of natural language) and their conciseness (in mathematics, for example, a single symbol may translate a whole page of natural language text).

In fact we may summarise and say that, typically, artificial languages:

(i) Are less ambiguous than natural languages.

(ii) Cannot express the range of concepts of natural languages.

(iii) Are smaller than natural languages. They may have smaller vocabularies and they may have a more limited set of ways of combining the elements of the vocabulary.

(iv) Are much better suited than natural languages for describing certain kinds of concepts and for certain applications.

(v) The fact that they have often been designed with certain aims in mind makes them more efficient when used for those aims.

(vi) They usually have more rigid syntactic requirements (as anyone who has programmed a computer will testify).

Inverting these properties tells us that natural languages are ambiguous, powerful, large, and general – all of which present obvious problems to anyone exploring the possibility of machine understanding of natural language.

At this point, before we begin to investigate this possibility, it might be worthwhile noting why the branch of artificial intelligence concerned with natural language understanding is so important for psychiatry. There are a number of reasons.

Primarily, of course, there is the central role of language as a mode of human behaviour. As a behavioural window on the mind language takes a pre-eminent position. Language and linguistic interactions lie at the centre of psychiatry and psychiatric diagnosis – in the clinical interview, for example.

A second point is that language is fundamental to human intelligence. It is not an exaggeration to say that the problems of language comprehension and generation are the same as the problems of intelligence. Solve one and we have solved the other. In many ways this makes language a particularly attractive area within artificial intelligence since it is more precisely defined and delimited than 'intelligence'. We know what it is we are trying to do, without being distracted by fruitless discussions of what 'intelligence' is.

As far as psychiatry goes, an exciting third reason for exploring natural language processing is the use of computers for interviewing patients. This is, of course, controversial and we will discuss it later.

Throughout the remainder of this chapter we will be faced with a number of interwoven threads. Two of them are so important that we briefly describe them here. They are the two approaches to studying language understanding arising from, on the one hand, linguistics and on the other hand computer science. The former tends to focus on linguistic features and particular structures, while the latter has primarily addressed global models and concentrated on how language is processed. There is, of course, a parallel here between this situation and more general work on understanding human mentation, where psychologists have tended to address small domains – attempting a bottom-up approach – while artificial intelligence researchers have ignored the details and attempted to construct global models. Proponents of the first approach would probably maintain that concentrating on small manageable areas leads to better grasp of fundamentals – and that when enough such areas have been explored one has a sound foundation for a general theory. Against this, proponents of the second, global, approach might argue that the first leads to a tendency to focus on the easier problems, glossing over the hard. The second approach, while not exploring any particular aspect of language as deeply as the first, by necessity has to make a stab at all problem areas. Moreover, a further important advantage of this approach is that the success of the global theory can be assessed by comparison with human language processing. Validation of the first, linguistic, approach is more difficult.

The reader will no doubt also appreciate something of the science/ engineering distinction creeping in here. The first approach is very much science: trying to understand some aspect of nature (in this case, the human brain). The second approach is drifting towards engineering: trying to build a system which performs in a recognised way and might even do useful work.

Another point which applies to artificial intelligence work in general but is perhaps most striking in language work is that, only naturally, published accounts of programs tend to emphasise the achievements rather than the shortcomings. Until recently most natural language programs were research projects rather than marketable products and as such, once the Ph.D. had been gained, in most cases the researcher went on to other things leaving the program to become outdated and gather dust. The result was an unverifiable distorted impression of the abilities that such programs had. In addition to this – pushing from below, as it were – we have the impact of advances in computer technology, permitting researchers to build more powerful systems with larger vocabularies, more complex grammars, and a more sophisticated world model. Current programs would have been totally infeasible only twenty years ago, so we must naturally ask what language understanding systems will look like in twenty years time. The prospect is clearly very exciting.

Of course, the property of programs arousing considerable interest and then dying through lack of developmental support, leaving published accounts only of their virtues, is not something which is peculiar to language work. It occurs throughout artificial intelligence. Rare exceptions, discussing systems' weaknesses, are the INTERNIST project (see Chapter 5), Tennant's (1981, p. 10) honest discussion of his Automatic Advisor program and Winograd's (1973) criticism of SHRDLU (see below and see also Boden, 1977 for further criticism). It should also be noted, in this general context, that the fact that programs fade away has the beneficial result that the epistemological ideas represented within them can also be replaced. New and better ideas can be explored.

In discussing natural language processing systems we are faced with a categorisation problem. Some way must be found to split the collection of systems into sensible subclasses so that the techniques they use can be addressed in a coherent and structured way. The difficulty arises because, firstly, systems tend to use a multiplicity of ideas, not just a single easily classifiable approach, and secondly, the different approaches themselves do not have rigid boundaries, but merge into each other. We shall see examples of this below.

Winograd (1976, a reprint of his 1972 Ph.D. thesis) distinguished four categories of natural language processing program:

(i) *Special format systems*. Systems which only accept input sentences of a certain kind or kinds. Such systems are only suited to the type of domain for which they were designed but despite this they give impressive performance on those problems because of the match of formalism and problem area.

(ii) *Text-based systems*. Systems in which raw input text is stored and questions are answered by finding closest matches between the question and the text. Such an approach has the advantage that it is not restricted to a single domain, as is (i), but it clearly has severe limitations. In no way could such a system be described as intelligent, and it is clear that the human brain does not function in this way.

(iii) *Limited logic systems*. Limited logic systems take a step in the right direction by transforming the input to a uniform representation. Questions in the form of one of a set of standard formats can then be answered, with the question-answering procedure specially encoded as part of the control mechanism.

(iv) *General deductive systems*. The problems with limited logic systems were simply that they were limited and could only handle information or questions in certain ways. The natural extension is to adopt one of the general knowledge representations outlined in Chapter 2. General deductive systems adopt this idea and, moreover, they also use the idea that human knowledge *about* knowledge (about how to solve problems, for example) should also be represented by the same scheme.

Other categorisations would be possible and all will overlap to a greater or lesser extent. The one we have adopted is basically delineated by the subheadings within this chapter and we outline it below. First, however, note the important point that effective language understanding requires processing at many levels. The endings of words must be matched, words must occur in acceptable order in the sentence, and sentences must combine to give a meaningful whole. This will become more clear as we work through the chapter.

We begin our outline in the next section, with the very basic idea of *pattern matching* systems. These are simply sequential lists of words or word types which are compared with an input string. Such patterns can be encoded as *transition networks*, structures which, as we shall see, can be extended to lead to extremely powerful formalisms for natural language processing.

The notion that there are patterns – regularities – in sentences, which can be matched, suggests that we should search for more universal sets of patterns. Indeed, that we should attempt to reduce the whole language to a set of rules which generate all valid sentences and which only generate valid sentences. This leads us to the study of *syntax* and *grammars*. Such a study can go in two directions. One is that taken by linguists, which is the path of context-free, context-sensitive, and transformational grammars. We shall discuss this path since it is important to understand these ideas in order to appreciate the artificial intelligence work and to relate it to work in computer science.

The second direction, predominantly the work of artificial intelligence researchers, was developed in parallel with the above. Whereas linguists were concerned with formulating grammars which could generate syntactically correct sentences, artificial intelligence workers were concerned with analysing sentences – splitting them into their component parts and identifying the relationships between these. Such analysis can be carried out using extensions of transition network ideas, namely *recursive transition networks* and *augmented transition networks*.

Of course, syntax alone does not make a natural language. In addition to syntax, describing structure, we must also consider *morphology*, describing the form of the words, *pragmatics*, describing world knowledge, and *semantics*, describing the mapping between the language and the world. Again this division into four classes is not perfect. Thus Raphael (1968, p. 39) says:

> The boundary between syntactics and semantics is hazy. For example, some linguists classify the so-called 'mass-nouns' (e.g. 'water') as a separate grammatical group because they do not take the article. However, the distinction between 'I want meat' and 'I want a steak' seems to be basically a semantic one.

Semantics, concerned with meaning, is clearly of central importance and has had an impact on computer natural language processing systems second only to that of syntax.

Note that although many (perhaps most) natural language understanding systems split the process into several subprocesses (e.g. word recognition, syntactic analysis, and semantic analysis), this is not necessary. Work on humans suggests that we utilise knowledge from several different types of analysis simultaneously. Some of the more advanced computer systems have also adopted this strategy. A major difference between human and machine processing is, of course, the parallel versus serial distinction. I believe that the current development of parallel central processing units and interacting processors will stimulate great advances in machine language work. For purposes of exposition, however, it is, of course, much easier to keep things separate. (SHRDLU, described below, integrates syntactic and semantic processing, and ELIZA (Weizenbaum, 1965) integrates semantic analysis and simple pattern matching. The latter accomplishes it by matching patterns and keywords and by ordering keywords according to their likely semantic importance.)

As we note below, early work (stimulated by an interest in translation) did not recognise the essential requirement for a natural language understanding system to have some kind of internal world model. In retrospect this oversight seems absurd – but we have the advantage of knowledge of the developments described below, most of which have taken place in the last twenty years. (There is an unfortunate tendency in popular literature to decry early mistaken scientific theories as foolish – as if Henry Cavendish, for example, must have been a borderline idiot not to see how ridiculous phlogiston was. Needless to say, it is easy for us, with the benefit of hundreds of years of work by men of genius, to point out where the early workers went wrong. But this does not imply that their interpretations and ideas were not the most appropriate to make in the context of their own time and knowledge.)

A cautionary note that the reader should bear in mind while reading the discussion below is that it is naive to expect a perfect natural language processing program. Even humans are not perfect: they misinterpret sentences, are confused by ambiguity, and argue about 'correct' syntactic forms (for example, when is it appropriate, if ever, to split an infinitive?). Assessment of computer programs, in fairness, should only be in terms of the type and frequency of their mistakes compared to those of humans.

A fitting remark with which to end this introductory section would be to note the advances of the last two decades, to invite the reader to speculate on the next two decades, and to observe that there are useful systems now commercially available which use a subset of natural language.

3.2   Simple pattern matching

The very simplest kind of pattern with which an input sentence could be compared would be one consisting of words – a *literal pattern*. So, for example, if our program had stored within it the sentence pattern 'The cat sat on the mat', then whenever the input was 'The cat sat on the mat' it would be recognised. Whenever the input was not this sentence the pattern would fail to recognise it and, since it simply recognises or fails to do so, it would give no further information.

This is clearly of limited value to say the least. One of the defining concepts of natural language is that it is unbounded; a user can formulate a sentence that nobody has ever created before. So even if a system based on simple pattern matching was astronomically large it would ultimately fail.

One extension, permitting more powerful pattern matches, is through the use of *wild cards*. These are simply spaces in the pattern, which can be filled by any word. Thus

> The .... sat on the mat.
> The .... sat on the .....
> The .... on the .....

Such *open patterns* are clearly much more powerful, allowing a wide range of input sentences to be matched with just a single pattern. (SIR (Raphael, 1968), one of the systems described at the end of this chapter, uses open patterns.)

Going yet further, we introduce the concept of *lexical category*. A lexical category is simply a class of word. Thus noun, verb, and adjective are distinct lexical categories. Using these we can create *lexical patterns*, consisting of sequences of words, wild cards, and lexical categories. Thus

> The *noun* sat on the *noun*.
> The *noun verb* on the *noun*.
> The *noun verb preposition* the *noun*.

Compared with open patterns, lexical patterns help us refine the match. For example, the last open pattern above will accept

> The sit hop on the red,

while the third lexical pattern above rejects this because 'sit' and 'red' are not nouns.

This is a convenient place to make an important point about lexical categories. It is important because not only does it apply to word classes but – as we shall see – an exactly analogous point applies to more general structural elements of grammars. The point is that *there is no such thing as the grammar of a language*. At school we learn about English grammar: how different words are of different kinds, play different roles in sentences, and how sentences can be decomposed into various clauses in a methodical and algorithmic way. But the fact is that there is more than one way in which such a structural decomposition may be carried out. Certain ways are suitable for certain objectives and may be rather poor for others. Thus one can choose or even design a grammar to suit oneself. There is no natural partitioning of a language into subcomponents. Winograd (1983, p. 52) further says: 'It is now accepted as obvious by linguists that the categories applying to one language cannot be applied directly to a different language, even one that is related or a derivative'. (He then slightly relaxes this by adding: 'However, there appear to be some fundamental similarities among the structures of all languages, for instance the presence of categories corresponding roughly to our notions of noun and verb'.) Incidentally, Winograd (1983) is to be thoroughly recommended. It influenced this present discussion of pattern marching systems.

Literal patterns, open patterns, and lexical patterns are all *simple patterns*. A further extension introduces the class of *variable patterns*. These permit several spaces in a pattern, and have the spaces labelled to indicate that the word occupying some space must reappear elsewhere. For example, the pattern

The *1* over there is my *1*

would match the input sentences

The cat over there is my cat,

The house over there is my house.

but it would not match

The cat over there is my oldest

The cat over there is mine.

One can extend the power of these simple pattern matching devices in a number of ways. For example, one could store a list of legal endings (-ed, -ing, -est, etc.) and split any of these off from a word before trying to match the stem. The term for the basic unit of meaning derived from such a splitting is a *morpheme*. Thus 'book' is a single morpheme, 'quickest' has two (quick and -est), and 'disambiguation' has three (dis-, ambiguous, -ation).

Simple pattern matching systems can also be easily extended to generate responses to input sentences. The trick is to match an input sentence, binding certain words of the input to labels, and substitute these words for the matching labels in a template of an output sentence. Thus the pattern

I am *1* most of the time

would match the input

I am sad most of the time

and cause the output template

Do you think it's good to be *1*?

to be completed as

Do you think it's good to be sad?

Fig. 3.1. A very simple transition network.

Or, a more complicated example,

    1 and *2* like *3*

would match

    Jack and Jill like John

and the output template

    And does *3* like *1* and *2?*

would produce

    And does John like Jack and Jill?

  This is, of course, not restricted to nouns.

  Patterns such as those above are all very well, but it is clear that they are quite limited. A very large number of patterns would be needed to cover even a moderate domain of discourse without the inadequacies of the mechanism showing through. The basic problem is that we need a separate pattern for each sentence structure. A more effective approach is to take advantage of regularities between the patterns. A common way to present this idea is through the use of *transition networks*.

  Fig. 3.1 is a transition network which would match the input sentence 'The book is interesting'. One can imagine a pointer passing along the numbered states whenever a word in the input matches a lexical category connecting two states. Thus the transition from state 1 to state 2 occurs because 'The' is in the lexical class of determiners. A successful match is indicated by arrival at the fifth, terminal node.

  The string 'The book wit interesting', on the other hand, would not be accepted. 'Wit' is not a verb and so would not permit the transition between nodes 3 and 4. The process would fail.

  So far, of course, we have introduced nothing which is not in the lexical pattern idea outlined above. But now consider Fig. 3.2. An extra loop, labelled 'adjective' has been added, which both begins and ends at node 2. Thus, in matching a string, we come into node 2 from node 1 using a determiner. We can then leave node 2 in two ways: either by a noun to node

Fig. 3.2. A transition network with an iterative loop.

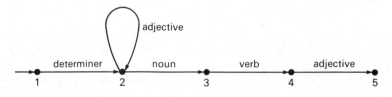

3, as before, or by an adjective – which returns us to node 2. Thus input sentences without adjectives before the noun (as before) and input sentences with adjectives before the noun will both be matched by this network. Moreover, input sentences with an arbitrary number of such adjectives will be matched – the loop from node 2 to node 2 will simply be repeated. Thus the transition network of Fig. 3.2 will match

The book is interesting.

The big book is interesting.

The small brown book is interesting.

For illustration, Fig. 3.3. shows a more complicated transition network. This would match all of

The big man hit the ball to the dog.

John hit the ball.

John hit Jack.

With additional power comes additional complexity and extra problems. The network in Fig. 3.3 shows multiple entry points and two cases where states have more than one outgoing arc with the same label. How is the transition network to choose which arc to match against an eligible input word? And worse, what if an input word belonging to two lexical categories (e.g. a ring and to ring, his hate and to hate, lead the metal and to lead) happened to occur at a node with an arc for each of these categories? How, then, to choose? The answer, unfortunately, lies in a more complicated control structure.

There are two common approaches. One involves choosing one of the eligible arcs arbitrarily and backtracking if it turns out that a mistake was made (because the process terminates in failure). The second involves developing all possibilities in parallel. Other schemes are possible – such as looking ahead to try to identify which interpretation is correct and then adopting this on a deterministic basis. Semantics also has a role to play here, as we outline below.

Pattern matching systems as outlined above are simple – but simple does not mean poor. Consider, for example, the human ability to recognise ungrammatical sentences and to attribute to them the correct meaning. A considerable proportion of human conversation is conducted in ungram-

Fig. 3.3. A more complicated transition network.

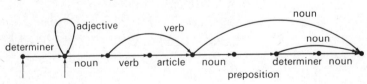

matical terms. Pattern matching systems can also have such strengths (by making use of those pattern components that they *can* recognise and ignoring the remainder). This is in contrast to highly structured parsers of the kind we see below. Of course, pattern matching systems lose out by not being able to pick up all of the subtleties which can be teased out from a formally correct sentence. This can at times lead to errors in understanding which makes the system appear stupid.

Chapter 6 describes PARRY, a very impressive natural language understanding system which is fundamentally based on pattern matching ideas.

3.3 Syntax

Since practically everyone else seems to quote Lewis Carroll's *Jabberwocky*, I may as well do so too to illustrate a point. The first verse goes:

> 'Twas brillig and the slithy toves,
> Did gyre and gimble in the wabe,
> All mimsy were the borogroves,
> And the mome raths outgrabe.

This is nonsense since 'brillig', 'slithy', and so on are fabricated and do not actually mean anything. And yet in a curious way it is very sensible nonsense. It is as if only a dictionary were needed to make it all become crystal clear. Now consider

> Sat sit house down and in out coves,
> And and and and and and and babe,
> Book drunk float grumble burnt sighed loaves,
> And mother astrolabe.

This is much more nonsensical nonsense – appearing to require a mammoth disentangling effort to make sense of it. And yet in the latter example all the words are common English words. Certainly no dictionary would be needed to understand individual words.

Clearly the distinction between the two passages lies in the way the words are put together. The first passage has a structure that the second lacks. Since the first passage seems almost sensible while the second is simply rubbish, this 'structure' property is clearly of major importance in interpreting English sentences. This structure property is called *syntax*. Syntax addresses the way words are strung together to make sentences.

The syntax of a language is described by means of a *grammar*. A grammar is the specification of a procedure for generating and testing sentences to identify those which are allowed in the language. A grammar has four components:

(i) A set of *syntactic categories*, also called *non-terminal* symbols.

(ii) A set of *terminal symbols* (words).

(iii) A set of *rewrite rules* (compare the production rules of Chapters 2 and 5).

(iv) A *start symbol* (e.g. 'Sentence').

The syntactic categories include nouns, verbs, prepositions and so on (i.e. the lexical categories) and they also include higher level structures such as noun phrases, verb phrases, and prepositional phrases. A noun phrase might consist of a determiner, some adjectives, a noun, and perhaps some prepositional phrases. Thus the following are all noun phrases:

> Jack.
>
> The big dog.
>
> The big dark house on the small hill near the radar station in South Wales.

The final example above shows that prepositional phrases consist of a preposition followed by a noun phrase:

> . . . in *the house*
>
> . . . by *the side of a river*

and so on.

Note that this means that *recursive* structures are possible: a noun phrase might have a prepositional phrase as a component, and this in turn might have a noun phrase as a part, which in its turn . . . An example is given in Fig. 3.4.

The rewrite rules are applied to the non-terminal symbols (beginning with the start symbol) until only terminal symbols remain. This is just as in a backward chaining production system where the start symbol is the goal state and the terminal symbols are all elements in the database.

Fig. 3.4. Recursive nesting of syntactic phrases. NP: noun phrase; PP: prepositional phrase.

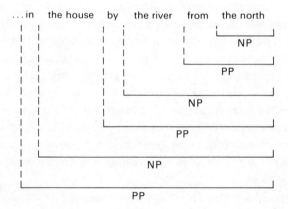

Fig. 3.5 gives an example of a grammar and Fig. 3.6 an example of applying it to a sentence. The symbols used in Figs. 3.5 and 3.6 are to be interpreted as follows: S = sentence, N = noun, V = verb, P = preposition, A = adjective, D = determiner, NP = noun phrase, VP = verb phrase, PP = prepositional phrase. Thus the first rule in Fig. 3.5 tells us that a sentence is composed of two parts, a noun phrase followed by a verb phrase. There are two types of noun phrases indicated (NP and NP1) so that matches can be made both to noun phrases containing determiners and those without.

The language generated by the grammar of Fig. 3.5 is then defined as the set of strings of words which can be produced by applying the rules in Fig. 3.5 (iii) to the terminal symbols. We could thus operationally define syntactically based natural language understanding systems by saying that they use grammatical rules to decompose the sequence of words comprising an input sentence in order to determine the relationships between words in the sentence and the role played by each of them.

At this juncture perhaps it is useful to remind ourselves that there can be many grammars – more than one way to describe a language. Apart from the possibility of different sets of lexical classes, mentioned in § 3.2, there is also the possibility of different syntactic structures – the trees (as in Fig. 3.6) might have different shapes. Indeed, as we shall see below, several different grammars have been adopted for use as the basis of English understanding programs.

There is one other term which we must introduce. A *parser* tests a sentence against a grammar to see if it has a formally correct syntactic

---

Fig. 3.5. A simple grammar. For key see text.

(i) Syntactic categories: N, V, P, A, D, NP, VP, PP.

(ii) Terminal symbols: words, including those used in the sentence decomposed in Fig. 3.6.

(iii) Rewrite rules:

    1.   S → NP VP
    2. NP → NP1
    3. NP → D NP1
    4. NP1 → A NP1
    5. NP1 → N PP
    6. NP1 → N
    7. VP → V NP
    8. PP → P NP

(iv) Start symbol: S

structure and to produce a representation of that structure, such as the tree in Fig. 3.6.

Now that we have introduced the notion of grammars we can go on to investigate different types of grammar. Noam Chomsky, in the 1950s, produced a categorisation of four types:

Type 0: A structure containing the four components (i) to (iv) above, with no restrictions on the form of the rewrite rules in (iii).

Type 1 (Context sensitive grammars): As for type 0, except that the rewrite rules have right hand sides containing at least as many symbols as the left hand sides. In such grammars all rules are of the form

$$aXb \rightarrow aYb$$

Type 2 (Also called *context-free grammars, immediate constituent grammars, Backus normal form*, or *recursive patterns*): Here each rewrite rule contains a single element as its left hand side. (With a side reversal, this is analogous to pure production systems (Chapter 2) in which multiple conditions produce a single action.) It will be clear that the generation process of a type 2 grammar can be represented as a tree.

Type 1 and 2 grammars are often called *phrase structure grammars*.

Type 3 (Regular grammars): Every rewrite rule has the form

$$X \rightarrow aY \qquad or\ X \rightarrow a$$

where X and Y are single variables and a is a terminal.

If a language can be generated by a type i grammar but not a type j grammar with $j > i$ (where i and j refer to the 0, 1, 2 etc. of Chomsky's types above), then the language is said to be of type i.

It is important to note that while practical parsing algorithms can be written for type 2 and 3 grammars to test a given sentence for membership, unfortunately English and other natural languages are not type 2 (and hence also not the more restrictive type 3).

Fig. 3.6. The grammar of Fig. 3.5. generating a sentence.

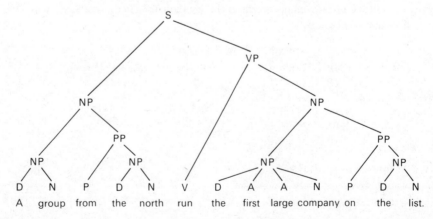

3.4 Context-free grammars

Simple ideas of pattern matching are inadequate for understanding natural language. This is because they do not adequately represent the structures occurring within natural languages: they can recognise a structure, but not analyse it into its component parts so that general descriptive schemes can be applied.

In this section we will introduce the ideas of *phrase structures*, expanding on the reference in the preceding section. Such structures go further than simple pattern matching, but unfortunately even these ideas are not sufficiently flexible to handle all the complexities of real natural languages. For this they must be extended (see below). However, they do have the merit of being straightforward to program. (This does not only mean that programs can be easily written. It also means that programs will run relatively quickly. This is clearly very important in, for example, psychiatric interviewing, where a subject cannot be expected to wait for half an hour for his statement to be processed. Far better a system which is not perfect, but which operates in a realistic time. One might regard this as an engineering approach.)

We should note at this juncture that a number of structural types have been used for describing the syntactic aspects of language. Amongst these are:

(i) *Dependency trees* (The *head-and-modifier* approach). Each structure to be decomposed is regarded as consisting of a *head*, which is a single word, and one or more modifiers, which are also single words and which say something about the head. These modifiers may in turn be modified – so that the top level modifier comprises the head for another modifier. This may be repeated to several levels. Thus a particular sentence may be regarded as a noun modified by a verb, which is in turn modified in some way and so on. For example, in 'the cows run quickly' the head 'cows' has modifier 'runs' which acts as a head for the modifier 'quickly'.

(ii) *Role structure trees* (The *slot-and-filler* approach). The pattern of any particular kind of phrase can be described by a set of slots (*vide* the use of the word 'slot' in the context of frame structures in Chapter 2), each of which can be filled by words of a certain type (e.g. a certain lexical category) and each of which plays a particular role in the phrase. For example, in 'the large brick house' there are three slots, one for determiners (filled by 'the'), one for adjectives (filled by 'large' and 'brick') and one for a noun (filled by 'house'). In fact, of course, noun phrases can be more complex than this, so a realistic set of slots would be more complicated.

(iii) *Phrase structure trees.* Here the elements of a pattern need not be simple words but can be other patterns – even to the extent that the elements may be patterns of the same kind as the parent, so that the process can be recursive. The tree structure, as in Fig. 3.6, is a common way of representing such analyses. Note the recursion between noun phrases.

Our primary interest here is in (iii), since these seem to have been most widely used in computer natural language understanding systems.

We have already noted that a context-free grammar can be regarded as being a set of rules each mapping a single symbol to a sequence of symbols, as in Fig. 3.5. However, we must note that in order to define completely the *generation* process using such a grammar it is necessary to specify how to choose which rule to apply and which particular words to use. These are largely semantic issues. *Recognition* and *identifying structure* can, however, be tackled using syntactic methods.

Parsers come in many shapes and forms. One important distinction is between top-down and bottom-up systems and another, referring to the way they tackle choices and ambiguities, is between sequential and parallel methods (this is analogous to the problem of choosing from a set of candidate arcs in a transition network).

Top-down systems begin with the sentence, represented by the start symbol, S, and expand it by replacing appropriate rules' left hand sides by their right hand sides. Bottom-up systems begin with the individual words in the sentence and try to replace groups of these which conform to rules' right hand sides by the rules' left hand sides. The first begins with a single node and ends with many terminal nodes while the second does the reverse. We give examples below.

The question of choice can arise in different ways during a parse. For example, a word may belong to more than one lexical class, so that one must be selected, or there may be more than one applicable rule in the grammar. These both occur in the example below. Parallel methods process all such possibilities in parallel, so that their number is increasing exponentially and might be very large. Sequential methods tackle them one at a time, by backtracking if a mistake is discovered. Choosing between these two approaches will depend on questions of efficiency and speed.

For our example we shall parse the sentence 'The large man hates the small man', using the grammar of Fig. 3.5. The steps followed by a top-down procedure using backtracking are shown in Fig. 3.7.

The sequence begins in line 1 with the initial S node. Only one rule has S as its left hand side so, as line 1 shows, this is used to split S into a noun phrase and a verb phrase. The number following S $\rightarrow$ NP VP indicates which rule has been applied. After a rule has fired (using production system terminology), the system cycles through the rules again, attempting to decompose any of the current elements. In this case rule 2 will fire, replacing NP by NP1. Before cycling through the rules, in each case the system checks to see whether any elementary lexical classes (N, V, A, D, P) exist in the string and if they match the beginning of the input sentence. In line 3 rule 4 produced A NP1 which, since the word 'the' does not belong in category A (adjective), fails to match. The system thus tries a different rule in place of rule 4. Line 4 shows rule 5 being tried, and failing, while line 5 shows rule 6 failing. There are no other rules with NP1 as their left hand side so the system backtracks, abandoning the line which produced NP1. This was line 2. An alternative rule with NP as its left hand side is tried. The first (and only) alternative to rule 2 is rule 3, yielding, in line 6, D NP1. The D (determiner) here matches 'the' – indicated as 'OK' in Fig. 3.7. The D and the word 'the' are henceforth ignored and the process continues until finally, in line 18, rule 6 produces N (noun), which matches the final word 'man' of the sentence.

Our bottom-up example parses the same sentence. The process begins by trying to find a right hand side string of lexical categories which matches a string of categories in the sentence. Since, initially, all the sentence elements are in fact words, no match is found. When no match is found the system replaces one of the chosen categories by another possible one. Initially this

Fig. 3.7. Top-down backtracking parse of 'The large man hates the small man' using the grammar of Fig. 3.5.

Step			*Rule no.*	
1	S → NP	VP	1	
2	NP → NP1		2	
3	NP1 → A	NP1	4	fail
4	NP1 → N	PP	5	fail
5	NP1 → N		6	fail
6	NP → D	NP1	3	OK **The**
7	NP1 → A	NP1	4	OK **large**
8	NP1 → A	NP1	4	fail
9	NP1 → N	PP	5	OK **man**
10	PP → P	NP	8	fail
11	NP1 → N		6	OK
12	VP → V	NP	7	OK **hates**
13	NP → NP1		2	fail
14	NP → D	NP1	3	OK **the**
15	NP1 → A	NP1	4	OK **small**
16	NP1 → A	NP1	4	fail
17	NP1 → N	PP	5	fail
18	NP1 → N		6	OK **man**

means simply choosing a category for one of the words. In Fig. 3.8 the word 'the' has been replaced by the category label D. Repeating this process results in 'large' being replaced by A and 'man' by N. Now rule 6's right hand side does match, and N is replaced by rule 6's left hand side, NP1. Recycling, rule 2's right hand side matches, replacing NP1 by NP, and then unfortunately nothing matches any substring of D A NP so the system has to backtrack. This results in rule 2 being usurped by NP1. Rule 3 then quickly matches D NP1, yielding NP. No rule has just NP as its right hand

Fig. 3.8. Bottom-up backtracking parse of 'The large man hates the small man' using the grammar of Fig. 3.5.

	D	**large man hates the small man**
	D	A			
	D	A	N		
Rule 6:	D	A	NP1		
Rule 2:	D	A	NP		

Ultimate failure because no match to D   A   NP
Backtrack
D   A   NP1

Rule 4:   D   NP1

Rule 3:   NP
                 NP   N

Ultimate failure because of wrong category choice.
Backtrack

	NP	V	D	A	N
	NP	V			
	NP	V	D		
	NP	V	D	A	
	NP	V	D	A	N
Rule 6:	NP	V	D	A	NP1
Rule 2:	NP	V	D	A	NP

Ultimate failure because of wrong category choice
Backtrack

NP   V   D   A   NP1

Rule 4:   NP   V   D   NP1

Rule 3:   NP   V   NP

Rule 7:   NP   VP

Rule 1:   S

side so the system substitutes a category for another word. 'Hates' becomes N, because 'hates' can be a noun. Rule 6 replaces N by NP1 and then failure occurs because no string has NP NP1 as its right hand side. Again new words are replaced by their categories but to no avail since, as we can see, 'hates' here serves as a verb, not a noun. Ultimately the system recognises that it is getting nowhere and backtracks to replace the N for 'hates' by the alternative lexical category V and the process continues.

Problems can arise and unfortunately extra complexities have to be introduced to circumvent them. For example, in a grammar mapping some symbol to itself followed by another a loop is set up: $X \rightarrow XY$ recycles to give XXY and XXXY and so on. Similarly, there are techniques for making parsers more efficient – again at the cost of loss of simplicity.

Structures other than those above have also been explored. Some even begin at the end of the sentence and work backwards, while others attempt to build up islands of recognised phrases and coalesce them to form complete sentences. These are described in the further reading references given at the end of the chapter.

Perhaps a fitting way to conclude this section is to glance at the various advantages and disadvantages of the two basic approaches we have considered.

In some circumstances (e.g. connected discourse) the ends of sentences are not clear. This can naturally cause difficulties, especially for top-down parsers. An advantage of top-down systems is that they generate *expectations* about what sort of word is to come next. Bottom-up systems do not do this. Conversely, bottom-up systems can make sense of bits of malformed sentences which would clearly be useful in an automated psychiatric interview. Bottom-up systems, however, propose many potential parses that could never comprise part of a sentence (perhaps the NP N group in Fig. 3.8 is an example). The reader might like to consider the relative merits of top-down and bottom-up systems in parsing the two sentences:

'Is the book with a cover?'

'Is the book with a cover good?'

and the sentences

'John decorated the house and the shop'

'John decorated the house and the shop needed decorating'

and, indeed, what extensions would be needed to the simple grammar in Fig. 3.5 to accomplish this.

3.5   Transformational grammar

It is not difficult to see that English has neither a regular (type 3) grammar nor a context-free (type 2) grammar. Further, even context-sensitive (type 1) grammars have major disadvantages (in that they require complicating features to analyse natural languages). In fact, phrase structure languages in general, as outlined in the preceding section, encounter difficulties when presented with the full range of English sentences. Consider the following examples:

(i) *Morphological difficulties*. For example, choosing the correct form of the verb 'to be'.

(ii) *Embedding*. A classical example of a difficult structure for phrase structure grammars involves the word 'respectively', as in 'John, Jane, and Mary are a psychiatrist, a computer scientist, and a mathematician, respectively'.

(iii) *Matching separated subject and verb*. Phrase structure grammars experience difficulty in matching endings when the subject and verb are separated, as in

Which *sentence* of these *agrees* with this one?

Which *sentences* of these *agree* with this one?

(iv) Sometimes two words represent a single compound word, and yet can be split up: 'He split the phrase up'.

Attempts to tackle such shortcomings while retaining the phrase structure concept were not altogether successful, and in response to this Chomsky (1957) proposed an extension. He suggested that the rules comprising a grammar could be of a more general form than those applied to a sequence of words or symbols as with context-free or context-sensitive grammars. In particular, he suggested that the rules should operate on structures which were themselves derived by a more restricted type of grammar. This led him to propose that language generation proceeded through three levels, as shown in Fig. 3.9. The context-free grammar produces simple declarative sentences and their phrase structure trees. The transformation rules manipulate these sentences, modifying them so that they cover the full range of natural language sentences. Finally, the morphophonemic rules tidy things

Fig. 3.9. Levels in sentence generation in transformational grammar.

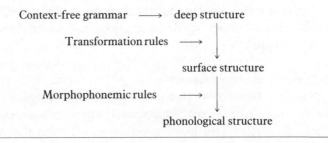

up and produce the terminal phonological structure used in speaking or writing.

As an example, a transformation rule for the passive construction might take the simple declarative sentence 'John hit the ball' and transform it into the sentence 'The ball was hit by John' by transposing the position of the two noun phrases and introducing 'by' and the auxiliary.

Such transformation rules require that some component of the phrase structure tree match the 'left hand side' of the transformation rule and also often require that other conditions be met (for example, that two noun phrases in different parts of the sentences be identical). There are systems of notation for representing transformation rules in a precise manner (see Winograd, 1983).

Some transformations are optional, in the sense that while applying them changes the sentence's form, the sentence is grammatically sound whether they are applied or not. In contrast, others are mandatory – they must be applied to yield a grammatical sentence.

Since transformational grammar was influenced in its early days by Skinner's behaviourism, it was natural for researchers to try to identify things such as transformation rules and deep structure in the human mind. Initially it seemed as if they might succeed: sentences involving a transformation were grasped less quickly than those without, and sentences requiring two transformations took longer still. Unfortunately, however, as the theory became more complicated – as more of the transformations necessary to replicate natural language were included – so the cracks began to show. Put bluntly, although transformational grammar represented a major advance, it did not solve all the problems, and an acceptable compromise needed to be maintained between comprehensiveness and the size of a reasonable set of rules. This has directed the focus of work on transformational grammar away from attempts to identify its psychological reality. (Is this another instance of the situation described by Paul Meehl, quoted in § 2.5?)

It will be obvious to the reader from this that there are different versions of transformational grammar, each supported by its own school. As with almost every other major scientific theory (take as examples evolution, quantum theory, and statistical science), there are differing interpretations within the general body of the theory.

Problems of choosing between alternative transformational grammars motivated some workers to take a step back and look at the criteria on which such a choice should be based. One such criterion poses the choice in the form of a question asking whether the grammars in question can actually be learnt from examples (the 'projection problem'). Study revealed that, under common assumptions about the learning procedure, context-free grammars cannot be learnt. This is rather unfortunate, since, as we have noted above, a context-free grammar lies at the base of transformational grammar. This has led to the suggestion that some basic part of grammar is physically encoded in the hardware of the brain – part of its physiology.

The artificial intelligence community and the linguists working in transformational grammar have not always agreed. This is, of course, to be expected since their objectives are subtly different. One example is a consequence of the emphasis that linguists put on the independence of syntactic processing from other mental functions concerned with language manipulation. In general they stress that the syntactic processes may be quite different from the processes used elsewhere in the brain. In contrast, artificial intelligence researchers seek powerful general formalisms – as we have demonstrated in Chapter 2. Controversies between the two groups have sometimes derived from a basic misconception of their differing aims.

3.6   Augmented transition networks

While linguists were developing transformational grammar based on ideas of derivation of legitimate sentences, artificial intelligence researchers were tackling things from the other end and developing one of the most important concepts for parsing: the *augmented transition network* (ATN).

We introduced the basic ideas of transition networks (TNs) in § 3.2. TNs can be shown to be equivalent to type 3 (regular) grammars and have the limitations mentioned above. We can relax some of the restrictions by allowing *recursion*. A *recursive transition network* (RTN) is like a TN with the extension that arcs between states can be labelled by the names of other networks. Thus, in place of simple words or elementary lexical categories, composite categories are allowed. For example, an RTN might have an arc labelled NP. NP will be the label or name of a separate RTN. Whereas the simple TNs of § 3.2 consisted of straightforward templates against which a sentence was matched, RTNs comprise collections of networks, each of which may have the others (or even itself) as a subnetwork.

Fig. 3.10 gives an example. The symbols are as before except for 'Jump', which is a new one. A jump arc lets the system pass from one state to another without matching a word. Thus the noun phrase network in Fig. 3.10 can cater for such phrases as 'the dog', 'these large dogs', 'a large black dog', 'those dogs in the shed', which have a determiner and can also handle such phrases as 'Jack', 'meat', and so on without a determiner. The recursion here should be clear enough. S contains NPs as arcs. These arcs are traversed, not by matching single words to them, but by matching the NP network to a sequence of words. NP itself calls the network PP and PP calls NP – allowing recursive nesting.

RTNs have the power of type 2 (context-free) grammars.

Networks, as described above, are ideal for pattern matching purposes but they do not store the structure of the parse. If we are to go further than simple pattern matching – if we are to manipulate the knowledge contained in the input sentences – then we have to store this structure.

This leads us to augmented transition networks (ATNs). An ATN is an RTN with the following extra properties:

(i) It has a set of *feature slots*.
(ii) It has a set of *role slots*.
(iii) The arcs have associated *conditions*.
(iv) *Actions* can be carried out when an arc is taken.

Let us examine these extensions one by one.

When a phrase is parsed the feature and role slots are filled by values describing the network. Examples of features are voice (which may be active or passive), number (singular or plural), determiner (definite or indefinite) and mood (declarative, interrogative, or imperative). Each lexical category also has a set of features, these being filled in when that arc is traversed.

An example of a role slot is one labelled 'subject'. When a sentence is parsed some noun phrase will be allocated to this slot.

Conditions on the arcs must be satisfied before the arc can be traversed. Thus, for example, a verb may be checked to see that it is a possible auxiliary (will, has, was, . . .) before it is added to the list of auxiliaries.

Fig. 3.10. An example of a recursive transition network for handling transitive verbs.

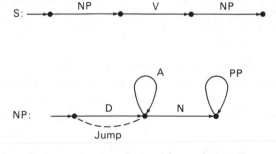

Actions are processing operations which occur as an arc is traversed. Thus the number slot of a feature register may be set, the subject of a role slot may be indicated, or a verb might be added to the list of auxiliaries.

As with transformational grammars, ATNs represent a very significant advance but they do not yet solve everything. The fact that the conditions and actions are chosen with respect to a particular order of parsing makes things easier to think about and program but limits the system's power. Transitivity has not yet been adequately resolved using ATNs (or, to be fair, using any other grammatical formalism).

Special difficulties also arise with what Winograd (1983) calls 'long-distance dependencies' in which (p. 478): 'some element of the structure is constrained by features of another part of the structure that is not its parent or one of its children, but appears at a distant place in the tree'. Examples are:

> 'The song I like to sing'
> 'The song that the man we knew liked to sing'
> 'What do you believe his opinion was?'

Several methods have been proposed for tackling such difficulties but none is perfect, a particular problem being that the distant phrases do not always serve the same purpose.

Difficulties also arise with conjunctions (Jane wrote a book *and* published it), comparatives (Jane is *older than* John), and ellipsis (an understood item, as in: Jane likes John but Mary doesn't).

We have stressed above, perhaps to the point of boredom, that there are as many versions of grammars, parsers, and so on as there are researchers. It will thus come as no surprise to learn that there are various shapes and sizes of ATN formalism. There is a foundation theory and then different workers develop things in different directions as they attempt to cater for the peculiarities of English. Woods (1970) seems to have been one of the first to propose ATN ideas.

3.7   Systemic grammar

As we have demonstrated above, many approaches to grammar are based on a merger of ideas about cognition and mathematical formalisms. In contrast, *systemic grammar* has its origin in anthropology and sociology in addressing questions relating to the social role of language. Thus speech acts fulfil certain *functions* – they occupy certain roles within the context of larger units. Perhaps a basic role division of entire sentences would be into statements, commands, and questions, and within each of these divisions further classification would lead to a hierarchy of roles.

This emphasis on roles means that systemic grammar is not solely concerned with syntactic structure as are the grammars above, but has a stronger relationship to pragmatics, i.e. knowledge of the world being described. So, for example, different ways of structuring sentences are recognised to have distinct meanings. The sentences

Jack hit Mary with the ball

Jack used the ball to hit Mary

have the same underlying interpretation but subtly different meanings.

Systemic grammar has inspired considerable interest in the artificial intelligence community and underlies two of the systems we describe at the end of this chapter (Winograd, 1976 and Davey, 1978). It was originally developed by a group of linguists at University College, London, beginning with Halliday (1967, 1970), and has subsequently developed in several directions. It is based on a three level classification of the units of language (some would describe five levels, adding *morphemes* and *sentences* to the three below).

At the lowest level we have *words*. These are the fundamental atoms. If we start at this level, then systemic grammar, unlike other grammars, does not split words into meaningful subunits (as, for example, a verb may be split into root and ending morphemes, the latter indicating tense, or a noun may be split into a stem and an ending indicating plural). Instead these modifications of the basic word are described by a system of features attached to the word. Thus in 'Mary kicked the ball' and 'Mary kicks the ball' a corresponding point in the structural analysis represents 'kicked' and 'kicks', with the difference being indicated by 'past' and 'present' features attached to 'kick'.

The next level up in the hierarchy consists of *groups*. There are four types of group: noun groups, verb groups, preposition groups, and adjective groups. Each group has function slots for the words making it up. Thus a noun group has (mostly optional) slots for determiners, ordinals, numbers, adjectives, classifier nouns, a noun, and qualifier (such as a prepositional group). Just as with the lower level words, each group has a set of features describing particular aspects of it: whether it is singular or plural, definite or indefinite, and so on.

The top level of the hierarchy consists of *clauses*. Clauses are comprised of groups filling roles of subject, predicator, complement, and adjunct. Of the clause Winograd (1976, p. 47) says:

> The structure exhibiting the greatest variety in English is the
> CLAUSE. It can express relationships and events involving time,
> place, manner, and other modifiers. Its structure indicates what
> parts of the sentence the speaker wants to emphasize, and can
> express various kinds of focus of attention and emotion. It
> determines the purpose of an utterance – whether it is a question,

command, or statement – and is the basic unit which can stand alone. Other units can occur by themselves when their purpose is understood, as in answer to a question, but the clause is the primary unit of discourse.

Although the structural components are put into one of three classes, the structural decomposition of a clause may be more complicated than the simple hierarchy this might seem to imply. The point is that groups often contain other groups, clauses can be parts of groups, and clauses can occur within other clauses. Noun groups, for example, occur within prepositional groups, which occur within noun groups (as is the case several times in our earlier example: 'A group from the north run the first large company on the list' in Fig. 3.6).

The features describing a unit are not just a collection of isolated attributes but form a structure of definite interrelationships. A simple such structure is a set of alternative features, only one of which may be chosen. Such a set of mutually exclusive features is called a *system* (hence *systemic*). A simple example of a system is the pair *major* and *secondary* for a clause. The feature *major* serves as an *entry condition* to the system composed of the three features *question, imperative, declarative*, since if and only if a clause is a major clause does it make sense to choose between these three features.

In addition to such sets of mutually exclusive features, there are also systems running in parallel. For example, as well as classifying a clause as *major* or *secondary*, it is also necessary to classify it as *passive* or *active*. These two features thus comprise an independent system running in parallel with the *major, secondary* system.

In transformational grammar (§ 3.5) transformation rules work on the same deep structure to produce different surface structures. In systemic grammar such sentences with different surface structures would be found to have almost identical feature sets, differing in only one or two particulars. *Realisation rules* describe the differing word orders needed to indicate these feature set differences. In understanding text, rules working in the opposite direction, mapping from the text to appropriate features, are needed. That is, *interpretation rules*.

It is also worth noting that, when modelling human language functions, systemic grammar seems to have a number of merits. For example, of the particular form of systemic grammar that he uses, Davey (1978, p. 3, and see Example 3 below) says: 'Another advantage of systemic functional grammar is that it seems to be psychologically more plausible than transformational grammar'. Certainly, one of the arguments in favour of this kind of *functional* representation of syntactic structure is that it is a more natural approach. This can be seen when one attempts to compare analyses between different languages. The constituent methods described earlier tend to force the text into a structure rather than let it produce its own.

3.8   Semantics

Semantics is concerned with *meaning*. That is, with the correspondence between the symbols of the language and the objects, events, and actions of the outside world. Thus syntax describes the formal symbol manipulation of the language, and semantics the relationship or mapping of those symbols to reality. The distinction might seem clear enough when stated so boldly but in fact it is a somewhat fuzzy one, as we remarked at the beginning of this chapter. However, for us it is a useful one for it enables us to carve the problem of language comprehension into manageable chunks. Certainly syntax and semantics have been treated separately by most builders of natural language processing systems. This does not mean that they have merely considered one or the other aspect of language but rather that they have regarded the distinction as being a real one. In perhaps the majority of systems syntax plays the dominant role, although there are one or two exceptions. Where the two aspects come together is to narrow down the range of possible interpretations which have to be examined. This discovery, that using extra properties of a system can be helpful in eliminating ambiguity, is one of the major findings of artificial intelligence work. We expand on it in the context of language comprehension below, but to indicate its more general applicability it is worth noting that the same effect also applies to work in vision. There, it was thought initially that introducing extra complications such as shadows into scenes would increase the computational burden dramatically and make robot vision that much more difficult to achieve. In fact it was discovered that these extra 'complications' simplified things since now fewer possible orientations of objects could match the observed scene. (For example, without considering shadows two possible configurations might have been feasible. Shadows effectively let us also look at things from another viewpoint and help eliminate one of the configurations.) In practice what happens is that as the interpretation of a scene is built up ('this is a corner – is it an inner or an outer corner?' etc.), so the extra constraints let us eliminate possibilities and so help to reduce the exponential explosion of possibilities. An exactly analogous situation applies in language understanding. As a sentence is parsed many possible interpretations are generated for components of it (and, as we shall see, sometimes for the entire sentence). Most of these are eliminated at later stages by syntactic constraints but semantic constraints let us eliminate them early on – with a considerable saving in computational effort. We discuss this in more detail below.

In discussing meaning we are, of course, in danger of making circular definitions. (My *Concise Oxford dictionary* defines 'meaning' as 'what is meant'.) The way semantic concepts are integrated into computer language processing programs is via links specifying relationship between words. A simple approach of this kind is the *classification* approach. Here a number of *semantic categories* are defined (animate, human, solid, abstract, . . .) and each noun is assigned to one or more of these classes. A similar operation can be carried out for verbs. These categories restrict the way words can be used – so, for example, since 'thought' is abstract it cannot be screwed to a wall.

One of the problems with this is that the set of categories may be chosen in many ways, each of which has its shortcomings. There is, of course, also the complicating problem that the categories will overlap and may form a hierarchical tree structure.

Going beyond semantic categories, we have the notion of semantic nets introduced in Chapter 2. Rather than simple subclass or membership relationships such networks allow many kinds of relationships to be represented. This is potentially a very powerful approach and has been the centre of much research, although it seems to have gone out of fashion at present. Perhaps with the continued development of ever more powerful computers it will experience a resurgence of interest.

The remainder of this section examines ways in which semantic constraints may be used in conjunction with syntactic parses to reduce (or, ideally, eliminate altogether) ambiguity.

We begin with the general observation that *semantic markers* attached to words, describing their properties and relationship to other words, provide a *context* which can serve to reduce ambiguity. (This notion of context applies more generally: words within a phrase, phrases in clauses, clauses in sentences, sentences in discourse, and so on.) These markers indicate the possible uses of a word in conjunction with other words. Thus, for example, in 'He struck him on the temple' the semantic markers associated with 'struck' will make it clear that it is the part of a head interpretation of 'temple' which should be used, rather than the place of worship interpretation. In examining possible word meanings (such as in this 'temple' example) to see which is appropriate there are two basic strategies which can be employed. The first is to put the possible meanings into some kind of sensible order and simply take the first one. Consider, for example, the three sentences:

(1) Jack paid by check.
(2) Jack moved his king out of check.
(3) The advance received a check.

In (1) the context induced by the semantic markers attached to 'paid' suggests the pecuniary interpretation for check. In (2) the context induced by 'king' makes us think of chess. (3) is perhaps rather more ambiguous, but, to me, at least, 'advance' induces the notion that it can be arrested, or 'checked'. Perhaps the sentence is describing a military campaign.

Thus in each of these three sentences the possible interpretations for 'check' can be ranked. If a 'stop-on-success' strategy is being employed the first of the interpretations in the list will be taken.

The advantage of this sort of approach is, of course, that it is relatively quick. Of course, it might get it wrong. Perhaps sentence (3) above refers to a payment received in return for early submission of a delivery of goods. In this case the system has to backtrack and work its way down the list of interpretations. In doing so it can take advantage of anything it has learnt in attempting to match the first meaning.

The alternative to the 'stop-on-success' strategy is the parallel approach in which all possible meanings of a word are investigated. Thus in (1) above, each of the three meanings of 'check' (and any others stored) would be examined and the most appropriate one chosen. Obviously this will take longer to arrive at its initial choice than the other method. This method can be extended so that if no interpretation fits perfectly the closest is chosen. More generally, such extending relaxation will allow us to interpret successfully such sentences as 'the house floated down the river' in a story about floods, despite the fact that houses are not normally floating objects.

Apart from ambiguities involving individual words, semantic considerations can help us to resolve other possible confusions. Consider, as an example, the prepositional groups in

> Jack greeted the girl by the door in a skirt.

Here semantic markers allow us to eliminate

> (1) While Jack was wearing a skirt he greeted the girl

and (2) The greeting occurred near the skirted door.

But semantic markers attached to individual words do not solve everything. In

> Jack greeted the girl by the door in the barn

was it the door in the barn that the girl was standing next to when Jack greeted her, or was she in the barn, near the door? Or was Jack in the barn when he greeted the girl near the door? Or were both of them near the barn door when the greeting occurred?

This sort of ambiguity has to be solved by the larger context – that in which the sentence as a whole occurs.

Pronouns pose particular problems of ambiguity since there may often be more than one possible referent. (And, indeed, more than one pronoun: so he hit him with it in front of her.) The most common use of pronouns is to represent some concept that has occurred earlier, though this is not their only use, and they can also be used to refer to concepts mentioned later. (Jack wasn't in the habit of kissing everybody, but because he was particularly fond of *her*, he kissed *Mary*.) Things are further complicated by the fact that pronouns can refer to entire sentences or clauses (I told you to clear up the books; do *it* now) or even to concepts not explicitly mentioned. For example, in 'Before Jack chose a book to read, he stacked *them* on the shelves' 'them' refers to an understood set of books.

Fortunately things are not as bad as this might seem to suggest. Several systems which effectively handle pronouns have now been built (see examples in § 3.10.) The situation is eased by the fact that, as Hobbs (1976) showed, 98% of the pronoun references in text refer to concepts in the current sentence or the immediately preceding one. It does not seem unreasonable to suppose that in dialogue a similar proportion (if not larger one) holds.

Determiners (a, the, those, some, any, etc.) impose very useful semantic constraints on noun phrases:

> One of the two apples in the basket was poisoned. She gave him the basket and the man chose *the* apple.
> One of the two apples in the basket was poisoned. She gave him the basket and the man chose *an* apple.

A particular problem for syntactic analysers arises from ellipsis. This is the practice of leaving part of a sentence understood:

> Jack asked Mary to come and she said she would (come).
> Jack ate a cake but Mary didn't (eat a cake).

In such cases some kind of semantically directed completion can help before a syntactic analysis is attempted. Tennant (1981) describes two types of ellipsis which are common in conversation. He calls them *superstructure ellipsis* and *substructure ellipsis*. In the former a major part of the sentence is omitted, with only a small part remaining. For example;

> Jack: Mary, how many cream cakes did you eat?
> Mary: Only one.

In substructure ellipsis, the global structure of the sentence is retained, but some component is implied. For example,

> Jack: Mary, how many cream cakes did you eat?
> Mary: I ate three.

Sometimes, just to complicate things further, both types can occur simultaneously.

Winograd (1976, p. 23, and see Example 2 below) observes that syntax and semantics seem to work in parallel in humans. He gives an example of such an operation from his own program:

As a concrete example, we might have the sentence 'I rode down the street in a car.' At a certain point in the parsing, the NG program may come up with the constituent 'the street in a car'. Before going on, the semantic analyzer will reject the phrase 'in a car' as a possible modifier of 'street', and the program will attach it instead as a modifier of the action represented by the sentence. Since the semantic programs are part of a general deductive system with a definite world-model, the semantic evaluation which guides parsing can include both general knowledge (cars don't contain streets) and specific knowledge (for example, Melvin owns a red car). Humans take advantage of this sort of knowledge in their understanding of language, and it has been pointed out by a number of linguists and computer scientists that good computer handling of language will not be possible unless computers can do so as well.

Of course, some situations are more difficult than others, and their resolution relies on constraints imposed from several different directions simultaneously. And some can never be resolved in this way – all natural languages are full of idioms (what would an uninformed computer make of the expressions 'the man in the Clapham omnibus' (as used by our legal colleagues), 'he was over the moon', 'she was in the pink', or 'when the balloon goes up'?).

A fitting conclusion to this section seems to be a brief examination of a famous 'artificial intelligence sentence' parsed by an early syntactic analysis program. The sentence

Time flies like an arrow

produced the following possible interpretations

(1) Time moves quickly, just as arrows do.

(2) An imperative to measure the speed of flies, perhaps with a stopwatch, as one might measure the speed of an arrow.

(3) To measure the speed of those particular flies which resemble arrows, again perhaps with a stopwatch.

(4) The species of fly known as 'time flies' (analogous to house flies and horse flies) like to eat arrows.

Clearly semantic analysis would have a major contribution to make here, but resort to a dictionary of idioms may ultimately be necessary.

3.9 Other points

An obvious application for natural language understanding programs in psychiatry is to interview patients, perhaps to obtain history, perhaps to carry out some kind of behavioural therapy, or perhaps to follow up some therapeutic regime. As yet, however, no language processing system has been applied in this way. Having said that, we should mention two applications of computers in these domains.

The first is ELIZA (Weizenbaum, 1965). This was a simple pattern matching system which accepted natural language input and produced responses using the sort of techniques described in § 3.2. The system maintained the upper hand by continually asking prompting questions in the manner of a Rogerian psychiatrist. In no way can it be said to understand language, and indeed it has been described as a toy. (It should be noted, however, that there were several versions of ELIZA, the later ones being relatively sophisticated and embodying some interesting concepts. Nevertheless, Weizenbaum (1976, p. 188) says: 'I chose the name "ELIZA" because like G. B. Shaw's Eliza Doolittle of *Pygmalion* fame, the program could be taught to "speak" increasingly well, although, also like Miss Doolittle, it was never quite clear whether or not it became smarter'.) From our view, two decades on, the basic system seems woefully inadequate and its simple mechanism means that it can produce absurd conversations. Despite this the system attracted considerable interest, not least because it demonstrated how willing people were to be deceived. Even people sufficiently knowledgeable about computers to appreciate the severe limitations of ELIZA would insist that it understood them – sometimes asking to communicate with it in private.

More serious is the use of computers to take patients' histories, not via subtle processing of all of natural language's complexities, but by the simple expedient of asking the patient a string of questions to which the answers are yes, no, or don't understand. (Perhaps even giving the patient a keyboard with only three keys.) Chapter 5 discusses, in some depth, the use of this kind of system to infer a diagnosis. Here we are solely concerned with extracting information from a patient, with no interpretive aim in mind. The results, for example, could be printed out in a standard format and passed to the consultant. We emphasise that this is not in fact an application of either artificial intelligence or natural language processing technology.

One might imagine that this more restricted use of computers would inspire far less controversy than the possible use in diagnosis. In some situations, at any rate, such appears not to be the case. We quote from an editorial by J. D. Matarazzo in *Science* (Matarazzo, 1983). He is discussing psychological testing:

> There is a danger that wholesale use of automated tests by people
> without a knowledge of their limitations will be a disservice to the
> public. Compounding this danger, the tests have a spurious
> appearance of objectivity and infallibility as a halo effect from the

computer, and their ease of use may cause them to be more widely
employed than are current tests.

My experience as an expert witness leaves me in no doubt that a
flood of litigation involving unqualified users of the products of this
new technology is just around the corner.

While his comments may be directed at psychological testing, the issue is
clearly one which should be watched.

A schedule of questions could be presented to a patient on paper, but the
use of computers has a number of advantages. The primary one is that a
complex hierarchical structure of question modules can be followed. That
is, the subject's answers influence the next questions to be asked (if a patient
says he is male then questions asking about pre-menstrual tension can be
avoided). The computer steers the patient through the question net
automatically, not requiring him to sort out the meaning of directions such
as 'If the answer to question 2.3 was "yes" go to question 4.0, otherwise
proceed to 2.4".

Examples of publications describing such systems are Slack, Hicks, Reed
& Van Cura (1966), Slack & Van Cura (1968), Mayne, Weksel & Sholtz
(1968), Card *et al.* (1970, 1974), Grossman, McGuire, Barnett & Swedlow
(1971), Lucas *et al.* (1976), Lucas (1977), and Lucas, Mullin, Luna &
McInroy (1977).

Lucas *et al.* (1977) describe a psychiatric example for obtaining information relating to alcohol problems. Two points are particularly worthy of
note. The first: 'It would appear that computer interrogation is at least as
accurate as interrogation by psychiatrists working in a specialist alcohol
clinic in eliciting indicants relating to alcohol problems from male patients'.

The second is the support that their results give to the statement made
elsewhere (e.g. Slack & Van Cura, 1968; Card *et al.*, 1974) that patients are
more willing to give accurate information to a computer than to a doctor
when 'difficult' questions are involved (an example being questions relating
to how much alcohol they consume).

Needless to say, the possible financial saving (perhaps measured in terms
of a highly qualified expert's time) makes this an important area to watch.

It would be an oversight in a chapter on natural language processing not
to say something about machine translation. As a practical field of research
this really started with the advent of the computer after the Second World
War, largely in response to recognition of the tremendous growth in
scientific literature (so that, for example, it was desirable to translate from
Russian to English). To the early investigators it seemed that the basic
problem of translation lay in amassing and matching suitably large vocabularies. This, however, was a mistake. In the United States a study of the

effectiveness of machine translation published in 1966 (National Research Council, 1966) led to the recognition that progress had not been as great as some people were claiming and this resulted in a drastic reduction in US funding. (One cannot help but be reminded of the general situation prevailing in the United Kingdom after publication of the 'Lighthill report' (Lighthill *et al.*, 1973). A similar cutback in funds resulted, letting other countries take the lead.)

Interest in machine translation continued in the Soviet Union, however, and in Europe the EEC, with its problems of multiple languages requiring tons of documents to be translated, stimulated further interest (King, 1981). It is generally recognised nowadays that a prerequisite for machine translation of natural language is a machine understander of natural language. That is, the system must have an implicit world model and must make use of the syntactic and semantic knowledge discussed above. We should remark, however, that a proposition which is already feasible is to use a machine to *aid* a human translator. Basically, the machine can do the hard work, leaving the subtleties to the human.

For completeness we should also say a few words about speech recognition and understanding – as distinct from keyboard input language understanding. It might be thought that the problem of recognising spoken words is very much one of electronic hardware, divorced from the subtleties of artificial intelligence. However, this is not altogether true. The reason parallels the situation described above of sorting out meanings of ambiguous words in language understanding. To interpret phonemes, the basic units of speech, effectively, one must take account of context and overall structure. Higher level analysis can guide and illuminate lower level analysis. A good example of this is the HEARSAY project, which makes use of syntactic and semantic structures (Reddy, Erman & Neely, 1972; McCracken, 1981).

It does not require much imagination to see that speech understanding systems could play a very important role in everyday life. Such machines could talk to the blind, enable the physically disabled to control machines, provide information (such as from timetables) over the phone, and provide a general input channel to computers. Coupled with speech producing systems – technically an easier problem – the possibilities are endless.

Systems which recognise some tens of isolated words can now be purchased 'over the counter' for attaching to home microcomputers. Developing systems which can handle the connected speech of ordinary conversation, however, has proved much more difficult because of the way words tail into each other. Despite this, such systems do exist, though at present they only run on large computers in research laboratories.

A useful introduction to speech recognition and synthesis technology is given by Poulton (1983).

3.10 Examples

Example 1: SIR (Raphael, 1968)

SIR (Semantic Information Retrieval) was an early pattern matching program. Raphael expressed a belief that question answering systems 'capable of intelligent, humanlike behaviour' must lie between the two extremes of systems in which the processing occurs while text is fed in, so that questions of an expected form can be easily answered, and systems which barely process the initial text at all, carrying out the necessary computation as each question is presented. He therefore included in his design criteria for SIR:

(i) that the representation should be sufficiently general to be useful 'in a wide variety of subject areas' while requiring that the 'stored information should be specific enough to be of real assistance in the question-answering process' and

(ii) that the computational work-load be split between the initial transformation of text and the examination of individual questions.

These two criteria, he felt, were best met by systems based upon words and word associations. He quotes Walpole (1941) 'Words do not live in isolation in a language system. They enter into all kinds of groupings held together by a complex, unstable and highly subjective network of associations; associations between the names and the senses, associations based on similarity or some other relation. It is by their effects that these associative connections make themselves felt; . . . The sum total of these associative networks is the vocabulary'. Because of this: 'SIR uses an approximation to those associations as its basic data store'.

SIR is designed only to tackle simple sentences – sentences consisting of words representing objects or classes of objects and the relationships between these objects. This is achieved by describing each word by a list of attribute-value pairs. For example, the class of dogs might be described by the list

(legs: 4) (sound: bark, growl) (ears: two) (eats: meat) . . .

Each attribute here defines a relation between the original word (dogs) and the word which acts as the matching attribute. Thus a network of interrelations is built up.

This structure was accumulated by selecting a particular relationship (such as set inclusion) and developing programs for recognising sentences containing that relationship by studying their syntactic structure and strategic use of token words.

The relationships SIR covered were

(i) Set inclusion.

(ii) Part/whole relationship.

(iii) Numeric quantity associated with the part/whole relationship.

(iv) Set membership.

(v) Left-to-right spatial relations.

(vi) Ownership.

The full set of patterns SIR used in recognising sentences is shown in Fig. 3.11. The list is simply processed sequentially to find the first match (and the sentence is basically ignored if no match is found). Note that this set could easily be expanded. The process of analysing an input sentence thus involves three stages:

(i) Compare the pattern with the sentence. If dissimilar, try the next pattern. If similar continue to step (ii).

(ii) Examine the slot fillers (i.e. the sentence word sequences which match the blanks or wildcards in the pattern) to check that they have the correct form and lexical class. If acceptable go to (iii).

(iii) Carry out the associated action for this pattern – create a relationship, see if a relationship exists, etc.

Fig. 3.11. The patterns SIR can recognise. (Adapted from Raphael, 1968.)

X is Y

Is X Y?

X owns Y

Does X own Y?

How many Y does X own?

X is Y part of Z

X has as a part one Y

There are Y on X

There is one Y on X

Is X part of Y?

How many Y are there on X?

How many Y are parts of X?

X has Y (Y an object)

X has Z (Z a number)

How many X does Y have?

X is just to the right of Y

X is just to the left of Y

X is to the right of Y

X is to the left of Y

Is X just to the right of Y?

Is X just to the left of Y?

Is X to the right of Y?

Is X to the left of Y?

Where is X?

What is the X of Y?

SIR's output uses a set of built-in responses, which may be either completely 'canned' (as in 'I understand' in Fig. 3.12) or which might require words from the triggering sentence to be supplied. Fig. 3.12 gives a short example of a SIR dialogue (adapted from Raphael, 1968).

Example 2: SHRDLU (Winograd, 1976)

One of the most famous natural language understanding systems was that produced by Terry Winograd for his Ph.D. work. This was published in the journal *Cognitive Psychology* in 1972 (vol. 3, no. 1) and has been reproduced in Winograd (1976). It has been described in a number of places. Its impact may be gauged by the passage on the dust jacket of Winograd (1976) from Professor Max Clowes:

'Asked to say what Artificial Intelligence has to show for its first 15 years, any practitioner is bound to say, Terry Winograd's program'.

One reason for its importance is that it simultaneously tackled many aspects of language understanding. It did not just consider syntax or semantics but integrated both these and references to context and problem solving issues in a single unified whole.

Fig. 3.12. An example of SIR output. (Adapted from Raphael, 1968.)

```
User:  Every boy is a person
SIR:   I understand
User:  A finger is part of a hand
SIR:   I understand
User:  Each person has two hands
SIR:   The above sentence is ambiguous. Please rephrase it
User:  There are two hands on each person
SIR:   I understand
User:  How many fingers does John have?
SIR:   The above sentence is ambiguous, but I assume 'has'
       means 'has as parts'. I don't know whether finger
       is part of John.
User:  John is a boy
SIR:   I understand
User:  How many fingers does John have?
SIR:   The above sentence is ambiguous, but I assume 'has'
       means 'has as parts'. How many fingers per hand?
User:  Every hand has 5 fingers
SIR:   The above sentence is ambiguous, but I assume 'has'
       means 'has as parts'.
User:  How many fingers does John have?
SIR:   The above sentence is ambiguous, but I assume 'has'
       means 'has as parts'. The answer is 10.
```

Needless to say, no program short of one which is indistinguishable from a human will be perfect (and, to some, even the latter will be imperfect). Thus, only naturally, Winograd's program SHRDLU has received its share of criticism. Much of this suggests that the program only achieves the success it does because it so highly constrains its domain (see below). This seems a little unfair to me. It seems unrealistic to expect more from a system running on a highly constrained processor (as were the computers of the late 1960s and early 1970s compared with the human brain or even modern machines). Winston (1977, p. 178) indicates the flavour of SHRDLU's reception with his somewhat backhanded compliment: 'A thesis of very great influence, which unfortunately treated some problems so well that it gave the impression that all problems were solved'. (In fact Weizenbaum, 1976, p. 196 says of criticisms that Winograd himself has made of SHRDLU: 'It really must be said that this expression of humility is enormously refreshing, especially since it comes from within the priesthood of the artificial intelligentsia, and so is virtually unique'. Boden (1977) gives an excellent discussion of the shortcomings of SHRDLU.)

As we have remarked elsewhere, focussing attention on small domains is one way to make artificial intelligence feasible. Winograd applies this general principle to language understanding (p. 2): 'We feel that the best way to experiment with complex models of language is to write a computer program which can actually understand language within some domain'. The domain he has chosen is the blocks world. This consists of a table top containing a number of blocks of various colours and simple shapes (cubes, pyramids, boxes, etc.). The robot SHRDLU had a hand using which it could pick up, move, and put down the blocks. Thus it was able to rearrange the configuration of the blocks on command. In fact this blocks world was simulated in a computer, which leaves us free to concentrate on the language understanding part of the program and not be concerned with mechanical details such as slippage of the robot arm drive mechanism, or perceptual details such as how it recognises a red cube when it sees one.

SHRDLU is based on systemic grammar as outlined in § 3.7. Its parser is written in PROGRAMMAR, a language specially designed for writing grammars. One may think of SHRDLU as being a collection of interacting programs for handling aspects of syntax and semantics. Each program may interrupt others and be interrupted itself and this allows the system to avoid pursuing futile parses. Winograd gives as an example the sentences 'He gave the boy plants to water' and 'He gave the house plants to charity'. Interpreting the phrase 'boy plants' in the same way as 'house plants' is clearly something we would want to avoid, and such an interpretation is rejected by a semantic analysis program. This sort of idea applies generally.

So, for example, a subprogram for parsing noun groups may call a semantic routine for analysing noun groups. If no semantic interpretation is possible some alternative parse is tried. This sort of process avoids the need to examine all possible parses: in effect the system functions in an intelligent way in choosing a single parse. If an interpretation of a sentence fails, the reasons for failure are remembered and can help in choosing an alternative interpretation. As Winograd (1976, p. 23) says: 'Few sentences seem ambiguous to humans when first read. They are guided by an understanding of what is said to pick a single parsing and a very few different meanings. By using this same knowledge to guide its parsing, a computer understanding system can take advantage of the same technique to parse meaningful sentences quickly and efficiently'.

Any intelligent system needs some kind of internal representation of the external world, which it can manipulate and to which it can refer its perceptions. SHRDLU is no exception, and in order for it to be able to carry out commands and instructions relating to the blocks world, it has to be able to plan. For example, if asked to place the green cube on top of a red one it has first to determine which red one (is there one which has nothing on top of it?) and second it has to work out how to move anything which may be on top of the green cube (and which is preventing the hand from picking up the green cube).

SHRDLU's internal model is described in the PLANNER language. This represents a relationship between two objects as an ordered triple. Thus 'Mary kicked Jack' becomes (kick Mary Jack). 'Relationships' involving a single object (i.e. properties), and relationships involving more than two objects, are similarly represented: e.g. (lazy Jack) and (threw Mary ball Jack). Clearly the order of elements is important in this representation. The objects involved in such relationships might be relationships themselves, and by this means more complicated models can be built up.

An important feature of SHRDLU is its *procedural* representation. For example, nouns are called as programs, which set up standard forms of data structures. Thus if the noun group 'a green pyramid' occurs, the procedure triggered by the noun 'pyramid' sets semantic markers indicating the type of object, the procedure triggered by 'green' checks that pyramids can be green (it would reject 'green ideas'), and the procedure for 'a' sets an appropriate feature to 'indefinite'.

Using a procedural representation in this way has the advantage that it yields an extremely flexible system, but it has the associated disadvantage that it is difficult to maintain consistency if the procedures need to be modified.

The sort of thing the system was capable of is illustrated below. (This is extracted, with permission, from 'Understanding natural language' by Terry Winograd in *Cognitive Psychology*, **3**, 1972, published by Academic Press. The full text of the dialogue and accompanying diagrams of the blocks world is given in that reference, and also in Winograd, 1976.) The commands from the human follow the numbers (and are in bold print). SHRDLU's responses are given in capitals. The other passages are parenthetical notes to the reader.

1. Pick up a big red block.

OK.

The system answers 'OK' when it carries out a command. In order to pick up the red block, it had to clear it off by finding a space for the green one and moving the green one away.

2. Grasp the pyramid.

I DON'T UNDERSTAND WHICH PYRAMID YOU MEAN.

There are three pyramids in the scene, so the program does nothing.

3. Find a block which is taller than the one you are holding and put it into the box.

The system has to figure out what is meant by 'one' and 'it', as well as using deduction to decide which block it is holding.

BY 'IT', I ASSUME YOU MEAN THE BLOCK WHICH IS TALLER THAN THE ONE I AM HOLDING.

Printed out to keep us informed.

OK.

The hand has to set down the red block to pick up the taller blue one.

4. What does the box contain?

THE BLUE PYRAMID AND THE BLUE BLOCK.

5. What is the pyramid supported by?

Earlier the system responded to 'the pyramid' by saying 'I don't understand which pyramid you mean.' Now, it assumes that we mean the one just mentioned.

THE BOX.

6. How many blocks are not in the box?

Negatives such as 'not' and 'no' are handled whether they appear in clauses or noun groups (such as 'no boxes').

FOUR OF THEM.

7. Is at least one of them narrower than the one which I told you to pick up?

The phrase 'at least one of them' must be analyzed to refer back

to the previous question, and 'the one which . . .' must also refer to
blocks. Noun groups can have complicated numbers such as 'at
least one', 'more than three', 'exactly seven', etc. The memory of
past events is used to deduce which block is 'the one which I told
you to pick up'. Notice the complicated syntactic structure in
which 'the one' is actually the object of a clause embedded two
levels deeper.

YES THE RED CUBE.

8. Is it supported?

Passives can be used without a 'by . . .' phrase.

YES BY THE TABLE.

9. Can the table pick up blocks?

NO.

The semantic rules make this a nonsensical question which
therefore must be false.

10. Can a pyramid be supported by a block?

YES.

The deductive system finds an actual example, so it knows this
possible.

11. Can a pyramid support a pyramid?

I DON'T KNOW.

The question makes sense, but there is no example in the scene,
so there is no easy way to tell without being able to examine the
robot's programs.

12. Stack up two pyramids.

I CAN'T.

The robot tries and fails.

13. The blue pyramid is mine.

I UNDERSTAND.

This data is added to the data base.

**14. I own blocks which are not red, but I don't own anything
which supports a pyramid.**

I UNDERSTAND.

Two new theorems are created for proving things about
'owning'.

15. Do I own the box?

NO.

The box supports whatever it contains, including a pyramid.

16. Do I own anything in the box?

YES, TWO THINGS: THE BLUE BLOCK AND
THE BLUE PYRAMID.

17. Will you please stack up both of the red blocks and either a green cube or pyramid?

OK.

Logical connectives such as 'and' 'or' 'either' etc. are handled in both the grammar and semantics. A command is executed even if it looks like a question. The command is carried out by the following series of steps: it puts a green cube on the large red block (note that it chooses the green cube with nothing on it), then removes the small pyramid from the little red cube, so that it can use that cube to complete the stack as specified.

18. Which cube is sitting on the table?

THE LARGE GREEN ONE WHICH SUPPORTS THE RED PYRAMID.

Ordinarily the system would be satisfied with calling this 'a big green cube', but since we asked 'which cube' it has to be more specific in naming it. The use of substitute nouns (such as 'one') and pronouns in answers makes the discourse more natural.

19. Is there a large block behind a pyramid?

YES, THREE OF THEM: A LARGE RED ONE, A LARGE GREEN CUBE AND THE BLUE ONE.

20. Put a small one onto the green cube which supports a pyramid.

'A small one' must contrast with the earlier phrase 'a large block', so this means 'a small block'.

OK.

21. Put the littlest pyramid on top of it.

Words like 'littlest' are not in the dictionary but are interpreted from the root forms like 'little'.

OK.

22. How many things are on top of green cubes?

I'M NOT SURE WHAT YOU MEAN BY 'ON TOP OF' IN THE PHRASE 'ON TOP OF GREEN CUBES'.

DO YOU MEAN: 1 – DIRECTLY ON THE SURFACE
                       2 – ANYWHERE ON TOP OF?

When there are several interpretations and none is clearly better, the system has to ask the user for more information. The paraphrases were included with the dictionary definition of 'on', and the request for more information occurs automatically when the heuristics for resolving ambiguities aren't sufficient. A request like this can also occur when the meaning of a pronoun such as 'it' or 'they' is unclear.

2

THREE OF THEM.

23. Had you touched any pyramid before you put the green one on the little cube?

YES, THE GREEN ONE.

The system deduces from its memory what event is being referred to, and can relate other events to it in time. The analysis includes complex tenses of verb groups, and there are special facilities for keeping track of the various forms of irregular verbs like 'have'.

24. When did you pick it up?

WHILE I WAS STACKING UP THE RED CUBE, A LARGE RED BLOCK AND A LARGE GREEN CUBE.

A time is described by naming the main goal which was being worked on.

25. Why?

The system remembers immediately previous sentences to understand questions like this and the following ones.

TO GET RID OF IT.

By keeping track of selected parts of the original subgoal tree, the system has some understanding of its motives.

26. Why did you do that?

TO CLEAN OFF THE RED CUBE.

'That' refers to the action mentioned in the answer.

27. Why did you clear off that cube?

Here, 'that' means the one just referred to.

TO PUT IT ON A LARGE GREEN CUBE.

28. Why did you do that?

TO STACK UP THE RED CUBE, A LARGE RED BLOCK AND A LARGE GREEN CUBE.

29. Why did you do that?

BECAUSE YOU ASKED ME TO.

It remembers what it did, not how the request was worded.

30. How did you do it?

'It' refers to the action mentioned in the last question, rather than the answer.

BY PUTTING A LARGE RED BLOCK ON THE TABLE THEN LETTING GO OF IT; THEN PUTTING A LARGE GREEN CUBE ON IT; THEN LETTING GO OF THAT CUBE; THEN PUTTING THE RED CUBE ON THAT CUBE; THEN LETTING GO OF THAT CUBE.

This is a description of the top-level subgoals used to achieve the goal.

31. How many objects did you touch while you were doing it?

Time references can refer to a time span, using words like 'while'.

FOUR OF THEM.

32. What did the red cube support before you started to clean it off?

THE GREEN PYRAMID.

By remembering what has been moved, it is possible to deduce things about earlier states of the scene. We can use complex nestings of clauses like 'before you started to clean it off'.

33. There were five blocks to the left of the box then.

'Then' must refer to the time mentioned in the last sentence.

NO, ONLY FOUR OF THEM: THE RED CUBE, TWO LARGE GREEN CUBES AND A LARGE RED BLOCK.

Earlier in the dialog, new information about 'owning' was accepted at face value. But the system knows that it has complete information about the basic properties of objects, including location. It checks any statements about location or other such properties to see whether it agrees or disagrees.

34. Put the blue pyramid on the block in the box.

This is syntactically ambiguous, but is understood without ambiguity since the parsing corresponding to 'put the blue pyramid which is on the block in the box,' does not make sense in the current scene, while 'put the blue pyramid on the block which is in the box' does.

OK.

35. Is there anything which is bigger than every pyramid but is not as wide as the thing that supports it?

The system understands quantifiers such as 'every', 'any', 'some', etc., and structures such as 'bigger than', 'as wide as', etc. Here 'it' refers to a noun group within the same sentence but two levels up in the parsing tree.

YES, THE BLUE BLOCK.

36. Does a steeple

SORRY, I DON'T KNOW THE WORD 'STEEPLE'.

The system interrupts immediately when it sees a word it can't figure out.

37. A 'steeple' is a stack which contains two green cubes and pyramid.

The quote marks indicate that we are defining a new word.

I UNDERSTAND.

38. Are there any steeples now?

NO.

The new definition is used as a description to recognize steeples.

39. Build one.

OK.

The description given in the definition is enough to deduce a plan for building new objects as well as recognizing them. The word 'one' means 'a steeple', and the plan is carried out. First, one of the large green cubes is cleared off by removing the red cube and two pyramids. Then the two green cubes and the tall red pyramid are stacked up to fit the description.

40. Call the biggest block 'superblock'.

OK.

We can also give objects names.

41. Have you picked up superblock since we began?

YES.

42. Why did you drop it?

BY 'IT' I ASSUME' YOU MEAN THE SUPERBLOCK.
I CAN'T EXPLAIN A NONEXISTENT EVENT.

There is no record in memory of any block being dropped.

43. Is there anything to the right of the red pyramid?

YES, FOUR THINGS: THE BOX, THE RED CUBE,
THE BLUE PYRAMID AND THE BLOCK NAMED
SUPERBLOCK.

Once an object has a name, the name is used to help identify it in responses.

44. Thank you.

YOU'RE WELCOME!

Idioms can be defined without modifying the grammar.

It is interesting to contrast SHRDLU and PARRY (Chapter 6). PARRY seems to be able to respond sensibly to a tremendous range of inputs while SHRDLU's conversation is very limited to its blocks world. However, as we discuss in Chapter 6, one cannot infer from this that PARRY is the more intelligent system. It is fair to say that in some sense SHRDLU *understands* what it is talking about. It has an inner ('mental') model of its world and relates its communication to that model. It can plan, deduce, and infer. PARRY's internal representation is much shallower. Thus appearances can be deceptive.

Example 3: Discourse production (Davey, 1978)

Natural language processing has two poles. One is natural language *under-*

standing. Statements and questions must be analysed, decomposed and absorbed into the basic knowledge representation if the system is to take any kind of action as a result. In most understanding systems the action is fairly simple. It might be a straightforward physical action (or a simulation of it, as in SHRDLU) or it might be a retrieval from a database.

The other pole is that of systems which *generate* statements or questions. Of course, some systems, such as question-answering or database retrieval systems, must do both, but in general their output relies on 'canned' replies – answers which follow a limited set of precisely defined templates.

The system about to be described is different. Davey (1978) concentrated on producing discourse rather than accepting it. In fact, he took as his subject matter the restricted domain of the game of noughts and crosses and developed a program which could describe any such game in a connected sequence of English sentences.

Before describing his system perhaps we should emphasise the novelty of this approach. By far the vast majority of systems concentrate on the first pole. This should be reassuring for any Frankenstein watchers amongst the readers! It means that researchers have been concerned with getting a computer to do what it is told, rather than getting a computer to demand something or express an opinion!

Davey (p. 1) describes the aims of his system as follows:

> Our objective is to show how a speaker gets from what needs to be said to the words that say it. The model therefore specifies how to decide what has to be put into words, how to divide this information into sentences, how to arrange a sentence so that its parts fit their context and are easy to understand, and then how to pick words and combine them into phrases to mean the right things. It also specifies, and this is perhaps the most interesting bit, what can be left unsaid: it attempts always to avoid telling the hearer anything he knows already, anything more than he needs to know, or anything he might reasonably be expected to work out for himself.

And (p. 8):

> The program gives a commentary on a game, or part-game of noughts and crosses. It assumes that the audience understands the game and follows the commentary as it is given. In order to help the audience, the program arranges the commentary in such a way that each separate sentence describes a coherent episode in the game, a move or sequence of moves, which forms a 'play' in the struggle. The program has available certain sequential and contrastive conjunctions with which it signals to the audience the relation of one move to the next, and its deliberations about the arrangement

of move-descriptions into sentences are influenced by a preference for making the fullest possible use of these signals. The program's resources include subordinating conjunctions, and so the program may at this stage decide not only what moves the next sentence will describe, but also whether a particular move will be described in a minor clause.

Thus moves are explained in groups which form tactically meaningful chunks. Working in the opposite direction, and to counter any tendency to generate over-large sentences, a restriction to a maximum of three main clauses is imposed.

Davey acknowledges that the system is not perfect (it would be naive to expect it to be so at the current level of machine technology). He points out that the sentences generated are simple, consisting of subject–verb–complement structures, although the verb may be modified by an adverb and the complement may be an object, an adjectival phrase, or missing altogether. Subordinate clauses are, of course, generated.

The driving tension within the program arises from an attempt to reduce the gap between what the program knows about a particular game and what it believes the listener knows. It can attribute mistakes to its opponent (by comparing the opponent's moves with those it would have made under similar circumstances). Taking this attitude, rather than suspecting it might be wrong itself, is a very human attribute!

In explaining a game the program examines the immediate tactical implications of each move and then decides how to group moves. The product of these steps is a semantic specification for each sentence and not a direct syntactic specification. However, the semantic constraints are sufficiently rigid that the main clause is effectively determined.

The grammatical basis on which the design is based is derived from Halliday's systemic grammar (Hudson, 1971; see Davey, 1978 for a full list of references and see § 3.7). The basic structures of systemic grammar, outlined above (systems, words, groups, clauses, features, etc.), are extended by a set of rules which restrict the forms an item may take in accordance with the grammatical environment. This grammatical environment is defined by the feature list of the parent unit in a two stage process: (i) A set of rules note what features the parent has and determine from these features what functions must be performed and so what items are necessary to perform these functions. These rules are *feature realisation rules*. (ii) Re-order these functions and in some cases add further functions using *structure-building rules*. Once the grammatical environment has been defined *function realisation* rules determine the features of the constituents of the items. An example of this process would be the environment specifying that

a first person singular pronoun was to occur as the object of the verb so that
the rule sets would restrict the choice from the possible pronouns (*I*, *me*, *we*,
us, etc.) to *me*. An illustration of the whole process for a clause is given in
Fig. 3.13. Davey (p. 111) informally summarises the process as follows:

> The design procedure places the sentence design at the root of what
> will become the constituent structure tree of the sentence. The
> construction procedures then grow the tree until every branch
> terminates in a word. The root node is a sentence node, and the rest
> are clause, or group, or word nodes. For each type of node there is
> a specialist procedure that grows the immediate descendant nodes.
> A construction procedure receives a specification of its task in the
> form of a semantic representation and a partial or complete feature
> list for the item to be constructed. If the feature list is complete, the
> constructor simply invokes the realisation and structure-building
> rules appropriate to that type of item. Usually, however, the
> feature list needs completion. Each constructor specialises in
> traversing the systems sub-net for its type of item: it knows how to
> select the right feature from each relevant system. In making these
> selections, the procedure may use syntactic information, and
> semantic specialists that can report what game situation has been
> reached in the description so far, what has been mentioned
> recently, what other moves the current sentence will describe, and
> so on.

Fig. 3.13. The design procedure for a clause in Davey's system. (Adapted
from Davey, 1978.)

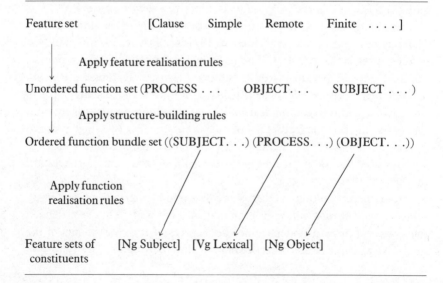

Before giving some examples of the text generated by the system, there is an additional point which should be mentioned. This is that, although this system generates sentences, it does so in the context of larger blocks of text. It is a true *discourse generating* system not one for producing isolated sentences. This is in contrast to most other grammatical work – notably transformational grammar, which focuses on generating individual sentences. As such, although the system naturally has severe limitations, it represents an important contribution to our understanding of natural language processing. (Davey's thesis (Davey, 1978) is also recommended for its wider discussion of natural language processing, as well as the details of this particular system.)

Demonstration 1 (Adapted from Davey, 1978, appendix 1)

The program plays 0 in both demonstrations.

Referring to Fig. 3.14, the program generated the following:

The game started with my taking a corner, and you took an adjacent one. I threatened you by taking the middle of the edge opposite that and adjacent to the one which I had just taken but you blocked it and threatened me. I blocked your diagonal and you forked me. If you had blocked mine, you would have forked me, but you took the middle of the edge opposite the corner which I took first and the one which you had taken and so I won by completing my diagonal.

Fig. 3.14. The game described in Demonstration 1.

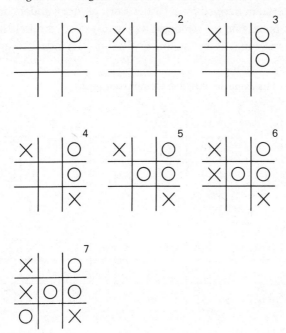

Demonstration 2

Referring to Fig. 3.15, the program generated the following:

The game began with your taking a corner, and I took the middle of an adjacent side. You threatened me by taking the end of the one adjacent to the corner which you had just taken and to the one which I had just taken the middle of but I blocked that, and you took the square opposite the one I had just taken. I took the middle of the board and threatened you. If you had blocked my line you would have threatened me, but you took the corner adjacent to the one which you took first and so I won by completing my line.

Not Nobel Prize winning style, perhaps, but a major feat nevertheless when one recognises that this is generated from raw words and morphemes and not from templates.

Example 4: QUALM (Lehnert, 1978)

When reviewing Lehnert's book in 1979, I stated that 'its specialised nature means that it is unlikely to be of wide interest or relevance to computer professionals' (Hand, 1980). How the field progresses! Now I would say that most professionals should have some grasp of the content of this book, and that it is of both interest and relevance to even a layman. Thanks to theoretical advances and hardware development, question answering systems are already available commercially and can be expected to have a major impact on our everyday lives before long.

The book basically describes Lehnert's Ph.D. work. The initial impetus for the QUALM system derived from earlier work on story understanding systems. Lehnert noted that the strongest way to test story comprehension, be it in man or machine, is by requiring the 'understander' to answer

Fig. 3.15. The game described in Demonstration 2.

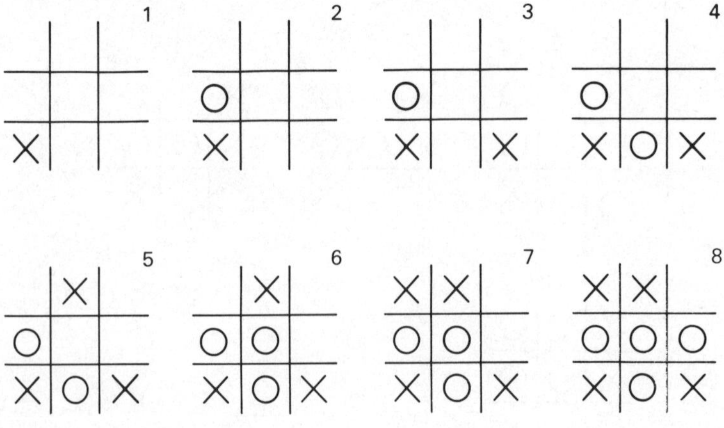

questions about the story. Questions, after all, can be posed to examine all aspects of comprehension.

QUALM, then, represents one in a series of systems related to text analysis. This makes it a stronger system – it is not just an isolated program but builds on and improves earlier theories (see also the remarks about INTERNIST in Chapter 5 and PARRY in Chapter 6).

In particular, QUALM runs in conjunction with SAM and PAM, larger systems which accept stories in English and generate internal representations. They can produce paraphrase output and (a very significant point), because of the modular nature of the systems, this paraphrased output can be in English, Spanish, Russian, Dutch, and Chinese (or, presumably, any other language, were one to write the output module).

Lehnert also briefly describes two other associated programs, COIL and ASP. COIL (Conceptual Objects for Inferencing in Language) was built to test how well a particular representation for physical objects lent itself to inference and retrieval. ASP (Answer Selection Program) took as an input a question about a story and a set of possible answers and then selected the most appropriate answer. The aim was to explore theories of the way in which suitable answers were chosen.

The underlying representation behind these systems, and that of QUALM itself, is *conceptual dependency* (see § 2.3). This represents meaning in terms of a structure composed of atomic elements termed *semantic primitives*. To understand a story the system has to translate the sentences comprising the story into a linked chain of events or ideas. Often, if not usually, items not explicitly included in the story have to be inserted in the linked chain (if we hear that Mary went to hospital after a car crash we infer that she was probably injured). Such inferences are derived from script and plan mechanisms (see § 2.4) within SAM and PAM.

QUALM may be regarded as consisting of two phases: understanding the question in the first place, and, having understood it, identifying an appropriate answer.

Let us look at each of these in turn.

Question understanding has four consecutive levels of interpretive analysis:

(1) A language dependent *conceptual parse* stage, which transforms the question into the conceptual dependency representation. Lehnert stresses the inadequacy of this stage as a complete understanding of the question. For example, she points out that the question 'Can you tell me where John is?' is expected to produce a location rather than the answer 'yes'.

(2) A *memory internalisation* stage which replaces nouns by pointers to tokens (see § 2.3).

Stages (1) and (2) can handle statements as well as questions. Stage (2) (and stages (3) and (4) below) are language independent, operating within the conceptual dependency representation.

(3) A *conceptual categorisation* stage which decomposes the internalised parse of a question into a 'question concept' and conceptual category. For example, in 'Did John hit Mary?' the first of these components is *verification* and the second represents 'John hit Mary'.

(4) The final stage is one of *inferential analysis*. This fills in the implicit inferences referred to above to find the correct interpretations. So, for example, the question 'What haven't I packed?' does not generate a list of everything in the Universe outside my suitcase.

Turning to the second QUALM phase we must now find an answer. Again this is a multi-stage process, but now of only two stages:

(1) The *content specification* stage identifies what kind of answer is needed (honest, misleading, detailed, brief, . . .). Lehnert says (p. 108): 'The factors that determine what people say and how they say it are motivational factors concerned with the context and purpose of conversation. If a model of Q/A does not acknowledge the role that these factors must play in the question-answering process, it cannot be viewed as a comprehensive model of human question-answering'.

And (p. 109): 'Content specification can be thought of as an interface device that takes information about the general attitude or mood of the system . . . and integrates this information into the retrieval instructions, which produce an appropriate answer'.

For a different purpose PARRY (Chapter 6) contains a similar mechanism.

(2) Having determined what kind of answer is needed and how to search for it, it remains actually to carry out the search. The heuristics to do this are guided by the results of the content specification analysis if such specification is present. If it is not, then a default is used. The heuristics are tailored to work well with the kind of memory representation produced by the scripts and plans applied when the story is understood. Lehnert notes that most questions can be answered directly from the stored representation but some (for example, questions relating to why someone did not follow some alternative course of action) may require information not explicitly within the stored representation. Special procedures are followed in such cases.

Sometimes the attempt to find an answer reveals that the initial question analysis was inadequate (perhaps because of a mistaken focus), and the process recycles. Finally, another module takes the conceptual dependency representation of the answer and generates an English response.

The examples given throughout Lehnert (1978) are particularly illuminating of the difficulties which will be encountered by anyone constructing a question answering system, and this book is recommended to anyone interested in natural language processing.

3.11　Further reading

One of the most comprehensive pattern matching systems is the PARRY series, described in Chapter 6. For historical interest in pattern matching Weizenbaum (1965) is recommended.

For formal theories from the computer side see Aho & Ullman (1972). Transformational grammar now takes many forms. The seminal work is, of course, that of Chomsky (1957, 1965), and see also Chomsky (1977). Other recommended work is Jacobson (1978) and Akmajian & Heny (1975). It should be noted that, as with systemic grammar, much of the work has appeared in unpublished duplicated note form.

The most influential early descriptions of augmented transition networks are given by Woods (1970, 1973) and Kaplan (1972, 1973, 1975).

For work on systemic grammar see Halliday's paper in Lyons (1970), Halliday (1978), Kress (1976), and Berry (1975, 1977).

Finally, an essential work for anyone's syntax library is that *tour de force*: Winograd (1983).

Semantics is discussed in Charniak & Wilks (1978) and in chapters 4 and 5 of Tennant (1981). Note that sometimes it is not possible to discuss syntax or semantics alone so often the two occur, intertwined, in the same publications. References to semantic networks and conceptual dependency can be found in Chapter 2 of the present book.

Discourse and text generation are further discussed in Brady & Berwick (1983), Mann & Moore (1980), and Clippinger (1975).

Work on machine translation is described in Snell (1979) and Hays & Mathias (1976), and a concise and interesting history of early developments is given in section IV B of volume I of Barr & Feigenbaum (1983).

Summaries of several natural language processing systems are given in Tennant (1981) and Winograd (1983), chapter 7.

4

Search and proof

4.1 Search

Chapter 2 introduced the concept of representation as a general notion which must be addressed either directly or indirectly when considering intelligent computer programs. A number of particular representations were introduced. In this section another general aspect of artificial intelligence is outlined, one which is again ubiquitous and one which appears in many manifestations. This is the concept of *search*. Moreover, since search is intimately connected with theorem proving (a dry term for planning, designing, deciding what to do, and so on), the second part of this chapter deals with proof in the powerful representation of the predicate calculus.

Search is a general term for choosing one item (route, solution, diagnosis, word, operation, etc.) from a set of such items. Frequently there is a premium on speed so that efficient techniques are desirable. Also it is often the case that the set of items is astronomically huge (or even infinite) so that some subtle or intelligent search procedure is needed if the search is to terminate in a reasonable time (or, perhaps, at all). Frequently, as we shall see below, this forces a compromise in which we abandon the effort to find the very best solution in favour of seeking a merely adequate one in exchange for the guarantee of a reasonable search time.

A general term for the domain over which the search occurs is *space*. We shall see examples of search spaces below. The search space may be composed of an infinite number of different elements, continuously linked to each other through other elements (just as all the points on a line are continuously linked via other points on the line). Often, however, the search space is composed of distinct and separate elements. These may be finite in number but they may be infinite (just as the integers are distinct and separate but are infinite in number). A common way of representing parts of spaces of the latter kind is by a graph: the distinct elements become nodes and the relationships between them become links (if there are such relationships – more on this below). Other names are often used (frequently derived more closely from the particular area of application a user has in mind). For example, the space may be called a *database* and the links or relationships between elements may be called *operators*, since, in some contexts, they show ways of moving from one element of the space to another.

To set the scene before we consider different search methods let us glance at the outlines of a few search problems:

(i) Finding a word in a dictionary to match a given input word. Clearly the search space here is finite.

(ii) Finding a proof of a theorem (or planning how to carry something out). Here the starting element of the space is known (the start *state*). It consists of the axioms and the theorems which have already been proven (or, if thinking of plans, it consists of the current state of the world). Similarly, the goal state is known. What is unknown is the sequence of steps connecting start and goal states. It is in this space of step sequences that the search occurs. This space is potentially infinite. It may be infinite in the trivial way that one can do and undo some action repetitively *ad infinitum*, but it may also be infinite in more subtle and interesting ways. Note that from any partially completed set of steps in a proof or plan chain one must decide what the next step should be. Thus again one is presented with a search problem, only now in the space of single steps.

(iii) Choosing a production rule from a list of eligible rules. The list will clearly be finite but speed may be very important.

(iv) Games can often be analysed as implicit tree structures: from this position player A has a choice of these moves, for the first of which player B must choose from these, and for the second from those, and so on. The objective is then to search for a path through the tree which culminates in a win.

What follows is a description of search methods in a roughly increasing order of the requirements they make of the search space.

(a) *Exhaustive search*

Perhaps the search method that a newcomer to the field would first think of is *exhaustive search*. This is merely the name for the process of examining the states of the search space one by one in a methodical manner until a solution state is found. Should there be no solution, the process continues until all the states have been examined.

Sometimes this is a perfectly reasonable solution. It might be fast enough when matching input words against a dictionary. Here the search space is of finite size so that the search is guaranteed to terminate in a finite time. Of course, 'finite' might not be small enough, since the language processing system might be operating in real time with a user waiting for an answer.

Unfortunately there are problem domains where this simple and obvious method is not feasible. One is where the search space, though finite, is very large. (This sort of situation often arises due to the *combinatorial explosion* – where one is seeking a best combination of elements.) An initial reaction to this might be that it poses no real problem – modern computers are immensely fast, capable of carrying out millions of additions and multiplications per second, and future computers will doubtless be even faster. However, take for illustration the game of chess. A very rough calculation gives the number of games as approximately 10^{120}. There are around 3×10^7 seconds in a year. Thus the trees of possible moves from any particular position can be so astronomically huge as to preclude the possibility of exhaustive search. Certainly, the question of whether chess, if played 'optimally' by both sides, is a won or drawn game is decidable in principle but not in practice. Some other – cleverer or more intelligent – way than exhaustive search must be found.

Sometimes things appear even more hopeless than merely very large search spaces. Sometimes these spaces are infinite. We referred above to the problem of choosing a sequence of steps to accomplish some objective. There will be an infinite number of possible sequences, so exhaustive enumeration is not just infeasible, it is impossible. Here the necessity for some more subtle approach is more pressing.

Exhaustive search requires that the elements of the search space be placed in some order so that current serial machines can examine the possible solutions one at a time without repetition or omission. This means identifying, or perhaps imposing, some structure on the space and then mapping this structure to a serial order. Note that no further use is made of the structure.

Fig. 4.1 A tree graph of solutions.

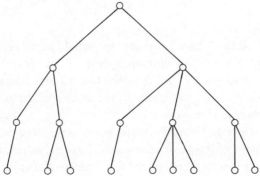

A common structure is a tree graph. An example is given in Fig. 4.1. We might be trying to match some input against parts of a semantic net. The nodes in the figure may be such parts, with descendant nodes perhaps being specialisations or particular types of ancestor node. Two broadly different kinds of exhaustive serial search processes may be applied to such trees (that is, there are two basic methods of mapping the tree structure to a linear sequence) although there are extensions which take from both approaches.

The first approach is the *breadth first* approach. This is illustrated in Fig. 4.2. All nodes at one particular level are examined before the search drops to the next level. The second approach, illustrated in Fig. 4.3, is the *depth first* approach. Here each branch is followed to its tip before back-tracking to another branch. Both methods are exhaustive – they examine every node and are guaranteed to find a solution should one exist. The depth first method has been described as *optimistic* because of the way it throws its resources into the first branch it encounters. In contrast, the breadth first method is cautious and *pessimistic*.

(b) *Random search*

There is a search method which is even more basic than exhaustive search in that it makes even less use of any structure in the set of potential solutions. This method, that of *random search*, simply randomly selects states of the search space for examination. The method is also known as the *British Museum Algorithm*. There are several suggested derivations for this name, but they are all of the kind: given a hundred monkeys randomly hitting the keys of typewriters they would eventually, by chance alone, generate the entire collection of books in the British Museum. Of course the Universe would have died a heat death long since, but that is not the point. Put this way the inefficiency of the method is rather obvious. Even so, there might be occasions when it can be of use. An example would be when a relatively

Fig. 4.2. Breadth first tree search.

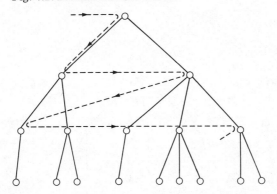

high proportion of the search space elements are acceptable as solutions. If there is no strong structure in the space it is conceivable that random search might be acceptably effective. Moreover, whatever its shortcomings, the method does serve as an absolute basis against which the performance of other methods can be assessed.

(c) *Evolutionary search*

A much more interesting random method is the method of *evolutionary search*. This makes use of local structure in the search space and, indeed, locally requires more structure than the exhaustive method. Put simply, it requires that, when two states are compared, it should be possible to say which of the two is better: which is closer to the (or a) solution.

The basic method is as follows. One begins with an arbitrary state (though the nearer one can make this to a solution the better) and randomly perturbs it to a nearby state. These two (the initial and perturbed) states are compared. The better is then chosen for the start of a new perturbation cycle. The idea is that the method will gradually inch its way towards the solution, getting nearer to it at each step.

The method has some weaknesses. It can be inefficient: because of the typical large size of the search space most suggested changes, even though they improve things, do so only very slightly. Moreover it has a tendency to pursue dead ends – if some state is better than those near it, though not a global best, the method may converge upon this local best. Of course, more sophisticated and complicated methods have been devised to tackle these disadvantages.

If more structure is present, which can be taken advantage of, then the method can be accelerated. A simple example is a space in which each state only has a few links to neighbours (or, one might say, there are only a few

Fig. 4.3. Depth first tree search.

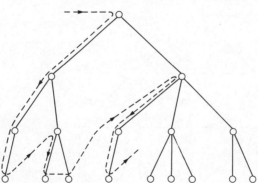

operators which allow transition from one state to another). In this case the links can be exhaustively searched and the best chosen at each step. A further simple example is that of a continuous search space. Fig. 4.4 illustrates contours in a two-dimensional such space. The aim is to find the point with the largest (equals best) value.

It is obvious to us that Y is the solution but a computer cannot see the contour map in its entirety. It can only see the height of single points and must proceed a step at a time. (That this should not be regarded as a weakness of the computer can be seen when we extend the problem to a hundred-dimensional search space. The human, who cannot conceivably visualise 99-dimensional contours in such a space, is now completely at sea. But the computer's stepwise method can proceed in just the same manner as in the two-dimensional space.)

The random search method described above randomly scatters points over this two-dimensional space and chooses the largest. In this example one might expect it to do quite well – choosing a final point somewhere near Y. In large dimensional spaces, however, unless the number of points examined becomes absurdly large, it will usually not do very well.

The evolutionary search method begins at some point X and considers an arbitrarily chosen point near X (call it Z). If the value of Z is greater than the value at X then Z is taken as the new starting point. Otherwise X is retained, the process generating a new random point near X. By this process an irregular path inches its way up the slope.

Now this example in fact allows us to take advantage of more structure. In particular, note that the space is *smooth*. A small step away from X (or any other point) leads to a small change in value. (This is perhaps in contrast to most of the search spaces encountered in artificial intelligence work.) One implication of this good behaviour is that the computer can examine the

Fig. 4.4. Contours in a two-dimensional continuous search space.

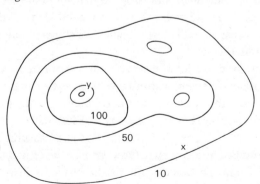

points near to X and determine the *best* direction to go. Then it can take a larger step in this best direction. The final result is a smoother path involving less computation. In general it is more efficient though it can still converge to local, non-global 'best' solutions.

This method, in the continuous space we have been describing, is known as *hill-climbing* (or, when the aim is to find the smallest rather than the largest value – perhaps if it is a measure of discrepancy – *steepest descent*). Classical mathematics has developed extremely powerful methods for searches in such continuous spaces, many of them extensions of this basic idea. References are given at the end of the chapter.

(d) *Accelerated search*

At the end of the preceding section we introduced the steepest descent method, showing how it made use of extra structure in the search space to lead to faster and more efficient searches. Unfortunately, relatively few search domains in artificial intelligence permit this method to be applied because they usually do not involve nice smooth continuous spaces. However, they often have other structural features which can be taken advantage of. In this section we outline one such feature and illustrate how it may be used. The resulting search method is called the *branch and bound* method.

We begin by partitioning the search space into a number of mutually exclusive regions. That is, we divide the set of potential solutions into a collection of non-overlapping sets such that every state of the search space lies in one set. The aim is to find that state which maximises some measure. This might be a measure of closeness of the match between the state and some other element.

We could certainly find this state by examining each state within each of our sets, choosing the best within each set, and then choosing the best of these best. But this boils down to the simple brute force method of exhaustive enumeration. However, suppose that we have identified some state as the best so far examined and suppose that for some set not yet examined we know that no state in this set can be as good as that one already identified (for reasons explained below). Then clearly there is no point in examining the states in this set.

This can obviously save us a lot of work. To carry it out we need to find some number such that no element within a given set can be better than that number. Precisely how this will be done depends on the details of the problem and the search space, but a typical way is as follows.

The objective is to find the state which maximises some measure. Suppose the space can be arranged as a tree structure, with all the elements in one state set emerging from one branch and all the elements in other sets emerging from distinct branches. The potential solution states are the final leaf nodes, the tips of the tree. The other nodes (the branching nodes) can be regarded as partial solutions. For example, suppose we were matching an input word against stored words. Then the branching nodes might consist of word frames, with some letters filled in and some left as wildcards (for example, a branching node containing the frame $AT would match both CAT and BAT perfectly). The tip nodes consist of completed words. Suppose now that every mismatched letter is scored -1. Then a word in the tree which does not match the input word at all well will have a large negative measure. A good but not perfect match will have a small negative measure. Our aim is to find the smallest negative match (i.e. the largest match) that we can. Now, by the nature of this matching process, as we go down the tree the numbers can only get less (more negative) because matching letters do not change things while mismatching ones add -1. This means that the number *at* a branching node can act as the number we require. If we already have a state whose score is better (larger) than that of the branching node then there is no point in examining the nodes which emerge from this branching node. Such nodes can only have smaller (more negative) or the same values. This can save a lot of work.

Usually the branching (splitting into subsets) and bounding (finding numbers such that all nodes in a subset have smaller associated values) are continued through several levels so that a true tree graph results. Note also that in general there is more than one way in which the branching tree may be arranged, some ways being much more efficient than others.

An interesting variant of this kind of accelerated search strategy is the *alpha-beta* method. This applies to situations in which there are two competitors (such as in games), with one competitor trying to maximise some value and the other trying to minimise it. The difference between this and the basic branch and bound method is an alternation of objectives as one works down the tree, switching from player A's move (to maximise) to player B's move (to minimise) and back. Again the basic principle followed is that if a route is identified as bad (worse than some alternative) then there is little point in finding out how bad or how much worse it is.

(e) *And/or trees*

An effective way of accelerating searches, which appears under various guises in this book, is based on the 'divide and conquer' principle. Some problems lend themselves to partitioning such that solutions to the components can be combined to yield overall solutions. A basic structure in this context is the *and/or tree*. Fig. 4.5 illustrates a very simple such tree.

In this figure an arc connecting two (or more) descendant nodes indicates that they must both (i.e. this one *and* that one) be solved for the ancestor to be solved. An absence of a connecting arc indicates that one *or* the other (or others) will suffice to establish the ancestor.

This decomposition results in replacement of the original single problem by a set of simpler problems which may well have smaller and more manageable search spaces. Note also that there may be more than one route through such a tree (ancestor nodes may be derived by more than one possible route) and that a search for an effective route may pay dividends.

Often descendant nodes can be achieved by more than one route. For example, a match to the word IN could be found by first matching I and then N, or the other way round. This would lead to a node for IN which could be reached by two different paths, so that the and/or tree is no longer a tree but is now a more general and/or graph. Note that in such general cases a node may be an *or* component of some ancestor through one route and an *and* component of some other ancestor – it is not the nodes but their relationships which determine their 'andness' and 'orness'.

(f) *Suboptimal methods*
The methods outlined above for tackling more extensive search problems help matters but many problems still lie beyond them. For example, it remains impossible to identify the best move from an arbitrary chess position. In such situations we can sometimes abandon the objective of finding the single best solution and satisfy ourselves with merely finding a good one, one that is adequate for the purpose to hand. Relaxing the aims in this way opens the problem to a much wider range of methods, and indeed gives scope for imaginative development of new methods. The basic aim

Fig. 4.5. A very simple and/or tree.

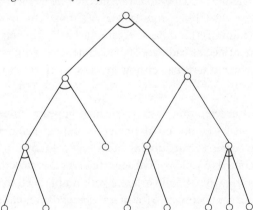

might now be stated as narrowing the search space so that a search becomes feasible and so that the reduced space still contains good solutions. This can be done in a number of ways. One way is to make use of additional task dependent (or *heuristic*) information. We have seen examples of this in Chapter 3, where the search for syntactically valid analyses was guided by constraints imposed by semantic knowledge.

A second way to narrow the search space is to adopt a cumulative search method. For example, suppose one wished to choose the best subset of 10 questions from a set of 200 for use in a psychometric measurement scale or a psychiatric screening instrument (see Chapter 5). There are 2×10^{16} such subsets and each of these would have to be examined if the crude exhaustive approach were being adopted. Assessing a single subset might well be a lengthy process so that assessing and comparing all of them is totally out of the question. Instead we could acknowledge the infeasibility of the exhaustive approach and adopt a cumulative *stepwise* procedure. This begins with an examination of all 200 questions to identify the best single one. Then one examines all remaining 199 questions to find that one which, when used in conjunction with the best one already chosen, gave the best results. Then one seeks a third, and so on, up to 10. It is important to understand that this procedure may not give the best set of 10 (See § 5.6). Indeed it is possible that it might not give a very good set. However, it is reasonable to expect it to yield a good set in most cases. Other approaches along these lines are outlined in Chapter 5. The point to note about them is that they constrain the search space and so make an impossible problem manageable. They can also be viewed from another perspective which allows us to introduce another general definition. This is the concept of an *evaluation function*. Such a function is an indicator of which branches of a search tree are most likely to be of value for pursuing. A typical occurrence would be in a game in which there are too many branches to develop all of them so that a quick (and possibly fairly crude) assessment of their relative merit for development must be made. The stepwise selection method just described can be seen as using such a function: it is used to decide which variable to add to those already selected.

4.2   Resolution proof

In § 2.2 the principles of the predicate calculus were introduced. This calculus has been applied in a large number of areas of artificial intelligence research for two main reasons. First, because it provides a very general representation which can be used to describe an extremely wide range of types of structure with ease. And secondly, because mechanical proof procedures for predicate calculus have been developed. In the language of § 2.2, this means that we can begin with some basic premises and automatically establish the truth of a theorem. In application domains it means that robots may plan sequences of actions to produce a desired effect, database systems can deduce an answer not explicitly stored, simulations can work out how their actions will affect their environments, and so on. In practice 'proof' is simply search in which properties of the formal system are used to constrain the search space. In this section we outline one very important type of proof method for the predicate calculus, that of *resolution refutation*.

The basic principle is straightforward and will be familiar to anyone with an elementary grounding in school mathematics: we begin by assuming the theorem to be false and show that this leads to a contradiction when combined with the premises. The steps are thus as follows:

(a) Negate the theorem.

(b) Add this to the set of premises.

(c) Convert this expanded set of formulae to a standard form (*conjunctive form*, consisting of a conjoined set of *clauses*, explained below).

(d) Derive a contradiction using the method of *resolution*.

A *clause* is a formula consisting of a disjunction of atomic formulae or their negations. That is, it consists of a series of basic elements connected by 'or's. Any syntactically correct formula can be reduced to a set of clauses by the following steps:

(i) Convert all connectives to their equivalent forms using only $\sim, \wedge$, and $\vee$.

(ii) Apply the simple equivalences known as De Morgan's laws so that each negation only negates an atomic formula, and nothing more complicated (e.g. $\sim(p \wedge q)$ becomes $\sim p \vee \sim q$).

(iii) Rename the variables so that each quantifier is associated with a different variable name.

(iv) Remove all existential quantifiers by replacing their associated variables by explicit functions (Skolem functions) with universally quantified arguments.

(v) Place all universal quantifiers at the beginning of the formula. Henceforth they are assumed to be present and ignored in future formal manipulations.

(vi) The formula may now be rearranged to be a conjunction of disjunct atomic formulae or their negations.

(vii) The $\wedge$ symbols are now dropped, so that the conjoined formula becomes a list of formulae.

(viii) Finally, variables are renamed so that each name appears in only one clause.

Resolution, in step (d) above, works on this conjunctive form as follows. Suppose we have two clauses, one being of the form $\sim p$ and the other of the form $p \vee q$. The first asserts p to be false and the second says that either p is true or q is true. The only way that both of these clauses can be true is if p is false and q is true. This is the basic principle: two clauses, each consisting of a series of disjunctions, are found such that one includes some atomic formula p while the other includes the negation of p . These two clauses can then be merged into a single disjunction of all the elements other than p and $\sim p$. Thus $p \vee q \vee s$ can be resolved with $\sim p \vee r$ to give $q \vee s \vee r$. Should one or both of the clauses contain variables (as might well be the case – recall that from step (v) above there might be universally quantified variables remaining in the clause set), then straightforward extensions are possible in which the terms with variables become instantiated by particular items.

The process is continued in this way, choosing two clauses to resolve to yield a third, until eventually two contradictory clauses (p and $\sim p$) are produced. This is the desired objective, for then it appears that the list of basic premises plus the negated theorem implies a contradiction.

This is only a very brief overview of resolution refutation and there remain many points we have not discussed. For example, the issue of how to decide which two clauses to resolve at each step. Some ways are more efficient than others. Similarly, a simple 'the theorem is true' may not be enough. Raphael (1976) gives an example in which a telephone answering system is asked 'Is there a number at which Dr Coleman can be reached?' and it uses resolution refutation to arrive at the answer 'yes'. What is wanted, in fact, is the number itself. A very simple extension of the above resolution refutation method produces a system which will also give the telephone number.

A great deal of work has been done in the area of automatic logical theorem proving and it is still a thriving area of research. References are given in the next section.

4.3   Further reading

An excellent introductory text on numerical optimisation in continuous spaces is Adby & Dempster (1974). A discussion of the branch and bound method, including several examples of its application in different circumstances, is given in Hand (1981*b*) and a discussion of the alpha-beta method is given in Knuth & Moore (1975).

Chapter 6 of Hand (1981*b*) contains a discussion of different types of search methods for choosing variables for statistical screening and diagnosis. Other references are given in Chapter 5 of this book.

Finally, a fairly comprehensive overview of search methods as used in artificial intelligence is given in Part II of Volume I of Barr & Feigenbaum (1983).

Turning to resolution refutation, Nilsson (1982) presents an extremely readable introduction, covering methods for deciding which two clauses to resolve and oriented towards a production system point of view. Other work covering this area includes Chang & Lee (1973) and Loveland (1978). Chapter 10 of Clocksin & Mellish (1981) also contains an introductory discussion.

5

Computer assisted diagnosis

5.1 Introduction

The *Concise Oxford dictionary* defines 'diagnosis' as the 'identification of disease by means of a patient's symptoms, etc. Formal statement of this', thus making clear both the aim and the information which is to be utilised in achieving this aim. Diagnosis in psychiatry, however, has had a less easy history than in other areas of medicine. Some critics have even gone so far as to reject the concept of diagnosis as being useful for psychiatry. I state this here so that I can point out that this chapter does not discuss this issue. This is not an appropriate place for a debate on (what I consider to be) sterile philosophical points. Here we concentrate on the diagnostic process itself, how diagnoses are made, how the process may be improved, and how the computer and the ideas of artificial intelligence may be applied. That is I take as the aim and method those given in the definition above. I take as a basis the usefulness of the concept of diagnosis – which is not to say that there may not be difficulties with the currently dominant classification. The reader interested in more fundamental issues will find Kendell's book (Kendell, 1975) a good introduction.

To set our task into perspective, let us first glance at some comments that have been made about the diagnostic process:

'Medical diagnosis is a difficult and complex task largely empirically based and poorly understood as an intellectual task' (Rogers, Ryack & Moeller, 1979).

Rogers *et al*. (1979) further quote Janis & Mann (1977) as characterising man as '. . . a reluctant decision maker – beset by conflict, doubts, and worry, struggling with incongruous longings, antipathies, and loyalties . . .' This sort of thing makes one wonder how one can even get up in the morning, let alone make diagnoses! And it is not helped by Goldberg (1970):

'He [the human] has his days: boredom, fatigue, illness, situational and interpersonal distractions all plague him with the result that his repeated judgements of the exact same stimulus configurations are not identical.'

These remarks all describe the difficulties men have in making diagnoses, and all apply to medical diagnosis in general. When we turn to the special case of psychiatric diagnosis, we find additional problems:

'The therapeutic prognostic implications of psychiatric diagnoses are relatively weak, and the diagnoses themselves relatively unreliable' and 'A related problem is that the majority of patients do not conform to the tidy stereotyped descriptions found in textbooks' (Kendell, 1975). (This last point is surely one which all practising psychiatrists must acknowledge.)

Kendell summarises nearly a century of thought on diagnosis in psychiatry in the following way:

> Eighty years ago Hack Tuke observed that 'The wit of man has rarely been more exercised than in the attempt to classify the morbid mental phenomena covered by the term insanity', and went on to add that the result had been disappointing. The remark remains as apposite now as it was then, and goes far towards explaining why many present day psychiatrists have lost interest in the whole issue of diagnosis, while others have suggested that it is an unnecessary, even a harmful exercise. This book was born of the conviction that such attitudes are profoundly mistaken, and that the development of a reliable and valid classification of the phenomena of mental illness, and of the unambiguous diagnostic criteria which are essential to this task, are two of the most   .
> important problems facing contemporary psychiatry.

The perceived weakness of psychiatric classifications arises in part because in other areas of medicine diagnoses can be confirmed by histological examination, biopsy, radiography, surgery, or autopsy. This is generally not possible in psychiatry with the consequence that, as Birtchnell (1974) puts it, 'there is no observable or measurable physical representation of mental illness so that its presence is largely a matter of the psychiatrists' opinion.'

If the diagnostic foundations are so unsound, it might appear as if the exercise of attempting to write computer programs for it was foredoomed. However, as Kendell says later in his book:

> It is undeniable that psychiatric diagnoses are often unreliable, and that it is commonplace for a single patient to be given three different diagnoses by three different psychiatrists, but this does not have to be so. It has been demonstrated several times that adequately trained psychiatrists can achieve acceptable levels of

agreement and that there are consistent differences in symptomatology, course and response to treatment between populations of patients from different diagnostic categories.

Clare (1976) makes a similar point in defence of psychiatric diagnosis (p. 113, 1st edition):

... the critics say ... the diagnosis of mental illness and particularly schizophrenia, as enacted by the average psychiatrist is as hard, objective and detached as the average man's estimation of the political perspicacity of his local MP. It is almost entirely subjective in both cases ...

Widely publicised as such a critical view of psychiatric diagnosis undoubtedly is, it is nonetheless false. It has served the critics well to exaggerate the amount of diagnostic dissent in psychiatry whilst comparing it unfavourably with an equally exaggerated view of the objectivity and scientific detachment of diagnostic practice in medicine in general. When the three stages of the diagnostic process (data accumulation, data interpretation, and data categorisation) are approached in a rational and competent manner, the results in terms of diagnostic agreement and all that follows it compare favourably with those in a comparable field of medicine.

It is perhaps worth remarking that the acknowledged subjective element in psychiatric diagnosis has stimulated a considerable research effort aimed at clarifying the categories and tightening up the diagnostic process – perhaps more so than in any comparable field of medicine.

Having established that psychiatric diagnosis is difficult, let us turn to considering how computers may be of assistance in this difficult task.

We can begin with the observation that modern medicine is incredibly complex. It would be totally out of the question to expect any single person to read, let alone take in, all the new research findings. (Or even turn the pages of the journals.) New research findings are published every day. The problem of complexity and sheer magnitude in modern medicine is currently tackled by creating specialities and sub-specialities. This is not an ideal solution: specialists require expensive specialist training and they are no solution for poor or large and sparsely populated countries (of what use is the expert if he is 2000 miles away and the only means of transport is a mule?). The creation of a hierarchy of specialities also raises the danger that multiple diseases will not be recognised.

The size and complexity of modern medicine has other aspects. The vast range of medicines currently available is a good example. Typically the choice is made from a small subset of those that might possibly be relevant – merely because the doctors cannot retain and recall information about all of them.

The complexity issue surfaces at a different level in De Dombal (1978, p. 32): 'Another reason why doctors from time to time make erroneous diagnoses is simply because they are totally unable to handle the volume of data which they elicit from patients.'

Computers, of course, are perfectly suited to storing and recalling large quantities of data. But more than this – they do it without error. Thus they can tackle the complexity issue at all levels. (This facility for manipulating large quantities of data in an error-free way is one of the properties identified by Gorry & Barnett (1968) as making computers appropriate for application to medical diagnosis.)

Secondly, apart from the complexity issue, we have the fact that doctors are not very good at making use of the known prevalences of diseases when arriving at a diagnosis. This point is discussed further below – but the thing to note is, again, that computers are ideal for this.

Thirdly, computers are accurate and reliable – contrast man, the reluctant decision maker, in the quote from Janis & Mann (1977) above.

The pressures and demands on psychiatric services are eloquently described in Clare (1976). This brings us to the fourth point – that computers can ease these pressures. Systems – programs – which can make reliable and trustworthy diagnoses will free the psychiatrist for more demanding (and more interesting) tasks.

Fifthly, we come to the question of cost. Computers can be highly effective at reducing costs – especially now that computer hardware has become so cheap. (Indeed, without this development many of the criticisms expressed above about humans – not always accessible and so on – would apply equally to computers.) In some cases expensive tests can be avoided by efficient utilisation (by computer) of what information is available. Humans tend to be conservative in their processing of information (Phillips, Hays & Edwards, 1966) and some clinicians require much more information than others (or their computers) before they are able to make a decision (Taylor, Aitchison & McGirr, 1971). This is discussed further in § 5.2, where we explore the means by which humans arrive at a diagnosis.

Finally (sixthly), a computer is immune from the boredom, fatigue, illness, and situational and interpersonal distractions listed by Goldberg (1970) as detracting from human diagnostic performance.

All of these difficulties make it apparent why Wagner, Tautu & Wolber (1978) stated: 'Medical diagnosis is no longer a strictly medical problem.'

Computers clearly possess a number of attributes which make them potentially extremely valuable for medical diagnosis in general and for psychiatric diagnosis in particular. Whether these attributes can be taken advantage of, and how one might go about doing so, are the subjects addressed by later sections of this chapter. However, at this initial stage I would like to make a plea for moderation. It is as serious a mistake to exaggerate the usefulness of computers as it is to underestimate the value of these tools. The lure of the shiny new technology must not mislead us into thinking (or fearing) that herein lies the answer to all questions, but neither must the occasional misuse of computers or their limitations in any particular application lead us to dismiss them as irrelevant.

5.2　　How humans structure diagnosis

We discuss below the question of whether or not the best way to approach machine diagnosis is by emulating the human approach. Whatever the answer to this question, modelling the human approach is certainly one natural starting point and by considering the human approach we can gain a useful perspective on the alternative approaches to be outlined later. Thus in this section we open the discussion by briefly examining how humans approach diagnosis.

Recent years have witnessed a number of studies of human problem solving skills and of diagnosis in particular. (To a considerable degree the interest has been motivated by the advent of the computer and the possibility of automating such skills.) A classic study of this kind is that of Newell & Simon (1972). They present a detailed discussion of how three clearly defined problem types are tackled by humans. Their conclusions are too lengthy to summarise here but what is important for the present discussion is an assumption underlying the work. The problems they examine are chess puzzles, symbolic logic problems, and cryptarithmetic puzzles. From this the reader will recognise that they are restricting their investigations to relatively precisely formulated problems. There is none of the imprecision or untidiness of the real world about them. They consider that this 'does not severely limit our analysis of problem solving, except at its physiological boundaries', but elsewhere they do acknowledge that studying well-defined areas of this nature represents only half of a problem as it would be encountered in real life. On p. 90, for example, they say:

> One part of the theory [of problem solving] will deal with possible
> representations, their selection and installation. The other
> principal part of the theory will deal with problem solving within a
> given representation . . . . The theory to be presented in this book

has much more to say about methods and executive organisations than about creating new representations or shifting from one representation to another.

The existence of these two aspects to problem solving has had major consequences for computer assisted approaches to medical diagnosis. We shall examine some of these later, but here we look at the relationship between the two aspects rather more closely. We shall see that to a certain extent the distinction is somewhat illusory – it is more a creation of man's mind, a structure imposed on reality, than a real distinction. But, despite this, it is of great value to preserve the distinction – the practical consequences are great.

We can describe the issue as being one of how *well-structured* problems are. Broadly speaking, a *well-structured problem* (WSP) is one which can be fairly easily mapped into a representation (see Chapter 2) which permits formal or mechanical problem solving techniques to be applied. Thus, for example, the game of noughts and crosses is a WSP – a simple set of algorithms can be written to play the game. On the other hand, writing a sonnet is not a well-structured problem, it is ill-structured. *Ill-structured problems* (ISPs) are relatively poorly formalised, and are usually regarded as a residual concept. As Simon (1973) puts it: 'An ISP is usually defined as a problem whose structure lacks definition in some respect. A problem is an ISP if it is not a WSP.'

So where does medical diagnosis fit on this WSP/ISP continuum? As we shall see later, in the past most approaches have regarded it as a WSP. This has had some interesting consequences, not only for the success or otherwise of computerised diagnosis, but more generally for the impact of computers on the practice of medicine. It is only relatively recently (as a consequence of growing interest in artificial intelligence methodology) that a recognition of its fundamentally ill-structured nature has dawned. Pople (1982) says: '. . . most existing diagnostic consultation programs . . . deal with the process of decision making in well-structured situations where the differential diagnosis is given *a priori*. These programs provide little if any assistance with respect to the more challenging business of *formulating* the differential diagnostic tasks that constitute the clinician's decision making context' (my italics).

Thus he is making the point that it is formulating the WSP from the ISP that is the difficult task. (The point made in the first part of this quote – that the diagnosis is given *a priori* – is an interesting one, and one which we shall discuss below.)

Simon (1973) has examined the relationship between ISPs and WSPs in some depth. Recalling the observation that ill-structuredness is usually regarded as a residual concept, he attempts to clarify things by first giving a set of criteria which a problem should satisfy to be well-structured, and then trying to give a 'positive characterisation of some problem domains that have usually been regarded as ill-structured, rescuing them from their residual status.' He attempts to show in this way that there is 'no real boundary between WSPs and ISPs'. Simon goes on to illustrate with two examples that 'definiteness of problem structure is largely an illusion that arises when we systematically confound the idealised problem that is presented to an idealised (and unlimitedly powerful) problem solver with the actual problem that is to be attacked by a problem solver with limited (even if large) computational capacities.' Chess is one of his examples. In principle chess is a WSP, there being only a finite number of possible games so that in theory one could always choose the best move from any given position. In practice this finite number is so vast that it is an ISP. Simon further states: 'In general, the problems presented to problem solvers by the world are best regarded as ISPs. They become WSPs only in the process of being prepared for problem solvers. It is not exaggerating much to say that there are no WSPs, only ISPs that have been formalised for problem solvers.'

The suggestion that it is the transformation from ISP to WSP which is the difficult aspect of problem solving is addressed thus by Newell & Simon (1972, p. 850):

> It is sometimes even argued that 'real' problem solving is not what we have called problem solving in this volume, but the preliminary sequence of processes that determine the problem space and program . . . The argument can be refuted simply by observing that if it were correct, and tasks from the same environment were presented sequentially to a subject, only the first of them would present him with a problem, since he would not need to determine a new problem space and program for subsequent tasks.

However, it seems to the present author that to a certain extent this is just what does happen. Familiarity with a problem type does lead to ease of solution – especially for those problems permitting a highly structured representation. An example would be school mathematics problems of the kind involving setting up and solving a system of equations.

Even for problem types defying very well-structured representations, familiarity permits the solver to tackle them more readily using the representations and strategies learnt in the past.

Summarising all this, some kind of filtering or transformation process is necessary to change a real world ISP into a WSP suitable for formal problem solving strategies. The difference between ISPs and WSPs is not so much one of kind as of degree, and the range of WSPs depends on the range of techniques available for tackling problems. Even Simon himself concludes: 'there is merit to the claim that much problem solving effort is directed at structuring problems, and only a fraction of it at solving problems once they are structured.'

Many classical studies of problem solving are based around puzzles in which the goal is known. The three problem types addressed in Newell & Simon (1972) are of this kind. Thus the start point and end point are set beforehand and all that is required is to find a path (in some appropriate space – see Chapters 2 and 4) from one to the other. Perhaps it is overemphasis on problems of this kind which has led to the exaggerated importance of formal methods of solution as a model of human methods:

> For some considerable time we cherished the illusion that [using formal logic to construct psychological models of reasoning] was the way to proceed and that only the structural characteristics of the problem mattered. Only gradually did we realise first that there was no existing formal calculus which correctly modelled our subject's inferences, and second that no purely formal calculus would succeed. (Wason & Johnson-Laird, 1972, p. 244.)

Perhaps then, these classical studies are inappropriate as models of the diagnostic process. They seem to assume in effect that the diagnosis is already known and that all that remains is to show that the evidence justifies it.

If a key feature of WSPs as opposed to ISPs is that in the former both the initial and goal states are known, then medical diagnosis seems to fall in the latter class, and some kind of transformation or formalisation is needed to change it into a WSP. We summarise below some of the studies which have suggested a basic mechanism for this formalisation. Rather than keeping the reader in suspense, we state now that the approach apparently used by medical consultants is to take the initial open-ended problem (What is wrong? What is the diagnosis?) and transform it into *a set* of closed problems (Is it this? Or this? Or this?). These can then be tackled by 'traditional' goal-seeking methods devised for WSPs. Thus in some ways it seems that Simon is correct as far as medical diagnosis goes.

Describing this mechanism in psychiatric diagnosis, Wing, Cooper & Sartorius (1974, p. *vii*) say: 'The good clinician, when he undertakes a diagnostic examination, knows what he wants to find out. He makes a systematic exploration of the subject's mental state, in order to discover whether any of a finite number of abnormal mental phenomena are present . . .' and on p. 2: '. . . all investigation and diagnosis still properly starts with interviewing the patient and making a provisional diagnosis . . .'

Of course, we now have to consider the question of how the potential diagnoses are chosen. It is not feasible to work through all possible diagnoses, eliminating them one by one, and it takes but a moment's thought to appreciate that humans do not approach diagnosis in such a brute force way. If the formalisation method described above is the human (presumably subconscious) approach, then we must still decide how the relevant subset of diagnoses is chosen.

First let us consider some of the evidence for the basic mechanism above. Elstein, Shulman & Sprafka (1979) describe a fascinating series of studies of the way in which medical doctors arrive at their conclusions. As they say (p. 65):

> The generation of hypotheses and utilisation of a hypothetico-
> deductive method seem to be a nearly universal characteristic of
> human thinking in complex, poorly defined environments. Work
> in the psychology of memory and thinking has suggested why this
> is so: the problem must be represented cognitively in the mind of
> the problem solver. While rational problem solving is characterised
> by a high degree of adaptation of this representation to the demands
> of the problem, there are limits to human capacity both in working
> memory and in respect to the number of operations that can be
> performed simultaneously (Simon, 1969; Newell & Simon, 1972).
> The function of early hypotheses, therefore, is to limit the size of
> the space that must be searched for solutions to the problem. Some
> way of progressively constraining the size of the search space must
> be found or else a clinical workup could never end in the time that
> is actually available.

Elstein *et al.* suggest that physicians do not blindly collect information until some hypothesis springs fully formed from the depths of the unconscious. On the contrary, very early on in the consultation they formulate hypotheses about what might be wrong and then they seek evidence relating to these hypotheses. This, of course, may not be an entirely rational and conscious process. The studies of Elstein *et al.* also reveal interesting information about how physicians choose and handle their hypotheses, and we shall discuss this later. By examining critically the types of errors commonly made, Elstein *et al.* were able to present a set of heuristics which they hope will lead to better diagnosis. Since these heuristics could well be used as a way to structure and resolve conflicts in rule-based diagnostic expert systems we shall outline them below. The creation of this set of heuristics is in many ways reminiscent of Donald Michie's 'knowledge refining', and might be regarded as a first step in that direction.

Apart from the fact of early hypothesis formulation, the work of Elstein *et al.* reveals the following points:

(i) The number of hypotheses under consideration at any one time is seldom more than five and virtually never more than seven. (This will come as no surprise to psychologists.)

(ii) Several types of error can occur in hypothesis generation and examination:

– inconsistent findings may be explained by using hypotheses which are excessively general.

– observations which are inconsistent with current hypotheses may be ignored – thus evading the need to generate new hypotheses.

– contrary to the above, current hypotheses may be made to seem more likely by exaggerating the apparent importance of some observations.

The reader will doubtless recognise these error types as all too characteristic of human frailties in debate!

In examining the diagnostic process in detail, it is necessary to consider four stages of the process:

(i) How the initial observations are chosen.

(ii) How the initial hypotheses are generated.

(iii) How hypotheses and observations are matched.

(iv) How hypotheses are evaluated.

Of these, (iii) and (iv) might be regarded as falling squarely within the WSP solution paradigm. (i) and (ii), however, lie outside it. The original ISP is thus split into a well-structured component and a component which still needs to be considered. The formalisation from ISP to WSP has been accomplished by this process of splitting the problem into a set of WSPs.

Pople (1982), too, has described this process (p. 122):

> One nearly universal finding is that the physician responds to cues
> in the clinical data by conceptualising one or more diagnostic tasks
> which then play an important role in the subsequent decision
> making process. This conceptualisation governs to some extent the
> acquisition of additional data and the range of alternatives
> considered in the eventual diagnostic decision making process.

The importance of steps (i) and (ii) above are made clear by Pople (1982, p. 122) when he says: 'One mark of an expert is his ability to formulate particularly appropriate differential diagnostic tasks on the basis of sometimes subtle hints in the patient record' and (p. 124) 'What distinguishes an expert is his ability to sense important omissions in the data that can often be filled in simply by asking the right questions.'

It is interesting to note here a parallel with human and machine chess. In chess the mark of a human expert is neither how many possible positions he examines nor how many possible moves ahead he looks. Rather, it is his ability to identify which of the possible moves are worth examining in detail. Chess playing programs which crunch through the examination of far more positions than a human can possibly consider have been found to play rather poor chess. Something more – or, at least, something different – is needed.

In the study described by Kassirer & Gorry (1978) one of the authors played the role of a patient, following a genuine patient record, and six clinicians were each asked to carry out a clinical interview, giving the reasons for their questions, stating what they learned from the answers, and reporting any hypotheses they may have been considering. They say (p. 247):

> Detailed analysis of protocols of the participating clinicians shows that the clinicians tried various hypotheses as explanations of the patient's problems – hypotheses that 'fit' the case at hand more or less well. Piece by piece, they assembled the evidence for and against competing hypotheses until one hypothesis seemed clearly better. When findings seemed inconsistent with a hypothesis, they searched for an explanation for the inconsistency or they rejected the hypothesis in question.

It seems fair to assume that this perception of the process the clinicians undertook has been refined somewhat, and that in fact the process was not so clean and certain. Hand (1984*b*) describes a preliminary investigation into how statistical consultants arrive at their recommendations (it seems to be a process bearing remarkable parallels to that of medical consultants arriving at diagnoses). In this I give condensed protocols of some of the interviews. Although the hypothetico-deductive model fits, it is certainly not blindingly obvious, and some filtering of the natural language camouflage is necessary before it becomes apparent.

Kassirer & Gorry also say: 'Specific diagnostic hypotheses were generated often with little more information than presenting complaints, that testing of diagnostic hypotheses consisted of various case-building strategies for corroborating and discrediting hypotheses', and 'At a time when the clinician was aware only of the age, sex, and presenting complaints of the patient, he often immediately introduced a hypothesis.'

Some light is shed on stage (ii) above (hypothesis generation) by this study. Simple response to early data items was apparently not the only trigger for hypotheses. New hypotheses were generated if current ones and new data conflicted and there was also some sequential hypothesis generation (for example, this datum suggests X might be true, and X could be caused by Y). It is interesting to note that some hypotheses were introduced only because of the potential treatment benefits which would result if they were true (wishful thinking?).

Kassirer & Gorry say that strategies for confirmation, elimination, discrimination, and exploration (i.e. refining) were used in stage (iv) above to test hypotheses.

They were able to study refinements of this basic hypothesis generate and test strategy because their subject clinicians came from three distinct disciplines (nephrology, gastroenterology, and cardiology). They state (p. 251):

> The expert nephrologists used a highly directed information-gathering method. Recognising quickly that the patient had a renal problem, these physicians focused on obtaining pertinent information regarding the kidneys and urinary tract, usually using an extended series of questions to assess the presence of manifestations of renal disease. In addition . . . the nephrologists asked fewer questions, mentioned the correct diagnosis earlier, made a firm diagnosis earlier, and maintained a smaller number of active hypotheses than the two physicians who were not expert in the patient's illness . . . Both [of the latter] clinicians asked most of the important questions asked by the nephrologists, but the pattern of questioning was not as directed. These physicians tended to explore more symptoms and findings unrelated to the urinary tract even when the questioning was producing little valuable data.

And even between clinicians from the same speciality differences in approach were observed (p. 255):

> The preliminary results show that although the clinicians we studied used the same basic strategies for evaluating hypotheses and for collecting information, they often used them in different ways. One style recognised was that of the clinician who directed all his problem solving efforts towards uncovering the core of the situation. In contrast, other clinicians approached the problem in a more methodical fashion by engaging in a systematic exploration of a variety of aspects of the patient's condition. A third style was that of the clinician who probed a number of different directions as if he were hoping to uncover some important fact almost by chance. This clinician interrupted one train of thought to jump to another area of investigation that superficially appeared to be rewarding. Finally, another approach is embodied by the clinician who began his analysis by going back as far in time as possible to obtain historical information, by dealing with the patient's problem from the point of view of its chronological development, and by considering recent problems only after obtaining a clear vision of past events.

Reading this, one is tempted to say that there seems to be a different style for each clinician, constrained by the common element of the basic underlying process of generating and testing hypotheses. This leaves us with great flexibility in designing programs for diagnosis.

One of the results of the study of Elstein *et al.* (1979), apart from the insight it sheds on the way humans arrive at their diagnoses, is the set of heuristics presented as suggestions by means of which the hypothesis generating and testing processes might be improved. As we have remarked above, apart from this they might also serve, as guidelines for structuring medical expert systems (§ 5.5). Because of this we include them below. They are derived from a list presented by M. J. Gordon in his 1973 Ph.D. thesis. We quote from Elstein *et al.* (1979, pp. 297–8, reprinted by permission):

> *Generating a list of alternative hypotheses or actions*
>
> (a) *Multiple competing hypotheses*. Think of a number of diagnostic possibilities compatible with the chief complaint and preliminary findings. Avoid making snap diagnoses. Key on 'good' symptom clusters; organ–system links are helpful. Nesting overcomes limits of working memory.
>
> (b) *Probability*. Consider the most common diagnoses first.
>
> (c) *Utility*. Consider seriously those diagnoses for which effective therapies are available and in which failure to treat would be a serious omission. Try to keep separate your estimate of the probability of a disease and the cost of not treating it.
>
> *Gathering data*
>
> (d) *Form a reasoned plan* for testing your hypotheses, one that reckons with probability and utility. Sequence laboratory tests to rule out first the most common diseases (probability), and next the diseases most needing treatment (utility).
>
> Corollary 1: Diagnostic decisions should be related to treatment alternatives. There is no reason to pursue a differential among diagnoses that will make no difference in the action to be taken, and your data gathering should reflect this.
>
> Corollary 2: There should be a reason for every datum gathered. For example, if a test result does not change your opinion about any of your diagnostic hypotheses, ask yourself why the test was ordered and what range of values could have changed your mind.
>
> (e) *Branch and screen*. History taking and physical examination should be branching procedures. Develop adequate screening tactics to help make overly detailed examinations unnecessary. For example, if a patient denies changes in weight, the physican can

omit going down the branch that relates to certain endocrinopathies.

(f) *Cost–benefit calculation*. Consider the harm tests might do and their cost. Balance these against the information to be gained.

(g) *Precision*. Strive for the degree of reliability needed for the decision at hand. More is not necessary.

Aggregating data, evaluating hypotheses, and selecting a course of action

(h) *Disconfirmatory evidence*. Actively seek out and evaluate any evidence that tends to rule out any hypothesis or action alternative as well as the evidence that tends to confirm it. Be aware of the tendency to discount or disregard evidence likely to disconfirm your favourite alternative.

(i) *Multiple diagnoses*. Don't forget the possibility that a patient with multiple problems or complaints has more than one disease.

(1) The joint probability of two common diagnoses may well be greater than one rarer diagnosis.

(2) When failure to treat both hypothetical diagnoses might have disastrous results, and neither can be confirmed or ruled out, act as if both were established.

(j) *Bayes' theorem*. Revise probabilities after collecting data.

(1) In assessing the probability of a particular diagnosis, give special weight if it is common.

(2) If the clinical findings are relatively more likely in diagnosis A than in diagnosis B, revise your opinion in favour of A.

(3) If hard data are missing about how common a disease is, or about how likely particular symptoms are in it, make rough approximations. It is usually possible to weight each finding as at least tending to confirm, disconfirm, or not change one's prior belief.

(4) If you rank order diagnoses on the basis of the predominance of findings in their support, weighted as described in (3), this ranking will correspond roughly to a probability scale.

(k) *Probability and utility should guide action*. When a course of action is finally selected, consider both the probability of the diagnosis for which this action is appropriate and the benefits/penalties that would accrue. Combine these two considerations to estimate expected value and choose so as to maximise expected value.

Corollary 1: Consider clustering diagnoses that would be treated identically. This nesting effectively reduces the number of alternatives to be evaluated.

Corollary 2: Among the benefits and penalties of medical action, consider quality of life and morbidity as well as mortality.

5.3   Taxonomies of computer assisted diagnosis

In order to structure the exposition, as well as to make it easier for the reader to appreciate the nature of the different approaches to diagnosis, some kind of systematisation is needed, some kind of taxonomy summarising the similarities and dissimilarities between methods. Several such taxonomies have been suggested, and we think it is worthwhile outlining some of these. This will help the reader to recognise the common threads; it will also make it clear that no taxonomy is perfect, and that all are to a certain extent artificial in that the boundaries between types of method are often violated. The particular classification that we have adopted to serve as the framework for § 5.4 to 5.6 is described last. Unfortunately, it is necessary to use one or two technical terms which may not be familiar to the reader in this outline of taxonomies. Any such terms will be explained in later sections.

Card's system (Card, 1970)

Type I: Allocate a complete symptom profile at one step. For example, a patient to be diagnosed will give values for 100 items, including simple questions (age, sex), symptoms, and complex biochemical test results. The program will be presented with all 100 results and will base its diagnosis on all 100. Standard non-sequential statistical pattern recognition (Hand, 1981*a*), including classical discriminant analysis, falls within this class.

Type II: Tests are conducted (or questions are asked) sequentially, one at a time, with the results of each test or question determining what is the next to be conducted or asked. A hierarchy of items thus exists, down which the diagnostic process works. The decision as to which branch to take at any point is made on the basis of the information the next test is expected to yield.

Type III: As type II, except that here the decision as to which branch to take at any point is made on the basis of the greatest expected *utility*. 'Utility' is a technical statistical concept which includes an assessment of the consequences of any decision. Thus drastic surgery may well be expected to reveal the cause (if, say, a brain tumour is suspected), but if it is likely to kill the patient then it will have low utility. Decision theory falls in this class. The differences between the three types are that type I assumes all information to be available before any classification is attempted (and so such methods might be more expensive and risky, but perhaps more accurate. We discuss these points below). Type III does not simply aim at the most accurate diagnosis but takes into account such things as the cost of carrying out a test or examination and the likely consequences if it is positive.

Shortliffe's system (Shortliffe, Buchanan & Feigenbaum, 1979)

Type I: Flowcharts. Flowcharts are branching protocols, as in Card's types II and III, which present a sequence of tests/questions to arrive eventually at a diagnosis.

Type II: Databank analysis. Computer database management systems applied to a large collection of past patient records can reveal relative probabilities of different types of diagnosis as well as information on prognosis and the likely effectiveness of therapy.

Type III: Mathematical models of physical processes. This category was not covered by Card's taxonomy. (At least, it was not identified as a separate type. The ideas in it will presumably be embedded in the hierarchies of Card's types II and III.) Of course, modelling approaches such as these can only be applied in those domains where a realistic mathematical model is possible – that is, where the phenomenon is well understood. Unfortunately, at present there seems little scope for this approach in psychiatry.

Type IV: Statistical pattern recognition. This falls squarely into our category of empirical systems (see below). Pattern recognition techniques have been applied with great vigour to a wide range of medical diagnostic problems, including psychiatry. We shall discuss them in some depth.

Type V: Bayesian methods. There seems to be a large amount of confusion in the medical literature over exactly what it is about a method that lends it the descriptor 'Bayesian'. We discuss this below.

Type VI: Decision theory. As we remarked above, decision theory differs from other methods in that it includes account of the consequences of decisions.

Type VII: Symbolic reasoning. At last we arrive at a fundamentally artificial intelligence approach. In types I to VI above the program manipulates numbers. In this type, however, symbols which are generally not numbers are manipulated. However, the reader should not be misled into thinking that the distinction is clear or precise. There is a considerable amount of overlap between all the methods: types IV and V have common members, type II's databases are essential for types IV and V, type I structures may be derived from type II databases using methods of types III to VII. And so on.

Elstein's system (Elstein *et al.*, 1979)

Type I: Process-tracing. These methods are an explicit attempt to model the mental processes used by clinicians. They are clearly artificial intelligence approaches and are in the mould of Shortliffe's type VII schemes. They fall into our 'mechanistic' category below.

Type II: Black-box. Elstein *et al.* describe such an approach as an 'attempt to model the processing . . . mathematically through studies of input–output relations'. No effort is made to simulate what goes on inside a clinician's mind as he makes a diagnosis.

Elstein's typology is near to my own, but not quite the same. A mathematical model of a well understood physiological mechanism, for example, fits into our 'mechanistic' class, but not easily into either of Elstein's types.

Rogers' system (Rogers *et al.*, 1979)

Rogers *et al.* adopt a basically two-faceted classification, categorising diagnostic systems according to the algorithm employed and the database used.

Algorithms are classed as statistical or logical. The former covers such approaches as methods based on Bayes' theorem, linear discriminant analysis, and pattern recognition. Logical approaches cover flowchart type methods.

In considering the database, Rogers *et al.* emphasise the source of information, the diseases covered, and the variables recorded.

No doubt each researcher or reviewer of the field will arrive at his own taxonomy of such systems. However, it is clear from the four described above that none can be perfect. The boundaries between the categories are tenuous. Often programs make use of ideas from several taxonomic categories, or concepts from one taxonomic type may be used as elementary components in another (examples of this will be shown below). Equally, it is clear that the taxonomies described above do not all cover quite the same ground. Presumably this is a reflection of the interests and predilections of the originators.

Despite all this, as I remarked at the beginning of this section, some kind of systematisation is needed in order to yield a coherent explanation. I have adopted what seems most suited to this text, dividing approaches to computerised diagnosis into *empirical* methods and *mechanistic* methods.

Type I: Empirical methods are predominantly based on databases of patient records (these collections need not necessarily be large: they might comprise only a few tens of records). Mathematical and statistical techniques, either simple or sophisticated, covering both hierarchical and non-hierarchical methods, are used to examine the databases to develop diagnostic rules. No information beyond that in the data is used – nothing about how men would use the information or how causative mechanisms may function to produce the results. These methods are very much in the mould of Elstein *et al.*'s type II black-box approaches. Note that although some statistical techniques are often termed 'model-building', it is better in the present context to think of them as empirical because they are not attempting to model in the sense of describe any known or hypothesised mechanism (be it psychological, physiological, biochemical, or whatever).

Type II: Mechanistic methods. In contrast to descriptive approaches we have what we have called mechanistic approaches. These include explicitly model-based methods such as those based on aetiological mechanisms and those based on human information processing theories. We also include in this class any approaches based on observations of clinical expertise which are not specific models of human processes. They are attempts to formulate mechanism and so belong here. They are not derived by statistical analysis of straightforward observations on a number of patients and hence do not belong amongst type I.

The term mechanistic should not be taken to imply reductionist, automatic, trivialised, and so on. Quite the opposite, in fact, implying mechanism in the sense of structure. Type I approaches, however, might justifiably be regarded as reductionist.

The two categories can also be usefully viewed as different levels of symbol manipulation. Empirical approaches are usually concerned with individual symptoms and with ways of combining them to yield a diagnosis, while mechanistic methods will usually be concerned with higher order symbol manipulation, involving patterns of symptoms. This will become clearer below when we consider examples.

The distinction between our type I empirical approaches and our type II mechanistic approaches is in many ways reminiscent of the distinction in psychology between 'statistical' and 'clinical' methods – see, for example, Meehl (1954) and Gough (1962).

Having attempted to outline the basic distinction I have adopted, it is worthwhile remarking yet again that the two orientations are not totally mutually exclusive. For example, some kind of decision has to be made regarding what symptoms might possibly be considered as relevant in an empirical approach, and this decision is fundamentally a type II decision – it depends on how one views the world.

Similarly, mechanistic approaches are based ultimately on subjective impressions derived in a loose type I way from experience; at the bottom level, information from empirical analyses often goes into mechanistic approaches.

5.4 Flowchart and hierarchical methods: empirical and mechanistic

Having spent § 5.3 drawing careful distinction between empirical and mechanistic approaches, we open our discussion of examples of the methods by considering the two types together. For flowchart methods this is convenient because the final structure is the same in the two cases, even though the route by which the structure is achieved is fundamentally different. Examples of both empirical and mechanistic approaches will be given below, but we can begin the discussion by examining the common structure.

Superficially there may appear to be two types of flowchart method. In the first a flowchart is used to determine the order in which questions are asked or tests administered. Fig. 5.1 illustrates an idealised version of one such flowchart. Referring to the figure we see that initially test A is carried out (or question A asked). If the result is positive, or if the question is answered in the affirmative, then test B is conducted, otherwise C is. If B is positive then diagnosis (i) is assigned, and so on. Note that either test A positive and test B negative or test A negative and test C positive will lead to test D being carried out.

Fig. 5.1. A simple idealised flowchart.

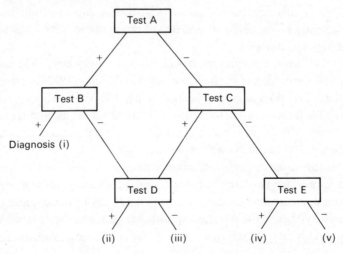

In the second approach all information is collected in one go at the start, but it is made use of in a sequential way. Thus, for example, a self-administered questionnaire may be completed by the subjects and then processed by a computer working its way through a structure such as that in Fig. 5.1.

From the outside the two approaches may seem very different, but from the inside they are clearly the same.

Usually some of the terminal stages of the structure will indicate that a human expert should be consulted, though clearly the approach will be more valuable the fewer such points there are.

The ideas implicit in the sequential data collection flowchart approach manifest themselves in various forms. Perhaps the simplest is when a printed flowchart (or an equivalent structure in text of the form: 'If the answer to question A is yes, then ask question B', etc.) is given to the diagnostician and he simply follows it. This is a relatively common use, especially amongst paramedical personnel, although in general it has been found that medical doctors are less prepared to adopt such systems.

The wish to provide basic medical care without requiring lengthy and expensive training is one of the motivations behind flowchart ideas – whether they are run on a computer or not. It is interesting to note that 'intelligent high school graduates, selected in large part because of poise and warmth of personality, can provide excellent care guided by protocols after only four to eight weeks training. This care has been shown to be equivalent to that given by physicians for the same limited problems.' (Shortliffe *et al.*, 1979.) Examples of such systems may be found in Komaroff *et al.* (1974), Grimm *et al.* (1975), Greenfield, Komaroff & Anderson (1976), Sox, Sox & Tompkins (1973), and Mesel *et al.* (1976).

Often the flowcharts are very simple indeed – fitting on to a single sheet of paper. In this case there is little to be gained by implementing the system on a computer – except, perhaps, mystification of the naive and a spurious air of high technology.

In other cases, however, the flowcharts can be very large. The computer listing of one version of the flowchart used in Bleich's (1972) electrolyte and acid/base disorders program occupies nearly 150 pages. Although it would be possible for someone to work through something as long as this manually, it would not be a very sensible approach – especially since a computer can do the same thing much more easily and quickly.

There are disadvantages to the flowchart concept compared to some of the other approaches we describe below (notably, of course, those more closely derived from artificial intelligence work). We shall discuss these in § 5.7 where we compare the different approaches. It seems clear, however, that these disadvantages are more serious in the manual case than in the computer implementation case. They are weaknesses of the method, but the computer can be jury-rigged to alleviate them, although obviously this is not an ideal solution.

The second type of flowchart method shares the property with the statistical pattern recognition methods to be outlined in § 5.6 that they collect all necessary information and then derive a diagnosis. The first type of method may thus arrive at a diagnosis using less information. (Referring to Fig. 5.1, for example, the second type will obtain results for tests A to E regardless. In contrast, to arrive at a final diagnosis of (i), the first type of method merely carries out tests A and B.) It seems clear that the first type of approach is closer to the unformalised human approach – human clinicians do not collect information on everything they can think of and then derive a diagnosis (as we discussed in § 5.2). However, this does not necessarily imply that it is better. For example, even when one has arrived at a diagnosis, further results – ones not absolutely necessary to reach the diagnosis – can increase (or decrease) one's confidence. Perhaps the trouble is that even the first type of flowchart methods are not sufficiently similar to the human approach. We discuss this and associated issues later.

Card (1970), as outlined in § 5.3, distinguishes between two types of flowchart methods on a different basis from that I describe. In his first type, branching decisions are based on the amount of information likely to be obtained from a test, while in his second type they are based on the cost and expected benefits as well as the amount of information expected (testing stops when it is considered that no test will reduce the probability of misdiagnosis by enough to justify its cost). This second approach has not been widely used in medicine. It seems closer to the human approach in that humans also seem to take some account of potential benefits (at least in that they have a tendency to hypothesise possible diagnoses which would have obvious treatments or other benefits – see § 5.2). Of course, assessing costs of tests and likely benefits and consequences in terms of more accurate diagnoses is by no means a trivial task.

Now let us turn to some examples. Fig. 5.2 presents an illustration of flowchart ideas applied to the diagnosis of schizophrenia. (I am indebted to Dr Paul Bebbington of the MRC Social Psychiatry Unit for permission to include this figure.) The diagram represents a hierarchical way of classifying the current mental state of patients, which would probably be roughly in agreement with the views of the majority of British psychiatrists. In the ordinary way, however, the diagnosis of schizophrenia is usually held to rest partly on other factors, such as the course and development of the condition. This is very much a mechanistic flowchart, the questions and branch points being derived from clinical expertise, not statistical extraction from data.

Fig. 5.2. A flowchart for the diagnosis of schizophrenia (in the absence of clear-cut symptoms or organic psychiatric syndromes).

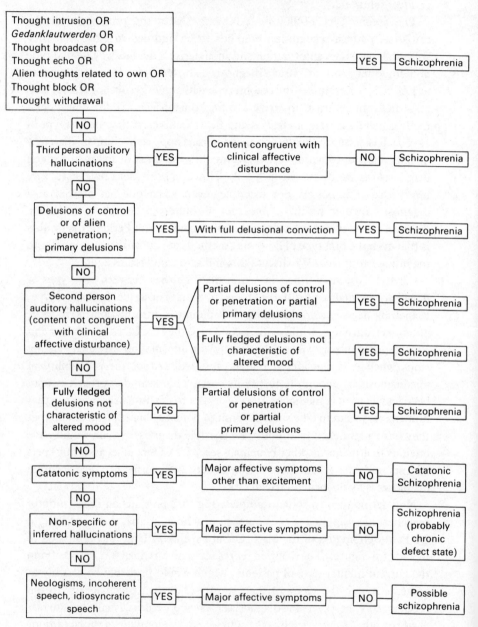

A second mechanistic example, one in which all questions are asked at the beginning before the diagnostic process is begun, is the Catego program described by Wing *et al.* (1974). Catego takes as input a set of ratings derived from a standardised psychiatric interview, the Present State Examination (PSE). It then uses a complex set of diagnostic rules to allocate each patient to a descriptive class, 'thus simulating the process of clinical diagnosis'. It is worthwhile stressing that this 'simulation' begins with all the data and progressively condenses it. It is very much not a sequential decision type procedure in the way it obtains the data. It might thus seem that the claim that it simulates clinical diagnosis is very much in contrast to Card's emphasis (Card, 1970): 'no doctor ever collects a whole set of all possible characters from the patients before making a diagnosis; he always acts sequentially.' Presumably the resolution of the contradiction lies in some confusion between collecting a whole set of data and using all the data simultaneously. Wing's approach is certainly not human in its initial evaluation of all 140 symptoms (or 500 items), but after this point it might at least be proposed as a simulation of some aspects of the human approach. Card is stressing the improbability that a human works with all of the data items simultaneously, in the manner of the pattern recognition procedures to be outlined in § 5.6.

Fig. 5.3 gives the general structure of a Catego analysis. Steps (i) and (ii) involve condensing symptoms or syndromes to yield more manageable descriptions. In step (iii) Wing *et al.* (p. 79) state: 'the main priorities are laid down by the degrees of certainty of each category but categories are also ranked in a hierarchy.' Note that from step (ii) a patient could be allocated

Fig. 5.3. The steps in a Catego analysis.

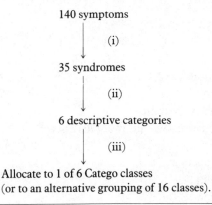

140 symptoms

(i)

35 syndromes

(ii)

6 descriptive categories

(iii)

Allocate to 1 of 6 Catego classes
(or to an alternative grouping of 16 classes).

to all six categories, though this would be unusual and would demonstrate an extremely mixed clinical character.

It is worth emphasising the mechanistic (my meaning) foundation of this system. The condensations and categorisations at various stages of the program are derived from clinical expertise and not from statistical manipulation. This reflects the backgrounds of the authors, who are psychiatrists rather than statisticians.

Another mechanistic flowchart approach, similar in many ways to Catego, is the Diagno system of Spitzer & Endicott (1968, 1969, and see Spitzer *et al.*, 1974). Spitzer & Endicott (1968) actually present a flowchart giving 'the basic logic implicit in the American Psychiatric Association nomenclature', but the system is run on a computer. The basic structure is a tree of binary choices 'similar to the differential diagnostic procedure employed in clinical medicine'. Input for the program consists of 39 scale scores of current psychopathology in the Psychiatric Status Schedule, age, sex, and number of previous admissions to a psychiatric hospital. Later versions include data from the patient's past. Output consists of 'one of 25 standard American Psychiatric Association diagnoses and qualifying phrases, as well as two unofficial diagnoses: not ill and nonspecific illness with mild symptomatology.' Each decision is defined in terms of the raw scale threshold points; it is worth giving two examples because of the similarities they show to the fundamental structure of production system rules which were described in Chapter 2 (and will be illustrated in § 5.5) and because they are so clearly decision points in flowcharts. In what follows the nouns and noun pairs are the names of different scales of psychiatric status (see Spitzer & Endicott, 1968).

Example 1

      If (Disorientation–Memory) > 3
      Then go to decision 2
      Else go to decision 11.

Example 2

      If (Delusions–Hallucinations) > 2
      or (Retardation–Withdrawal) > 4
      or (Inappropriate–Bizarre Appearance
      or (Behaviour plus Retardation–Withdrawal plus Speech
      Disorganisation)) > 7
      or (Elation > 0 or Grandiosity > 2)
      and (Agitation–Excitement > 2)
      or (Speech Disorganisation > 3)

    or (Social Isolation > 7 and Alcohol Abuse < 5)
    Then go to decision 12
    Else go to decision 20.

The version of Diagno described in Spitzer & Endicott (1968) uses 36 decision points.

A fourth example of a mechanistic flowchart program is described in Greist, Klein & Erdman (1976). This program is based on the Research Diagnostic Criteria (Spitzer, Endicott & Robins, 1975).

It should be noted that, as with virtually all other applications of computers, it is typical for such systems as those outlined above to undergo continuous development. The latest versions may well differ from the above.

So far we have been discussing mechanistic examples of flowchart methods. We now present three examples of empirical (type I) flowchart approaches. The first is from Sturt (1981a,b). In the examples above we have been implicitly assuming that costs, informativeness, and so on are derived from human experience. It is this which justifies us in categorising these approaches as 'mechanistic'. When these things are derived by objective mathematical methods then we have an 'empirical' flowchart. The basic idea of a branching structure of decisions is the same, but that structure may arise via either a clinical or a mathematical route.

Consider a set S of patients with known diagnoses (possible diagnoses being $d_1, \ldots, d_N$). Suppose that $n(d_j, i)$ patients in S with diagnosis d_j score i on some particular test. Then the 'discriminating power' of this test is defined by

$$D_S = \sum_i \max_j n(d_j, i).$$

That is, for each possible score on this test we find the class which has the maximum number of patients with this score. Then we add these maximum numbers over the possible scores. A test which had no overlapping scores between the diagnoses – that is, one in which each of the diagnoses produced different scores – would maximise this measure of discriminating power. And clearly such a test would be ideal since it would permit perfect classification of the patients. Thus this measure, D_S, takes larger values the better is the test. Of all the tests under consideration, that with the largest D_S value is selected as the first decision point of the flowchart. This divides the set S into several groups, one for each possible score. Each of these groups is then examined separately by the same process, in each case selecting that variable which has the greatest discriminating power on each group.

The process could be continued until all of the original set had been classified but there are disadvantages in this (see § 5.6). Instead a 'stopping rule' is applied – a rule which calculates when little advantage is to be gained by adding another test. Sturt (1981*a*) outlines several stopping rules. She illustrates the method with two psychiatric examples, one of 237 women living in south-east London and the other of 206 men and women living in two Ugandan villages. In both examples the aim was simply to devise a flowchart for classifying subjects as either psychiatric 'cases' or 'non-cases'. Fig. 5.4 gives the flowchart for the 237 women example.

The second example of an empirical method for flowchart construction is due to Quinlan (1982). This is based on Hunt's Concept Learning System (Hunt, Marin & Stone, 1966). Again there is a set of instances of the objects to be classified, along with a set of descriptors, each taking one of a set of

Fig. 5.4. Diagnostic key derived from a sample of 237 women living in south-east London by the method of Sturt (1981*a*). Class 1 means 'non-case' and class 2 means 'case'. A diagnosis is derived by first allocating the patient according to her value of symptom 11 (which was subjective anxiety) and then progressively splitting the groups further. *e* is the number of mis-classifications in each terminal division.

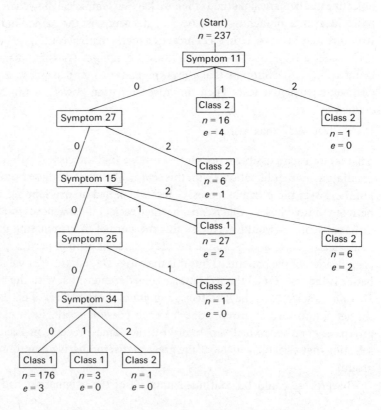

possible values. In the original Concept Learning System the sequence of descriptors was determined on a cost basis. Quinlan instead uses an information theoretic approach, choosing at each step that descriptor which adds the most information. He states 'This method of choosing the next attribute to test has been used now in a substantial number of different experiments, and does seem to give compact decision trees.' However, because the experiments he describes in Quinlan (1982) are not of a medical or psychological nature (they are concerned with subdomains of the chess endgame king-rook versus king-knight) we shall not dwell on them here.

For our third empirical example we turn to Goldman *et al.* (1982). This uses a flowchart derived by computer analysis (though which does not need to be run on one). It collects all of the information before making a decision (though this is not essential) and it takes the relative severity of the different kinds of misclassification into account. The background is as follows:

About two-thirds of patients admitted to hospital with myocardial infarction suffer from chest pain. Conversely, however, the presence of chest pain does not imply a myocardial infarction. Since it is obviously essential to try to avoid mistakenly refusing admission to infarct cases there is a natural tendency to admit all patients with chest pain. In some cases this has gone so far that only 30% of patients admitted to coronary care units turn out to be suffering from acute myocardial infarction. It is clear that considerable savings in both finance and resources could be made if identification could be made more precise. This is a natural role for the discriminatory and diagnostic tools described in this chapter.

Goldman *et al.* (1982) began with a large number of variables and examined them one by one to identify the particular variable which best separated the infarction and non-infarction groups. We define 'best separation' below. Splitting the patients into two groups using the variable yields groups containing (one hopes) predominantly infarction cases and predominantly non-infarction cases, respectively. Each of these two groups is then examined separately, searching for the variable which best discriminates between the two diagnostic categories within the group. This was repeated until sufficient accuracy was achieved. (The latter was measured in terms of keeping specificity as high as possible and bias as low as possible while maintaining sensitivity at 100%.)

Their measure of separation is particularly interesting because it takes 'cost' of misclassification into account. Their aim was to minimise what they called 'diversity':

Diversity = ((the probability of having had an MI [myocardial infarction] and being in the subgroup) × (the penalty of a false negative) × (the probability of a false negative))

+ ((the probability of not having had an MI and being in the subgroup)

× (the penalty of a false positive) × (the probability of a false positive)).

The resulting algorithm is shown in Fig. 5.5.

Feldman, Klein & Honigfeld (1972) give another example of an automatic flowchart generation method with a criterion based on the ratio of true positives to false negatives.

5.5   Expert systems

Conventional computer programs describe a branching and looping structure directing the flow of control and the operations to be carried out on the input data. All possible types of input data must have been foreseen, and routes through the program must have been determined for every eventuality. Suitable adjectives to describe this situation are 'rigid', 'fixed', and 'predetermined'.

It is, of course, not through accident or lack of foresight that such architectures have arisen. They are ideally well matched to the tasks that computers have been called upon to carry out in the past. Usually these have involved numerical manipulation or, at least, tasks which can be very precisely and clearly defined.

However, more recent task domains are not well served by such approaches. The simulation of human responses to various environments is an obvious example – here the data may be complex and rapidly varying. It may not be possible, even in principle, to foresee every possible combination of data that is likely to arise. The particular situation we have in mind here is, of course, psychiatric diagnosis.

In the past attempts have been made to tackle such complex domains using conventional methods. The flowchart approaches described above illustrate the application of conventional methods to diagnosis. In general, however, except when applied to an artificially constrained domain, the resulting programs are large, unwieldy, and extremely difficult to modify (these issues are discussed in § 5.7). What is needed is an alternative architecture, one which does not require the programmer to have worked out all possible paths for all potential input data. An architecture which is, in a word, flexible, and which is able to respond to any input datum in a sensible manner. A general term for such program structures is *pattern-directed inference system* (PDIS).

In Chapter 2 we described *production system* representations. Clearly such systems are PDISs. We noted in Chapter 2 that production systems, although originally proposed as a general computational mechanism (Post,

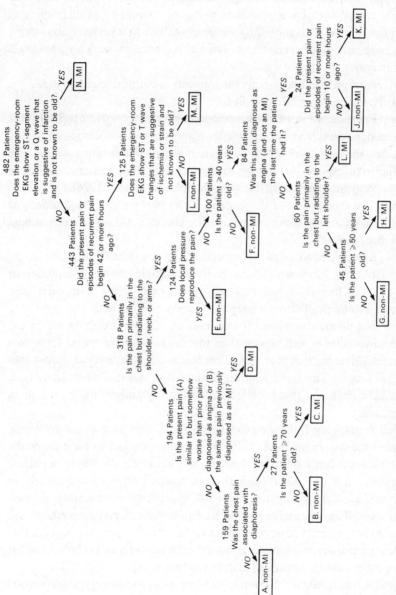

Fig. 5.5. Computer-derived decision tree for the classification of patients with acute chest pain. (Reprinted by permission of the *New England Journal of Medicine*, **307**, 588–906, 1982. Goldman *et al.*)

1943), had been adopted as a possible model for the way the human brain processes information (Newell & Simon, 1972). The use of a production system as a computer program for psychiatric diagnosis is thus very much an application of artificial intelligence techniques. Note that although one might regard such an approach as being an attempt to emulate the way humans carry out diagnosis, by virtue of the fact that production systems can be regarded as general computational mechanisms such a viewpoint is not essential.

Merits of production systems for application in this domain include:

(i) Their fundamental flexibility.

(ii) The separation of the knowledge about psychiatric diagnosis (the production rules) from the knowledge about the patient being investigated (the data the rules work on). It has been suggested that in humans long term memory corresponds to the rules themselves, and short term memory to the data upon which they work (see, for example, Anderson, 1976).

(iii) The modularity of the system. Rules may be modified, added, or deleted without the complex consistency checks required of conventional flowchart methods.

(iv) As a consequence of (iii) expertise may be gradually acquired over a period of time. Moreover this can be from multiple sources (from different experienced human consultants) or – more excitingly – from rules condensed automatically from a body of examples (see below).

(v) The human window. If the level of symbol manipulation of the individual rules is well chosen then the rules will make useful sense to a human. (Meaning that they should not be too complex, and nor should they be too simple. The input features to the rules, and the rules themselves, should be chosen so that knowledge is split into chunks suitable for human digestion.)

(vi) A mapping from the rules permits a simple trace of the reasoning process the system has used. This is a very important facility for it allows the system to explain why it has done what it has done. As I have remarked elsewhere, it is generally thought that one reason for the lack of sympathy in the medical community for statistical approaches to diagnosis is their bluntness. They are markedly non-human in their diagnostic methods and they do not present a reasoned deduction but merely a simple categorisation (or, more usually and somewhat better, a list of posterior probabilities that the patient belongs to various diagnostic categories).

(vii) As described in Chapter 2, each rule of a production system consists of a left hand side set of *antecedents* and a right hand side set of *consequents*. The antecedents represent conditions which have to be true for the consequent to be true. One advantage of production systems derives from this separation into conditions and assertions, namely that it makes it easier to debug the system – to sort out what has happened when an error occurs.

(viii) Following from (vii), if an error reveals a lack of a rule then this can be added in two parts – its left hand side conditions and its right hand assertion.

It was remarked in Chapter 2 that production systems could function in two ways: they could be either left hand side (antecedent) driven or right hand side (consequent) driven. In the first case the left hand side of the rules is matched against the data and when a match is found (when a rule 'fires') the right hand side carries out some action such as modifying the data or asserting something about the data (such as a diagnosis). In the second case a rule is chosen on the basis of its right hand side and the left hand side is examined to see if it matches the data. For example, if the right hand side represents a particular diagnosis then the rule's left hand side will be examined to see if all the conditions for this diagnosis are met. This right hand side driven approach is very similar to the human mechanism proposed by various authors and described in § 5.2. It also has the merit that in general, in contrast to left hand side driven systems, it requires only a simple conflict resolution strategy (see Chapter 2). Often a simple precedence list suffices. The example in Chapter 2 illustrates this. Here a likely (or possible) diagnosis is triggered by a very slight cue (as suggested in 5.2), and then right hand side driven rules are applied in an attempt to prove the diagnosis correct or to show it to be wrong. For example, suppose a diagnosis of delirium is suspected. Then the rule IF (overactive and unable to perform simple tasks) THEN (perhaps delirium) may be matched by its right hand side. This leads to attempts to validate the two components (overactive) and (unable to perform simple tasks). These might already have been established (be present in the database) or their absence may already have been established. If neither presence nor absence is known then the system will explore this. Perhaps – depending on the system's design – this will involve asking the user 'Is the subject overactive?' or it might involve trying to find rules which have these two components as right hand side goals and then seeing if it can prove the antecedent conditions of these rules.

It is worth reminding the reader at this point of an important division which has emerged in production systems, described in Chapter 2. The distinction is a consequence of how one views production systems:

(i) *Pure production systems* are characteristically simple, have a homogeneous rule base, and a simple executive and conflict resolution strategy. Typically they have been used for modelling theories of how humans think. Thus the aim is not to perform diagnosis (or whatever) as accurately as possible. Instead the aim is to match the way humans do this. One consequence of this aim which is worth remarking upon is that such a system is *designed to make mistakes*. If it is successful it should make the same sort of mistakes as a human.

(ii) In contrast to (i) are *performance production systems* in which the aim is to obtain the best possible performance. Clearly an ideal such system would make no errors – human or otherwise in kind. In medical diagnosis this seems the ideal to seek. Note, however, that a system which makes no errors is necessarily performing to some extent in a non-human way – and this might reduce its appeal to potential users. Recall the remark that their inhuman approach might explain the relatively poor reception of statistical pattern recognition diagnostic methods. Typically performance production systems are more complex than pure production systems, their rules are less homogeneous and the executive and conflict resolution strategy may be quite complicated. From a purist point of view they may be less aesthetically appealing, but from a functional point of view they are superior. (But see § 5.7, where we discuss the relative merits of human and non-human approaches to diagnosis.)

Chapter 2 explained the basic principles of production systems. Later in this section we give overviews of some examples of medical expert systems. As I have just remarked, we must expect these performance-oriented expert systems to exhibit considerably greater complexity than a simple pure production system. Hayes-Roth, Waterman & Lenat (1978) summarise some of the more sophisticated architectural techniques and principles that have been implemented. (It is perhaps worth reminding the reader of the dramatic rate of progress in the field of expert systems. The paper by Hayes-Roth *et al.* was published in 1978, since which time interest in the area has rocketed. Current systems make use of an even broader range of architectures and principles.)

(i) A need to make the pattern matching process faster. This arises from the increasing number of rules in modern systems, and the larger number of symbols (features, descriptors) which may be matched. Approaches to this include improved matching algorithms, new hardware architectures designed for rapid matching, and hierarchical groups of rules so that relevant subsets can be quickly identified.

(ii) Certainty factors have also been widely used. These are numerical 'probability' measures used to describe the likelihood of the implication of a rule being true – replacing the true/false dichotomy.

(iii) In large complex systems possessing knowledge about a number of different problem domains some method has to be chosen for activating the relevant aspects of the domain. This would certainly be the case for a general medical system but may not be necessary for one restricted to psychiatry.

Amongst methods which have been used are the *spreading of activation* (the knowledge base is structured as a network and a triggered area of knowledge also activates areas closely linked to it), *partial matching* (some conditions match), and the use of meta-knowledge (knowledge about what knowledge might be useful). The last of these is especially relevant to production systems since knowledge about knowledge can be encoded as rules, just like the original knowledge, producing a completely uniform representation.

The remainder of this section falls into three parts, describing the question-answering capacity of expert systems, automatic acquisition of rules, and finally presenting some examples of real working systems.

We have already noted that expert systems can typically ask the user questions. Usually this occurs when the system is trying to satisfy the left hand side conditions of a rule and is unable to do so by deduction from other rules. However, it is another characteristic of expert systems that the user can also ask questions of them. This potential for dialogue is undoubtedly one of the major strengths of expert systems and one which has led to their relatively enthusiastic reception in the medical community. A statistical system (as described in § 5.6) might say: 'The probability that the patient has disease A is 0.8 and the probability that he has disease B is 0.2'. There is little point the user asking how it arrived at this conclusion since the answer can only be 'I estimated these probabilities using the design set and mathematical and statistical techniques for estimating probabilities'. No *deduction*, of the form 'if W and X then Y and so Z' has occurred, so nothing can be explained. In contrast, when the expert system gives the diagnosis A as the most probable, the user can ask how it arrived at this conclusion. The mechanism enabling the system to answer the question is, in principle, straightforward. All it needs to do is map the rule which led to the diagnosis to the output terminal. If the rule was of the form 'If W and X and Y then Z' then the system simply replies:

'Rule number ** tells me that
 If W
 and X
 and Y
are true
 then Z is true.
And I have already established W, X, and Y.'

If the user wishes this can be pursued further – by the user asking how the system deduced W or X or Y.

Similarly, when the system asks the user a question the user can ask why the system wants to know, and again a simple mapping from the rule being used yields the answer:

> *System:* Is the subject disoriented?
> *User:* Why? (Meaning, why do you want to know that?)
> *System:* Because I suspect Korsakov's Syndrome
>   And disorientation is a further sign of this.

Note the remark above that this mapping from rule to explanatory text is simple in principle. In performance systems the extra sophistication can make it more complex.

We turn now to the question of how the rules are formulated.

One practical problem in building expert systems is the effort it takes to transfer the knowledge from the human expert to the program. Typically the human expert (the 'domain specialist') has little appreciation of artificial intelligence techniques and information structures and so has to work in tandem with an artificial intelligence specialist (a 'knowledge engineer'). For small demonstration programs involving at most a few tens of rules there is little problem (which is not to say devising suitable rules is easy). For large systems to be used in real applications, however (with hundreds or perhaps thousands of rules), the problem can be serious, requiring many man-years of effort. Because of this, attention has turned to ways to automate the rule acquisition process.

This process involves two stages. First, automatic acquisition of conceptual primitives. That is, ways by which the program can add to its list of the basic concepts comprising its rules, without requiring the mediation of a knowledge engineer. Secondly, it requires a method for automatic rule formulation – the ability to derive new rules by direct interaction with the domain specialist. We shall concentrate on the second stage here. An example of the first may be found in Davis (1978).

Several different approaches to the automatic rule formulation stage have been explored, of which perhaps the most popular two are as follows. First, take as raw data a set of examples of the objects to be classified and analyse these to extract class descriptions in rule form. (Examples of this are given below.) Apart from the difference in representation used for the final result this process bears close similarities to statistical methods – and also to automatic methods for generating flowcharts from examples. In fact, the distinction between flowchart systems and rule systems blurs when we consider automatic rule acquisition. We shall have more to say about this below.

The second popular approach is to present the existing system with a problem, observe its attempts to solve it, and add new knowledge to correct any mistakes. As Davis (1978) remarks, this approach assumes that the basic control structure and knowledge representations of the system are error free, and any errors arise from inadequate, or faulty, knowledge. In its simplest form this approach involves stepping through the trace of rules used by the system to identify that needing modification or to discover exactly what is missing.

The first type of approach – condensing a set of examples to a set of rules automatically – is still at an early age of development. However, as Michalski & Chilausky (1980) have observed: 'It is already possible to obtain practical results, if the problem is sufficiently well defined and specialised.'

Before presenting an example of this approach it should perhaps be noted explicitly that when the rule generation process is automated, the resulting system is arguably an empirical rather than a mechanistic system.

My example comes from Michalski & Chilausky (1980). This is not a medical application but it is such a good example that I consider it worth discussing in some depth. In view of the level and origin of indicators used as symptoms in psychiatry (see § 5.7), it seems very likely that the Michalski & Chilausky method could be applied in psychiatry.

Although not medical, Michalski & Chilausky's domain is concerned with disease: disease of soybeans. The example is particularly useful because not only does it illustrate a method of automatic rule acquisition, but it also shows how additional complications necessarily rapidly accumulate around the basic production system concept. The aim is to diagnose diseased plants as belonging to one of 15 disease classes. Particular instances are characterised by a list of attribute/value pairs, there being 35 such attributes (features, descriptors) chosen by consultation with an expert in soybean pathology. By letting the attributes in the left hand sides of the rules have more than one value, proliferation of rules is avoided. (For example the attribute/value list

> (damaged area = low areas, upland areas) (severity = minor)

replaces the two lists

> (damaged area = low areas) (severity = minor)

and   (damaged area = upland areas) (severity = minor.)

If it were necessary to have separate rules to cater for such 'internal' disjunctions then multiplication of the numbers of eligible values in each attribute could quickly lead to a very large number of rules.

Each attribute/value pair on the left hand side of a rule will have an associated number (a 'type (i)' number) indicating its importance. The weights may depend on the value and are determined by particular functions.

A second number ('type (ii)') indicates the degree of uncertainty of any particular attribute in a particular instance. Clearly this facility is extremely relevant to psychiatry.

Finally, a third number ('type (iii)') is added to each rule to indicate the strength of its implication.

Note that apart from any more fundamental learning, by creating or modifying rules, a simple kind of learning would be possible by modifying these numbers.

Automatic rule derivation was carried out using 290 cases with known diagnoses (determined by plant pathologists; compare the use of psychiatrists as the ultimate authority in diagnosing mental illness) and known attribute values. Some other information was also included – for example, structural information relating knowledge that a plant is healthy to the lack of disease in its component parts.

The program to derive the rules compared suggested rules with the examples, identified examples which were incorrectly classified, and then added correcting descriptive terms to correctly classify these. Michalski & Chilausky note that if any correcting terms explain only a few instances then it might be worthwhile replacing them by straightforward descriptions, and that situations like this may well be indicative of errors in the data. In statistical terms, they will be identifying outliers as worthy of close scrutiny.

Three examples of the derived rules are:

Example 1
    IF (leaf malformation = absent)
    and (stem = abnormal)
    and (internal discolouration = black)

    THEN (Diagnosis = *Charcoal rot*)

Example 2
    IF (leaves = abnormal)
    and (leaf malformation = absent)
    and (leaf mildew growth = on upper leaf surface)
    and (roots = normal)

    THEN (Diagnosis = *Powdery mildew*)

Example 3
    IF (leaf malformation = absent)
    and (stem = abnormal)
    and (internal discolouration = brown)

OR

    (leaves = normal)
    and (stem = absent)
    and (internal discolouration = brown)

    THEN (Diagnosis = *Brown stem rot*).

The authors also describe a rule set derived by consultation with experts in the area (requiring around 20 hours of discussion. This, just to develop 15 rules, demonstrates the problems associated with developing rule systems manually for large systems). For the human derived system a further sophistication was imposed on the basic production system concept, namely a grouping of the antecedent conditions for each rule into two sets: conditions which must be present in a plant with a particular disease (denoted Q_s) and conditions which, although generally present, merely reinforce the information given by terms in Q_s (denoted Q_c). Examples of these rules are:

Example 1

IF (time = July .... August)
and (precipitation $\leqslant$ normal)
and (temperature $\geqslant$ normal)
and (plant growth = abnormal)
and (leaves = abnormal) Q_s
and (stem = abnormal)
and (sclerotia = present)
and (roots = rotted)
and (internal discolouration = black)

and

(damaged area = upland areas)
and (severity = severe)
and (seed size < normal) Q_c
and (number of years crop repeated: a type (i) number,
    increasing with number of years)

THEN (Diagnosis = *Charcoal rot*)

Example 2

IF (leaves = abnormal)
and (leaf mildew growth = upper leaf surface) Q_s
    and
(time = August, September) Q_c

THEN (Diagnosis = *Powdery mildew*)

Michalski & Chilausky describe their comparative evaluation of the two rule sets, concluding: 'The comparison of 2 knowledge acquisition techniques indicates that decision rules derived inductively performed somewhat better than the rules derived by representing the knowledge of experts.' They offer several explanations for this result (which they say was contrary to their initial expectation):

(i) Insufficient information was obtained during the discussions with the experts.

(ii) The descriptors were inadequate.

(iii) The comparisons between the rule sets were based on inadequate inferential techniques.

(iv) The experts, though expert in making diagnoses, were not expert in explaining how they did it – not an uncommon situation. As Quinlan (1982) puts it: 'The expert is called upon to perform a most exacting task, with which he is also unfamiliar. He must set out the sources and methodologies of his own expertise.'

However, whatever the reason, the result is a most interesting one, with all sorts of implications.

Quinlan (1982) has also investigated automatic rule acquisition, as was mentioned in § 5.4.

Example 1: MYCIN

MYCIN (Shortliffe, 1976) was developed over a period of several years by a group of computer scientists and clinicians working at Stanford University. It is perhaps the best known of all medical expert systems. This is partly because, although MYCIN itself was designed to give advice on diagnosis and therapy in infectious disease, the basic structure can be applied in other domains. This basic structure, stripped of knowledge specifically relating to infectious disease, has been called EMYCIN, for Essential MYCIN (See Van Melle, 1979). Example 4 below, PUFF (Kunz, 1978), is another medical system which was built using EMYCIN. A psychopharmacology advisor has been built using EMYCIN and we briefly describe it at the end of the MYCIN description.

Before looking at the program perhaps we should look at the sort of situation in which it would be applied. Davis (1982) summarises it thus:

> A typical clinical situation begins with a patient showing signs of infection, and a specimen (of blood, urine, etc.) is obtained and cultured to check for the presence of disease-causing bacteria. While cultures may show some evidence of bacterial growth within twelve hours, typically 24 to 48 hours are required for positive identification of the organisms. Treatment often cannot be delayed that long, so the physician must base his decision on whatever information is available. This typically includes several easily observable characteristics of the bacteria in the culture (e.g. overall shape, response to oxygen, etc.), as well as the history of the patient

(e.g. previous infections, other clinical evidence of infection, or events that may make the patient particularly susceptible to a particular type of bacterium).

Shortliffe (1976) characterises therapy selection as a four part process:

(i) The physician must decide whether the patient has a significant bacterial infection which requires treatment. Bacteria which are normally present in the body must be excluded from consideration and bacteria from the atmosphere must be excluded from the sample.

(ii) The organism must be identified, or at least its range of possible identity narrowed down. As Davis has described, a sample taken from the site of suspected infection will be cultured and early data on the characteristics of the organism noted. The patient's clinical characteristics may also help to identify the organism.

(iii) Potentially useful drugs must be chosen. Biological populations are dynamic and resistant strains develop (partly due to indiscriminate use and overuse of antibiotics. The sensitive and targeted approach to their administration made possible through systems like MYCIN should ease this problem, which is a powerful argument favouring the use of such systems). Thus even when the identity is known it will be necessary to carry out *in vitro* tests to discover to which antimicrobial agents the bacterium is sensitive. The problem is that these sensitivity tests may take one or two days and decisions must be made before that.

(iv) The last step is to choose the most appropriate drug or combination of drugs. This choice is based on the likely effectiveness of proposed drugs, possible allergies, contraindications, route of administration, and other factors.

Bearing in mind these descriptions of the situation that the program must face, let us consider the properties that a clinical consultation program must have in order to be acceptable. These again are from Shortliffe (1976):

(a) *Useful.* There must be a need for the advice that the program gives, its advice must be reliable, and its advice must be easy to obtain.

(b) *Educational when appropriate.* The system must be able to explain to the user anything he may ask regarding the system's diagnostic strategies. On the other hand it must not gratuitously offer such advice – only when asked.

(c) *Able to explain its advice.* The system must be able to justify any recommendations it may make, so that the user can assess them.

(d) *Able to respond to simple natural language questions.* This may be an ideal, but it is an important one. Any tool is acceptable only proportionately to its ease of use. A screwdriver which needed six people to operate it would not gain wide acceptance. Similarly, a diagnostic system which required the user to learn a special language would not be popular.

(e) *Able to acquire new knowledge.* This is really self-evident in a field developing as rapidly as medicine. Note that the human medical expert must be able to instruct the system without requiring that he be an expert programmer as well.

(f) *Easily modified.* The system must be constructed so that any faulty knowledge can be corrected easily and new knowledge added easily.

The MYCIN system can be divided into three subprograms: the consultation system, which asks questions, draws conclusions, and gives recommendations; the explanation system, which answers users' questions; and the rule acquisition component. Fig. 5.6 illustrates the relationship of these components.

MYCIN's basic structure is a production system. Some examples of MYCIN's rules are as follows:

(i) IF (1) the gram stain of the organism is gram negative
and (2) the morphology of the organism is rod
and (3) the aerobicity of the organism is aerobic

THEN there is strongly suggestive evidence (0.8) that the class of the organism is Enterobacteriaceae.
(Note: the number 0.8 represents a measure of confidence in the conclusion and is discussed below).

(ii) IF (1) the gram stain of the organism is gram negative
and (2) the morphology of the organism is rod
and (3) the aerobicity of the organism is anaerobic

THEN there is suggestive evidence (0.7) that the identity of the organism is Bacteroides.

Fig. 5.6. Components of MYCIN. (Adapted from Shortliffe *et al.*, 1975.)

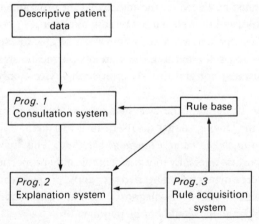

(iii) IF (1) the gram stain of the organism is gram positive

and (2) the morphology of the organism is coccus

and (3) the growth conformation of the organism is pairs

and (4) the site of the culture is one of: sputum, lung tissue.

THEN there is a suggestive evidence (0.7) that the identity of the organism is *Streptococcus pneumoniae*.

(iv) IF (1) the site of the culture is blood

and (2) the gram stain of the organism is gram negative

and (3) the morphology of the organism is rod

and (4) the patient is a compromised host

THEN there is suggestive evidence (0.6) that the identity of the organism is *Pseudomonas aeruginosa*.

(v) IF (1) the therapy under consideration is one of: cephalothin,

      clindamycin, erythromycin, lincomycin, vancomycin

and (2) meningitis is an infectious disease diagnosis for the

      patient

THEN it is definite (1) that the therapy under consideration is not a potential therapy for use against the organism.

(vi) IF the identity of the organism is Bacteroides

THEN I recommend therapy chosen from among the following drugs:

    1. Clindamycin (0.99)

    2. Chloramphenicol (0.99)

    3. Erythromycin (0.57)

    4. Tetracycline (0.28)

    5. Carbenicillin (0.27)

(Note: the numbers here are the probabilities that a Bacteroides isolated at Stanford Hospital will be sensitive to the indicated drug. They will be different for other hospitals and can easily be modified.)

(vii) IF the identity of the organism is *Pseudomonas*

THEN I recommend therapy chosen from among the following drugs:

    1. Colistin (0.98)

    2. Polymyxin (0.96)

    3. Gentamicin (0.96)

    4. Carbenicillin (0.65)

    5. Sulfisoxazole (0.64)

(viii) IF (1) there is an organism which requires therapy

and (2) consideration has been given to the possible existence

of additional organisms requiring therapy, even though
they have not actually been recovered from any current
cultures

THEN (1) compile the list of possible therapies which, based upon
sensitivity data, may be effective against the organisms requiring
treatment

and (2) determine the best therapy recommendations from the compiled
list

OTHERWISE indicate that the patient does not require therapy.

(Note: example (viii) differs from the others. It is called the 'goal rule' and
is discussed below.)

As we noted in Chapter 2, large collections of rules may have to be
structured in some way to facilitate searching through them. MYCIN does
this via a 'context tree'. MYCIN's rules might apply to the patient, a culture,
an organism, or a drug. These different domains of application are termed
'contexts', and MYCIN has ten of them. MYCIN's rules are classified as
belonging to one of a set of rule categories, with the categories defined
according to the contexts to which their constituent rules apply.

A particular context might be instantiated more than once in any
consultation. For example, there might be two cultures developed and
obviously the deductions about them must be kept distinct. The context
types instantiated during a consultation are put together into a tree structure, permitting the system to relate one context to another. (So that, for
example, it knows that 'organism-3' was derived from 'culture-2'.)

Davis (1982) characterises the data fed into MYCIN as both *incomplete*
and *inexact*. It is incomplete for the reasons given above – there are time
constraints, gaps in the records, and it is impracticable to give exhaustive
tests. It is inexact because many of the tests are qualitative and subjective.
Since these properties are also characteristic of psychiatric data this suggests
that expert systems may be ideally suited to recommending therapies for
mental illness.

Apart from the incompleteness and imprecision of the basic data, MYCIN
must also contend with uncertainty about some of the data. This can arise in
two ways. Firstly, because the user is not absolutely certain of the information he is supplying and, secondly, because the deductions embodied in
the rules are not always the crisp deductions of formal logic. As Davis puts
it: 'the system must have some means of representing the fact that "X and Y
seem to suggest Z" or "A and B *tend to rule out C*".' The numbers in the right
hand sides of rules (i) to (iv) above indicate how this uncertainty of
deduction is implemented. The numbers are *certainty factors*, indicating the
system's confidence that a conclusion is correct. As a deductive process
works its way through a chain of rules, so the certainty factors are com-

bined to yield a final measure of confidence in the conclusion. (See Shortliffe, 1976, chapter 4 and, for a very interesting result, Adams, 1976.) The certainty factors lie between $+1$ and -1 where $+1$ indicates that the value of a clinical parameter is correct and -1 indicates certainty that the value is incorrect. A value of 0 indicates that there is no evidence either way.

As the reader may have guessed, MYCIN begins by trying to establish the conditions of the left hand side and carry out the actions of the right hand side of the goal rule (number (viii)). A consequent-driven interpreter works on the other production rules to establish the left hand side of the goal rule. This has two interrelated mechanisms:

(a) MONITOR, which checks through a rule's antecedent conditions. If it discovers one for which the answer is not yet known MONITOR calls routine FINDOUT.

(b) FINDOUT. If the unknown item is a piece of laboratory data, FINDOUT asks the user. Otherwise it identifies rules with this item as their right hand side goal, chooses one (on a simple priority order basis), and transfers control to MONITOR to examine the chosen rule's left hand side.

To carry out the right hand side of the goal rule, MYCIN has a set of action rules (for example, rules (vi) and (vii) above). The possible organisms are listed and rules applied to identify suitable therapies. For example, we may get:

'My therapy recommendations will be based on the following possible identities of the organism(s) that seem to be significant:

Item 1: the identity of ORGANISM-1 may be streptococcus-group-D.

Item 2: the identity of ORGANISM-1 may be streptococcus-alpha

Item 3: the identity of ORGANISM-2 is pseudomonas.'

Each item has an associated therapy rule which is applied to give a list of possible drugs (for example, rule (vii) above corresponds to item 3).

The fourth step in Shortliffe's four stages of therapy selection, outlined above, is to choose the most appropriate therapy. This choice occurs in two stages. First, the most effective of the various drugs is chosen for each item, taking into account whether it is already being administered. Second, a rule-based screening for contra-indications is used and another choice made if appropriate.

In a great many application domains of expert systems it is important for the system to be able to handle the eventuality of the user making – and recognising that he has made – a mistake. This is certainly true of medicine and psychiatry. By the very nature of a production system architecture, a mistaken response can have all sorts of consequences before it is discovered.

Fig. 5.7(*a*)

PATIENT-1
1) Patient's name: (first–last)
** **FRED SMITH**
2) Sex:
** **MALE**
3) Age:
** **55**
4) Have you been able to obtain positive cultures from a site at
   which Fred Smith has an infection?
** **YES**

INFECTION-1
5) What is the infection?
** **PRIMARY-BACTEREMIA**
6) Please give the date and approximate time when signs or symptoms of
   the primary-bacteremia (INFECTION-1) first appeared. (mo/da/yr)
** **MAY 5, 1975**
The most recent positive culture associated with the
   primary-bacteremia (INFECTION-1) will be referred to as:

CULTURE-1
7) From what site was the specimen for CULTURE-1 taken?
** **BLODD**
= BLOOD
8) Please give the date and time when this blood culture
       (CULTURE-1) was obtained. (mo/da/yr)
** **MAY 9, 1975**
The first significant organism from this blood culture
       (CULTURE-1) will be referred to as:

ORGANISM-1
9) Enter the identity of ORGANISM-1:
** **UNKNOWN**
                       (typically the identity is not known and must be inferred)
10) Is ORGANISM-1 a rod or coccus (etc.):
** **ROD**
11) The gram stain of ORGANISM-1:
** **GRAMNEG**
12) Did ORGANISM-1 grow aerobically?
** **YES (0.8)**
13) Is the patient's illness with ORGANISM-1 a hospital-acquired
    infection?
** ?

Was the infection with ORGANISM-1 acquired while the patient
    was hospitalized?
Expected responses are: YES NO
Enter HELP list of user options.
** **Y**
(More questions follow to gather sufficient information
to infer possible identities of the infecting organisms)

Fig. 5.7. (*a*) Opening a session with MYCIN. (*b*) The final segment of a MYCIN session. (Reprinted by permission of Westview Press from *Artificial intelligence in medicine*, edited by Peter Szolovits. Copyright ©1982 by the American Association for the Advancement of Science.)

Fig. 5.7(*b*)

My therapy recommendation will be based on the following probable
      infection(s) and potential causative organism(s):
INFECTION-1 is PRIMARY-BACTEREMIA   (possible identities)
<Item 1> The identity of ORGANISM-1 may be PSEUDOMONAS-AERUGINOSA
<Item 2> The identity of ORGANISM-1 may be KLEBSIELLA-PNEUMONIAE
<Item 3> The identity of ORGANISM-1 may be E. COLI
<Item 4> The identity of ORGANISM-1 may be BACTEROIDES-FRAGILIS
<Item 5> The identity of ORGANISM-1 may be ENTEROBACTER
<Item 6> The identity of ORGANISM-1 may be PROTEUS-NON-MIRABILIS
     46) On a scale of 0 to 4, where higher numbers indicate
         increasing severity, how would you rate Fred Smith's
         degree of sickness?
  ** **3**
     47) Does Fred Smith have a clinically significant allergic
         reaction to any antimicrobial agent?
  ** **NO**
     48) Fred Smith's weight in kilograms (or <number> POUNDS):
  ** **70**
                    (note that 2 drugs cover for 6 potential
                    organisms)
[Rec 1] My preferred therapy recommendation is as follows:
     In order to cover for Items <1 2 3 5 6>:
     Give: GENTAMICIN
     Dose: 119 mg (1.7 mg/kg) q8h IV [or IM] for 10 days
     Comments: Modify dose in renal failure
In order to cover for Item <4>:
     Give: CLINDAMYCIN
     Dose: 595 mg (8.5 mg/kg) q6h IV [or IM] for 14 days
     Comments: If diarrhea or other GI symptoms develop, patient should
        be evaluated for possible pseudomembranous colitis.
Do you wish to see the next choice therapy?
** **Y**   (alternative choices are available)
Which, if any, of the above drugs do you wish eliminated from consideration?
** **CLINDAMYCIN**
[Rec 2] Next best therapy recommendation:
     In order to cover for Items <2 3 4 5 6>:
     Give: CHLORAMPHENICOL
     Dose: 1 gm (15 mg/kg) q6h IV for 14 days
     Comments: Monitor patient's white count
In order to cover for Item <1>:
     Give: GENTAMICIN
     Dose: 119 mg (1.7 mg/kg) q8h IV [or IM] for 10 days
     Comments: Modify dose in renal failure

Thus ideally one would want to return the system to the state it was in just prior to the error and restart from there. Unfortunately this would require storing an impracticably large amount of information.

At the other extreme we have the alternative of restarting the investigation from scratch. This is not an approach likely to be welcomed by the user since it will involve a lot of tedious repetition of correct answers to questions which have already been asked.

MYCIN's answer lies in the Patient Data Table. This is a record of all user responses describing a patient. When an error is discovered the analysis is restarted from the beginning but the Patient Data Table is first checked to see if each question has already been answered, before asking the user. By this means no question is unnecessarily repeated.

The Patient Data Table is also stored after a consultation and can be recalled at a later date. This has two uses. One is that any changes to the rule base can be evaluated by applying the modified rules to the same patient data as was used before. The other is that diagnoses and therapies can be re-evaluated as new information becomes available.

Fig. 5.7 illustrates the beginning and end of a MYCIN consultation and Fig. 5.8 illustrates MYCIN's facility for explaining its actions.

As the above implies, MYCIN is not a static system. It has undergone considerable modification and growth. The system described in Shortliffe (1976) has 200 rules, while that in Davis (1982) has 400 rules.

MYCIN is an important landmark in the history of expert systems. Shortliffe's book (1976) is to be thoroughly recommended as a thoughtful and stimulating account of a seminal expert system in the domain of medical diagnosis. Much of the material in the present description was based on the description given in that book.

MYCIN has two companion programs. TEIRESIAS, which by interaction with an expert builds the knowledge base that MYCIN uses (it displays a trace of MYCIN's deductive process and permits an authorised user to change the rules). Davis (1982) describes this as follows: 'The approach to knowledge acquisition used in Teiresias is modelled after a standard tutorial in which a student is given a difficult problem to solve, while the teacher observes and occasionally corrects the student's performance . . . . This means that the expert is faced with a sharply focussed task of adding a chunk of knowledge to remedy a specific bug.'

The other companion program is GUIDON (see Chapter 6), which utilises the same knowledge base to teach students.

Brooks & Heiser (1980) have used EMYCIN as the basis of an expert system for giving psychopharmacological advice. This is not a diagnostic system, but a system for choosing drug therapy. Selection of a medication

Fig. 5.8. MYCIN's ability to explain its actions. (Reprinted by permission of Westview Press from *Artificial intelligence in medicine*, edited by Peter Szolovits. Copyright ©1982 by the American Association for the Advancement of Science.)

(a) ** **HOW DID YOU DECIDE THAT ORGANISM-1 MIGHT BE AN E. COLI?**

I used RULE021 to conclude that the identity of ORGANISM-1 is e. coli. This gave a cumulative CF of (0.47).

Then I used RULE084 to conclude that the identity of ORGANISM-1 is e. coli. This gave cumulative CF of (0.55).

Finally, I used RULE003 to conclude that the identity of ORGANISM-1 is e. coli. This gave a cumulative CF of (0.74).

(b) ** **DID YOU USE RULE 163 TO FIND OUT ANYTHING ABOUT ORGANISM-1?**

RULE163 was tried in the context of ORGANISM-1, but it failed because it is not true that the patient has had a genito-urinary tract manipulative procedure (clause 3).

(c) ** **DID RULE 116 TELL YOU ANYTHING ABOUT INFECTION-1?**

No. RULE116 would be relevant to the primary-bacteremia when applied to ORGANISM-1.

But clause 2 ('the gram stain of the organism is not known') was already known to be false for ORGANISM-1, so the rule was never tried.

(d) ** **WHY DIDN'T YOU CONSIDER STREPTOCOCCUS AS A POSSIBILITY FOR ORGANISM-1?**

The following rule could have been used to determine that the identity of ORGANISM-1 was streptococcus: RULE033

But clause 2 ('the morphology of the organism is coccus') was already known to be false for ORGANISM-1, so the rule was never tried.

(e) ** **DO YOU RECOMMEND CLINDAMYCIN FOR BACTEROIDES?**

Yes.

RULE060

If the identity of the organism is bacteroides

Then I recommend therapy be chosen from among the following: CHLORAMPHENICOL, CLINDAMYCIN, RIFAMPIN, ERYTHROMYCIN, CARBENICILLIN, TETRACYCLINE, LINCOMYCIN

(f) ** **IS BLOOD A STERILE SITE?**

Yes, blood is one of these sites that are normally sterile.

(g) ** **WHAT ARE THE ORGANISMS ASSOCIATED WITH THE GASTRO-INTESTINAL TRACT?**

The likely pathogens associated with the gastro-intestinal tract are: ENTEROCOCCUS, CLOSTRIDIUM-GANGRENE, BACTEROIDES, KLEBISELLA, PSEUDOMONAS, E. COLI, ENTEROBACTER, PROTEUS.

between and within the five major classes of psychopharmacological agent (antipsychotics, tricyclic antidepressants, MAO inhibitors, lithium, and anxiolytics) depends on the severity and nature of the symptoms, the history of the patient and his present condition, as well as on diagnosis. As yet there are few theories relating underlying biochemical phenomena to the manifest psychological behaviour patterns. This means that it is not feasible to build a theoretical process model, so that an expert system approach, based on the loose modelling of human ways of selecting (as described above), seems an eminently reasonable approach. It is therefore particularly interesting to take note of one of the criticisms that Brooks & Heiser make about the application of EMYCIN in this domain. They suggest that physicians group their information about a patient into categories such as 'chief complaint', 'history of present illness', 'past medical history', and so on and that this grouping is used as a supporting skeleton to ensure that nothing of importance is omitted. The backward chaining structure of EMYCIN, however, does not group things in this way. The order of questions posed by the EMYCIN system will depend on the answers to previous ones in such a way that information from the different categories may be mixed. Brooks & Heiser claim that this can be disconcerting to physicians consulting the system.

Example 2: INTERNIST-I

The INTERNIST/CADUCEUS project (Pople, 1982) represents a particularly interesting series of medical expert systems for two main reasons:

(i) It differs from other such projects in that it is intended to be applied in a large domain (general internal medicine) rather than a restricted one.

(ii) The problem of structuring medical diagnosis is explored in a continuing series of systems. At least one consequence of this is that faults can be honestly acknowledged: they will be rectified in the next system. This is in contrast to much other artificial intelligence work in which single programs (perhaps leading to Ph.D.s) are constructed, after which the project dies. In such a case it clearly does not pay to emphasise the weaknesses.

INTERNIST-I's basic approach is a two-step one. Based on an examination of a patient's initial history, results of a physical examination, and laboratory tests, the system first formulates a system of differential diagnostic tasks (i.e. it identifies sets of competing diagnoses) and then it applies heuristic rules to choose from the competitors within each set. The first part is a way of imposing structure on the inherently ill-structured diagnostic problem, as discussed earlier in this chapter. Note that by identifying more than one set of competing hypotheses the program can identify multiple diagnoses.

At the heart of INTERNIST-I lie two interrelated lists: a list of diseases and a list of manifestations.

The disease list is structured as a taxonomic hierarchy. Miller, Pople & Myers (1982) give an example: 'acute viral hepatitis is classified as a hepatocellular infection, hepatocellular infection is a subclass of diffuse hepatic parenchymal disease, and diffuse hepatic parenchymal disease falls into the category of hepatic parenchymal disease, which is a major subclass of diseases of the hepatobiliary system.'

Unfortunately it was found that this hierarchy by itself was not sufficient to attribute accurately the various manifestations to particular diseases and to enable the system to formulate suitable subsets of competing hypotheses. Because of this, *ad hoc* algorithms were developed to aid in identifying suitable differential diagnostic tasks.

The disease and manifestation lists are connected in a number of ways, for example:

(i) *An evoking strength*. This indicates how strongly a patient should be considered to have a particular disease when it is known that this manifestation is present.

(ii) *Frequency*. Showing, simply, how often patients with the given disease have the particular manifestation.

Each manifestation also has an associated weight, termed its *import*, which simply indicates how important it is that it be explained by the final set of diagnoses.

Tables 5.1, 5.2, and 5.3 (from Miller *et al.*, 1982) show verbal interpretations of the numbers used to indicate the strength of evocation, frequency, and import.

As we have remarked elsewhere, and as is obvious in the very nature of the INTERNIST/CADUCEUS project being a developed series, expert

Table 5.1. *Evoking strength*

Evoking strength	Interpretation
0	Nonspecific – manifestation occurs too commonly to be used to construct a differential diagnosis
1	Diagnosis is a rare or unusual cause of listed manifestation
2	Diagnosis causes a substantial minority of instances of listed manifestations
3	Diagnosis is the most common but not the overwhelming cause of listed manifestation
4	Diagnosis is the overwhelming cause of listed manifestation

From Miller *et al.* (1982). Abstracted by permission of the *New England Journal of Medicine*, **307**, pp. 468–76, 1982.

systems such as INTERNIST-I rarely attain a 'final version'. They undergo constant change as they grow and are developed. This typically results in several descriptions appearing in the literature. That given in Miller *et al.* (1982) describes a system based on 15 man-years of work. It has profiles of 500 diseases and high level pathophysiological states. These profiles are inter-connected by 2600 links expressing causal relationships (of which more below) or, at least, the predisposition of patients with one disease to have another. The system has 3550 manifestations, themselves inter-connected by about 6500 links showing how the occurrence of each is influenced by the presence of others. Using this knowledge, INTERNIST-I works through the following steps:

(1) Patient data both positive and negative is entered. A single list is formed of all diseases which could have accounted for one or more of the observed manifestations.

(2) For each suggested disease, lists are maintained of manifestations it explains, manifestations one might expect it to produce but which it does not, manifestations it fails to explain, and manifestations about which one as yet knows nothing, but which are usually associated with the disease.

(3) Each disease in the single list formed in (1) is given a score derived from the evoking strengths of the present manifestations it explains, taking into account links to other identified diseases, and also taking into account expected manifestations which are not present, and manifestations which are present but are not explained by the disease.

(4) These scores are used to rank the diseases on this list.

(5) A set of competing disease hypotheses is then formed of the highest ranking one and those which, when individually taken with the top one, 'explain no more observed manifestations than either does when taken alone'.

Table 5.2. *Frequency*

Frequency	Interpretation
1	Listed manifestation occurs rarely in the disease
2	Listed manifestation occurs in a substantial minority of cases of the disease
3	Listed manifestation occurs in roughly half the cases
4	Listed manifestation occurs in the substantial majority of cases
5	Listed manifestation occurs in essentially all cases, i.e. it is a prerequisite for the diagnosis

From Miller *et al.* (1982). Abstracted by permission of the *New England Journal of Medicine*, **307**, pp. 468–76, 1982.

(6) If this set contains only a single member (the top ranked disease, by definition), or if the top one has a score sufficiently above the nearest competitor, then this is chosen.

(7) Otherwise a set of heuristic rules are acted upon to attempt (i) to demonstrate the top diagnosis is needed, (ii) to eliminate some diagnoses, or (iii) to discriminate between diagnoses.

(8) Questions are asked of the user in small groups, and the disease hypothesis scores are recalculated after each group has been answered. Miller *et al.* (1982) say: 'This *ad hoc* method for constructing a differential diagnosis gives INTERNIST-I seemingly intelligent behaviour, since the program will often change focus from one problem area to another when questioning in the first area has been counterproductive.

(9) When a diagnosis is accepted the manifestations it explains are removed and the process recycles.

(10) If a single diagnosis cannot be selected from within some competing group the program says so.

(11) If all remaining manifestations have a very low import the program stops.

Annotated examples of INTERNIST-I consultation sessions are given in Pople (1982) and Miller *et al.* (1982).

Miller *et al.* (1982) present a comparative evaluation of the performance of INTERNIST-I (described in Barnett, 1982 in the words: 'Their systematic evaluation of the model's performance is virtually unique in the field of medical applications of artificial intelligence.') The evaluation has the side-effect of making explicit some of the difficulties of carrying out such evaluations. Nineteen cases were chosen for the comparative study, cases which had not been examined before by the system and which were chosen

Table 5.3. *Import*

Import	Interpretation
1	Manifestation is usually unimportant, occurs commonly in normal persons, and is easily disregarded
2	Manifestation may be of importance, but can often be ignored; context is important
3	Manifestation is of medium importance, but may be an unreliable indicator of any specific disease
4	Manifestation is of high importance and can only rarely be disregarded as, for example, a false-positive result
5	Manifestation absolutely must be explained by one of the final diagnoses

From Miller *et al.* (1982). Abstracted by permission of the *New England Journal of Medicine*, **307**, pp. 468–76, 1982.

largely on the basis that all of the major diagnoses in these cases were ones which INTERNIST-I knew about – obviously a necessary requirement. (Even so, a statistician would not be too happy about the selection. For example, the test cases came from a single year, and temporal variation in clinical diagnosis is a well attested fact.)

Another difficulty in any such comparison is the problem of how to measure performance. For example, can something as crude as misdiagnosis rate serve, or must the confidence with which a diagnosis is made be included, and should the severity of misdiagnoses be taken into account? These points are discussed in Hand (1982*b*).

Furthermore, assessing performance implies that there is some absolute criterion against which diagnostic accuracy can be assessed. In Miller *et al.* (1982) the criterion used was the result of a pathological examination or universal agreement. While it seems difficult to come up with anything better, it would be a brave man who would claim there was no risk of error and the possibility of a mistaken criterion diagnosis must be borne in mind.

Miller *et al.* distinguished, very properly, between major and minor diagnoses, and between incorrect diagnosis and failure to make a correct diagnosis. On their test cases INTERNIST-I's performance appeared qualitatively similar to hospital clinicians' but inferior to that of case discussants.

It is worth mentioning again the particular value of the papers by Pople (1982) and Miller *et al.* (1982) in that they discuss the limitations of the INTERNIST-I system and do not simply stress its merits. They are well worth reading on that account alone by anyone with an interest in medical expert systems. Miller *et al.* identify the shortcomings of the program as:

(i) Arising from weaknesses in the knowledge base (for example, 'the absence of a manifestation required to describe an important finding; the use of overly simplistic manifestations for some circumstances; the inadvertent omission of a finding from a disease profile; the assignment of an incorrect evoking strength, frequency or import; and the failure of a manifestation to convey adequate anatomic information').

(ii) Deficiencies in the design or implementation of the program (for example, 'failure to incorporate temporal reasoning capabilities; problems resulting from the use of the scoring algorithm; the inability to take a broad overview in attacking a complex problem; and the improper attribution of findings to concluded diagnoses').

Since the program has identifiable weaknesses and yet already performs qualitatively as well as clinicians, the future looks bright.

INTERNIST-I uses, as its basic conceptual framework for organising knowledge, a nosological taxonomy. An alternative framework is one based on causal networks. Pople (1982) discusses this alternative in some detail.

Apparently one of the major disadvantages of this approach is that it requires excessive computational time. Their current work (on a program named CADUCEUS) is attempting to obtain the best of both the taxonomic and the causal worlds.

Example 3: CASNET

We mention CASNET because it represents the alternative approach to medical expert system design. That is, it is based on a causal association network rather than simulating (however weakly) human deductive processes. In psychiatry (except for a few specialised subdomains) this sort of approach would not (as yet) be feasible. It is only feasible with CASNET because enough is known about its domain of application – glaucoma – that most observed clinical phenomena can be explained in causal terms.

CASNET, developed within the Rutgers Research Resource on Computers in Biomedicine incorporates the knowledge of many clinicians and is an impressive example of collaborative work. Details may be found in Kulikowski & Weiss (1982) and Weiss, Kulikowski & Safir (1978) and Weiss *et al.* (1978).

Example 4: PUFF

PUFF is a system for diagnosing pulmonary function disorder (Kunz, 1978; Feigenbaum, 1979). Details of age, sex, smoking history etc. are taken, and measuring instruments connected to a computer record various parameters of breathing flow rates and volumes. The version Feigenbaum describes had 55 rules, for example:

     IF (1) the severity of obstructive airways disease of the
           patient is greater than or equal to mild
     and (2) the degree of diffusion defect of the patient is
           greater than or equal to mild
     and (3) the TLC (body box) observed/predicted of the patient
           is greater than or equal to 110
     and (4) the observed–predicted difference in RV/TLC of the
           patient is greater than or equal to 10
     THEN (1) there is strongly suggestive evidence (0.9) that the
           subtype of obstructive airways disease is emphysema
     and (2) it is definite (1.0) that 'OAD, Diffusion Defect,
           elevated TLC, and elevated RV together indicate
           emphysema' is one of the findings.

PUFF was built using EMYCIN (see above), and Feigenbaum reports that it took less than 50 hours by the domain expert and 10 man-weeks of effort by the knowledge engineers to encode the 55 rules.

The rules were derived from a set of 100 cases and were tested on a distinct set of 150 cases, yielding between 90 and 100% agreement between PUFF and human diagnosticians.

5.6   Empirical statistical methods

This section discusses objective methods of classifying patients into diagnostic categories – objective in the sense that the classification rules are obtained by applying formal mathematical rules to collections of 'measurements' describing patients. The techniques to be described are often termed methods of *discriminant analysis, statistical pattern recognition,* or *classification analysis.* At first, their objective 'non-modelling' nature might seem to suggest that they are unrelated to artificial intelligence work. In fact, however, the histories of pattern recognition and artificial intelligence are intertwined. One obvious overlapping field is the work on perceptrons. Moreover one frequently finds ideas from pattern recognition and artificial intelligence combined in a single system so that it is difficult to tell where one ends and the other begins. This is the case in speech understanding systems, for example, where initial low level characterisation of the words is in terms of a set of numerical descriptors and higher level recognition depends on relationships with context. Yet another example occurs within expert systems (§ 5.5): although most published descriptions concentrate on the rule-based nature of the formalism one can also approach them from a statistical pattern recognition orientation (see, for example, Naylor, 1983). If all of this was not enough, it would in any case be essential to have some discussion of statistical methods so that other symbol manipulation approaches could be put into a context as far as the implications for psychiatric diagnosis and therapy go.

Empirical statistical methods may be characterised in the following way. A number of variables are measured on each patient. The terms 'variable' and 'measured' here are used in a general way. They cover such things as height and biochemical concentration (both of which can be measured in the conventional sense), sex, religion, and social class (which are measured on categorical nominal or ordinal scales), answers to questions, presence or absence or degree of presence of specified symptoms, and so on. The choice of variables is a question we shall discuss below. The values of the variables, if they are well chosen, provide a summary of those aspects of the patient which are relevant to diagnosis. The same variables are measured for groups of patients known to come from each diagnostic class. Then we simply allocate our new patient into the category which he or she most closely resembles, where resemblance is determined by comparing his pattern of measures with the patterns of members in the various classes.

Although this is simple in principle, it can be quite complex in practice.

The variables may be interval, nominal, or have other measurement scales, or a mixture of different types of variables might be involved. Some may be more reliable than others. Not all may be measured on all patients or on all members of the samples from the various diagnostic categories. Sampling distortions may affect things. Perhaps there are not enough (or even any!) patients from some class. In addition to all this we have to define exactly what we mean by 'resemblance' – precisely when does one patient resemble a second more than a third? This section discusses some of these points.

Statistical pattern recognition has been the most popular method of computer diagnosis in the past, having been applied in virtually every domain of medicine (for some examples, see De Dombal *et al.* (1972), Titterington *et al.* (1981), Coomans *et al.* (1983), and Stern, Knill-Jones & Williams (1975)). At present, however, as we discuss elsewhere, it seems to be rather waning in popularity, being replaced by rule-based methods as the most popular.

We begin the discussion of empirical statistical methods by keeping things simple by initially supposing that there are only two diagnostic classes (called A and B), that only two measurements (x_1 and x_2) are taken on each patient, and that both of these measures are at least on interval scales. (Each of these restrictions will be relaxed below.) The process begins by taking samples of patients known to come from each class and determining their measurements. (In non-psychiatric medical disciplines the correct classification of these subjects may have been determined from histological or pathological examination, or perhaps by post-mortem, there being no reason why the measurements should not be taken before the class is known. In psychiatric work the correct classification is commonly determined by extensive statistically refined structured interviews.) These patients constitute the *design set* or *training set*, since the classification rule will be designed or trained using these examples.

Fig. 5.9. The design set for two classes measured on two variables.

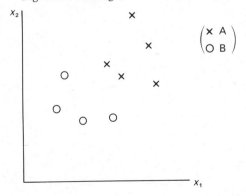

Fig. 5.10. Three possible classification rules.

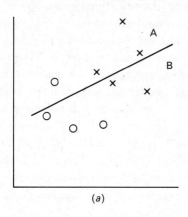

(a)

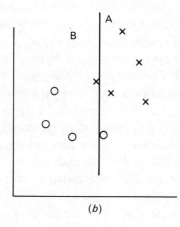

(b)

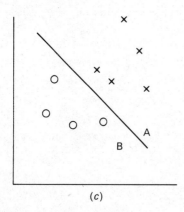

(c)

The data can now be displayed in the space spanned by the two x variables, as in Fig. 5.9. Crosses represent patients from class A and circles those from class B. From those patients we wish to devise a classification rule which can be used on future patients. A simple way to represent such a classification rule would be by a line; future patients falling on one side could be classified as belonging to class A and those on the other side of the line to class B. Fig. 5.10 illustrates three possible such lines applied to the data of Fig. 5.9. If we assume the design set to be a random sample from type A and B patients, then clearly we might expect the line in 5.10a to perform badly on future patients, that in 5.10b to perform better, and that in 5.10c to do best of all. This is based on counting the number of design set points each line correctly classifies: one would have little confidence in a line which misclassified a large proportion of them.

This example is rather idealised in that it is possible to find a line which perfectly separates the two classes in the design set. Usually this is not the case. Fig. 5.11 is more realistic in this regard.

There are several things one could do in such a situation. One could abandon the idea of using a straight line and use a quadratic curve or something even more complicated instead. We shall consider this option later. A second possibility would be to measure more variables – to look for further symptoms or predisposing characteristics, for example. Of course, with three or more variables we cannot work with a nice graphical representation, as in the above figures, so formal mathematical descriptions must be used. We shall return to this below. Another possibility would be to accept that perfect diagnosis cannot be achieved (as in the case with human psychiatrists) and do the best one can. If one could achieve a misclassification rate less than that of human psychiatrists then a great deal of value would have been achieved. Let us look at this possibility first.

Fig. 5.11. A case in which the classes in the design set cannot be separated by a straight line.

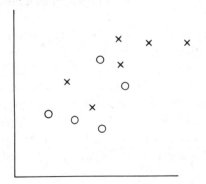

Given that the design set classes cannot be perfectly separated by a straight line, more care is necessary in choosing a line: it is certainly not so obvious which is the best. Still, with these simple examples, involving small design sets, it can be done. Even with large design sets (thousands per class are not unknown) it can, with patience, be done. However, we must also recognise that the design set points are merely a sample from some population. The sample will be subject to random fluctuation (if we had drawn some other set of patients – from the same classes, of course – then we would expect subtle differences in the distribution of points in the above figures). This has at least two implications. First, perhaps we need not be too concerned with getting our line exactly right – something close enough might do. Second, perhaps we can somehow take advantage of any extra knowledge or assumptions we may be prepared to make about the population of patients to determine a more reliable estimate of the position of the line. That is, perhaps some nearby position of the line would lead to fewer future misclassifications even though it did not minimise the number of misclassifications in the design set. This sort of thing again leads us to methods more formal than fitting a line by eye.

Over the last thirty or forty years a great many formal methods for fitting straight lines in problems of this sort have been suggested and their mathematical properties explored in great detail. Many have been summarised in chapter 4 of Hand (1981*a*). Because simple proportion misclassified has some disadvantages for formal optimisation algorithms (it has discontinuities, it does not yield a unique solution, it is not easy to optimise), many researchers have considered other criteria. One, of considerable historical significance, is the *perceptron criterion*. This is defined as being the sum of the distances, from the separating line, of all those design set points which are misclassified by the line. Clearly those points which are most severely misclassified, in that they are furthest from the line on its wrong side, contribute most heavily to the criterion. Points correctly classified do not contribute at all. The aim will be to find a line which minimises this criterion.

An early and elegant way is by *error correcting*. An initial position for the line is chosen and design set points are introduced one at a time. Each correctly classified point leaves things as they are, but each incorrectly classified point causes an adjustment of the line in the direction of the misclassified point. A big enough adjustment brings the point to the correct side of the line. It is simple to prove (see, for example, Nilsson, 1965; Hand, 1981*a*) that if the design set points of the two classes can be perfectly separated by a straight line then repeated cycling through the design set points using this method of adjusting the line will ultimately lead to a line which does perfectly separate the two samples. Of course, if the samples from the two classes cannot be perfectly separated by a line then this method leads to constant oscillation. One way round this is to progressively decrease the size of the correcting steps at each misclassification. Details are given in Hand (1981*a*).

The perceptron criterion may be minimised by other means. For example, Hand (1981*a*, § 4.3) describes how to minimise it by linear programming. This can be useful since it saves writing computer programs: linear programming algorithms exist as common standard packages.

The perceptron criterion occupies an important place in the pattern recognition literature – predominantly the work of electrical engineers and computer scientists. In classical statistics the pre-eminent position is occupied by Fisher's criterion. A nice (though not essential) motivation for this is given via modelling the shapes of the distributions of the populations from which the design set comes. Fisher's criterion is discussed in this context below. At this point, however, it is interesting to note that Fisher's criterion can be approached from a classical least squares point of view. This has the implication that classical statistical discriminant analysis can be carried out using a regression package. The details are in Hand (1981*a*).

Now let us consider the first approach to tackling overlapping design samples described above. This is the recognition that a straight line cannot perfectly separate the two classes and the suggestion that some more complicated shape might be adopted. Actually, this is a convenient point to introduce some terminology. The boundary that separates the classes is called a *decision surface*. In the two variable case it is a line (perhaps straight, perhaps not), but for more than two variables it becomes a surface or hypersurface. Decision surface is the generic term.

We could draw an arbitrary curved line by eye and use this for future classifications. Unfortunately this *ad hoc* approach has a number of disadvantages. One is the difficulty of communicating the shape of the line to other psychiatrists. A straight line in two dimensions can be completely specified by only two numbers. Clearly an arbitrary hand-drawn squiggle needs many more. Moreover any comment about capitalising on chance applies with a vengeance to such a procedure. Finally, the idea becomes infeasible in more than two dimensions (an arbitrary hand-drawn hypersurface in a hundred dimensional space?). I will return to the possibility of more complicated decision surfaces below. For now, however, a sensible possibility seems to be to generalise the line by taking a simple curve, say a quadratic, which can be easily defined in mathematical terms and so is subject to formal estimation approaches. Fig. 5.12 shows a case where a straight line cannot separate the design set classes perfectly but a quadratic can. Fig. 5.13 shows a more interesting situation. This sort of thing arises when, for example, class A represents normals and class B includes several subcategories of disease.

As it happens these quadratic surfaces, with no matter how many variables, can be handled by the same formal techniques as the multivariate planar surfaces. Again, details are given in Hand (1981*a*) or in the books cited in § 5.8.

There are several ways in which the above procedures can be extended to more than two classes. Some obvious ways are: to carry out c separate two class analyses (with c being the number of classes) to distinguish each class from all of the others; to carry out all $c(c - 1)/2$ separations between each pair of classes; to carry out a hierarchical approach, separating the c classes into two groups and then separating each of the groups into two and so on. These methods, however, are rather inelegant and may yield symptom (or variable) patterns which have ambiguous classifications. A more elegant approach, and one which always yields a unique diagnosis if such is desired, is described below.

The methods described so far might justifiably be called *parametric*. The diagnostic rules depend on the values of the parameters defining the decision surfaces (i.e. on the positions of the lines, curves, or hypersurfaces). These decision surfaces carve the space of the variables into two (or more) mutually exclusive regions such that a patient whose point falls into one of these regions is classified into one of the classes. The approach about to be outlined is, in contrast, *non-parametric*.

To introduce the idea, again consider the two class, two continuous variable case, to which we wish to apply a straight line decision surface. Rather than looking at each individual sample point when we estimate the separating line, we could simply use the averages of the two classes. That is, for class A we find the design set average scores for x_1 and x_2, and the same for class B and then we classify a new point according to which of these averages is the nearer to it. Fig. 5.14 illustrates this.

Whatever other merits this approach may possess, it is certainly easy. No problems with understanding sophisticated optimisation algorithms to find the decision surface; just calculate two means and the decision surface is immediately implicitly defined. Note also that the method generalises at once to the multiple class case. We just calculate c mean points and assign a new patient to the class with the nearest mean. The same immediacy applies to the case with more than two variables.

One drawback of this method is the lack of account it takes of the shapes

Fig. 5.12. A case in which a quadratic decision surface can separate classes which a straight line cannot.

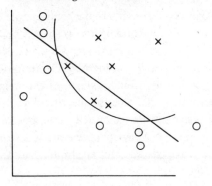

Fig. 5.13. The effectiveness of a quadratic decision surface. A straight line would fail hopelessly here.

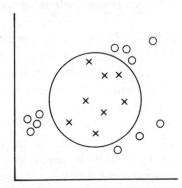

Fig. 5.14. Classifying according to the proximity of design set class means. A point at position p would be classified as class A because it lies nearer to the class A average than to the class B average. This is equivalent to seeing on which side of the dashed line the new point falls.

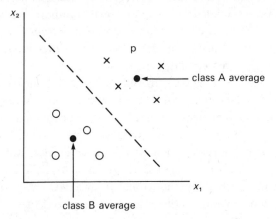

of the population distributions. The method would not be very effective with the data in Fig. 5.13, for example.

The method can be extended in a conceptually remarkably simple way by not bothering to calculate means before we find nearest points. A new point is simply allocated to the class of that point in the design set which is closest to the new one. This is the basic *nearest neighbour* method. Computationally, classifying a new point is more burdensome using nearest neighbour methods than using parametric methods because the distances from all design set points to the new one must be examined (as opposed to the distance to just *c* means or to a surface). Ways to accelerate this search for the closest point have been developed (see, for example, Fukunaga & Narendra, 1975 or Hand, 1981*b*).

In effect the nearest neighbour method induces a highly irregular decision surface, one which follows the data closely and one for which every design set point is surrounded by a small island such that any new point falling on that island is classified into its class.

The greatest neighbour method has been developed by many researchers in a great number of fruitful directions. For example, the fact that the basic method tends to overcapitalise on chance (as illustrated by the islands mentioned above) has led to the development of *k-nearest neighbour* methods. These find the class membership (diagnoses) of the *k* design set points nearest to the new point and classify the new one into the class of the majority amongst these *k*. For example, if amongst the five nearest points, three belong to class A and two to class B, then the new point will be classified as class A. Another extension reduces the number of design set points by eliminating superfluous ones. It does this by taking each point and seeing if it is correctly or incorrectly classified by its neighbours. If the former, it is deemed unnecessary and dropped. If the latter, it is retained. This *condensed nearest neighbour* method (Hart, 1968) leads to a smaller design set. This has been extended yet further by several authors, including Hand & Batchelor (1978) who eliminated isolated points from one class lying in regions densely populated by the other. This smooths out the decision surface to reduce overcapitalisation on chance.

We have introduced nearest neighbour methods in a simple informal way. It is now instructive if we look at them from another direction. A new point is to be allocated the same diagnosis as that of its nearest neighbour (or as those of the majority of its *k* nearest neighbours). Now clearly it is not unreasonable to suppose that regions densely populated by class A design set points and sparsely populated by class B design set points have a higher chance of generating new points from class A than from class B. Thus we can think of the nearest neighbour methods as *calculating estimates of this probability.* That is, for a given new point, these methods calculate the relative probability that it arose from each class and assign it to that with the larger probability.

This idea, that we are really concerned with estimating probabilities that points come from each class, provides a formal basis for the whole field of statistical pattern recognition (see Hand, 1981a). First let us re-examine parametric methods using this notion.

To illustrate, again take two classes and assume they are bivariate normally distributed with equal covariance matrices. Then it is shown in many places (e.g. Lachenbruch, 1975; Hand, 1981a) that the decision surface – which, the reader will recognise, is the surface at which the two classes lead to identical probabilities of generating a new point – is a straight line. In general, with d variables, a planar (hyper)surface separates the two classes. If the two classes have different covariance matrices then the decision surface is quadratic.

Fisher's classical method leads to this asymptotically optimal planar surface if the data really do derive from two multivariate normal classes with identical covariance matrices, but it is not necessary to assume such distributions for the method to perform well or even optimally (contrary to what many workers believe). One can think of Fisher's method as being a generalisation of the simple means method described above, which does take some account of the shape of the distributions. The method finds the direction such that the distance between the projections of the sample means on that direction, standardised for the within sample standard deviation in that direction, is a maximum. This standardised distance is Fisher's criterion. It has straightforward extensions to the multiple class case.

One of the first (if not the first) descriptions of discriminant analysis was given in 1936 and used this method. Since then the method has undergone a prodigious amount of development and is, beyond doubt, the most widely applied method, appearing in every general statistical package.

Returning to the idea of estimating the probability distributions of the populations from their design set samples, one could use distributions other than the multivariate normal. Hand (1981a) suggests the use of multivariate normal mixture distributions (see also Everitt & Hand, 1981). However, it is possible to take this avenue further and abandon the restriction to parameterised distributional forms. Hand (1982b) describes the use of the non-parametric *kernel method* for estimating the distributions of the classes.

This method is allied to the nearest neighbour method, but instead of simply considering the few nearest points, all design set points contribute to a kernel estimate at a new point. For each class we calculate an estimate at the new point by adding together contributions from the design set points in this class, with the size of the contributions being inversely related to the distance from the new point to the point in the design set. A new point falling in a densely populated region will have many large contributions, while one in a sparse region will have few large contributions. As with nearest neighbour methods, kernel methods involve quite extensive computation during the classification phase – though with modern computers this poses little problem in the domain of psychiatric diagnosis. (There are other problem domains in which classifications involving thousands of design set points must be made in very small fractions of a second.) Obviously the kernel method can be applied immediately to the multivariate multiple class case.

This is a convenient point to introduce two notions which generalise the probability estimation methods. These are the concepts of *prior probabilities* and *costs*. Prior probabilities are the relative sizes of the diagnostic categories in the population – the prevalences. Thus a very rare disease will have a small prior and a common disease will have a large prior. The samples from the classes (assuming random selection from within each class) indicate the shapes of the distributions but their relative sizes may not illustrate the priors of the classes. It is reasonable to assume they do if the entire population is randomly sampled but other procedures are possible. For example, random selection from an entire population might be expected to produce very few examples of a rare disease. To counter this, one might deliberately choose a larger non-representative sample from the rare class. Clearly, to avoid classifying too many new patients into this rare class, this must somehow be taken account of. This can be done by weighting the probability estimate for each class by that class's prior.

Costs represent a second dimension of difference between the various classes. Some misclassifications are more serious than others: misclassifying an operable cancer sufferer as healthy is worse than misclassifying a healthy subject as suffering from cancer. The relative severity of the possible kinds of misclassifications can be formalised as numerical *costs*, which can be integrated into the classification equations. This brings us into the realm of *decision theory* (see Hand, 1981*a*, chapter 1 for details).

Methods based on estimating population distributions from design sets and combining these with prior probabilities are often called *Bayesian* methods because they make use of Bayes's theorem. This is, in fact, a trivialising misnomer, since this elementary use of Bayes's theorem is fundamental to statistical pattern recognition. True Bayesian methods make use of a different philosophical basis for the concept of probability. Examples are given in Hand (1981*a*).

As it happens, probability approaches can be generalised in a useful way.

Note that for simple diagnostic purposes we may not need accurate probability estimates. Sometimes they can be useful: it is sometimes more valuable to have a list of possible diagnoses and their respective probabilities. Often, however, all we really need to know is which of two or more such estimates is the largest. Thus any function which is monotonically related to the probability estimates will serve just as well. Such general functions are termed *discriminant functions*. The reader will recognise that for the two class case the decision surface occurs where the discriminant functions for the two classes are equal (so that one function is the larger on one side of this surface, and the other function is larger on the other side).

Many of the variables used in psychiatric work derive from a psychological basis and are merely measured on ordinal or nominal scales. Examples are semantic differential tests and demographic indicants such as social class and religion. The methods described so far might reasonably be thought to be irrelevant to such cases. After all, the concept of distance is fundamental to the preceding and for ordinal and nominal variables it breaks down (or, at least, its definition needs extending). This has inspired a large amount of work for classification using categorical data. Summaries may be found in Hand (1981*a*, chapter 5), Hand (1982*a*), and Goldstein & Dillon (1978).

A basic method is simply to consider separately each cell of the multi-way cross-classification induced by the categorical variables. Thus with just two variables, sex (two categories) and social class (five categories), there are ten cells in the cross-classification to consider. Within each of these cells the design set provides samples which are used to give probability estimates. For example, perhaps in the male social class 1 cell there are forty patients with disease A and two with disease B. Future subjects in this cell would be classed as A. This type of approach is effective with large design sets and few variables but quickly breaks down as the number of variables increases. This is because the number of cells in the cross-classification increases exponentially. So, for example, if one had twenty variables, each having three levels and one felt that an average of ten design set points per cell was needed for reliable probability calculations then one would need 3.5×10^{10} design set patients!

What is needed to solve this problem is some way to simplify the description of the probabilities. Again the various approaches may be seen as either parametric or nonparametric.

For categorical data in complex cross-classifications there is nothing analogous to normal distributions which are an obvious choice for underlying population distributions. Thus the approach usually adopted is to choose some general model and gradually simplify it. Many different types of general model have been proposed.

A popular approach for statistically oriented workers is to use some kind of linear model of logarithmic transforms of the raw frequency counts in the cells. Logistic models and log-linear models (Bishop, Fienberg & Holland, 1975) are examples. These model the distribution by linear combinations of main effects and interactions of increasingly high order. Then interactions are tested to see if they are necessary to explain the shapes of the distributions. Gradually the higher order ones are eliminated and with luck a simple model which can explain the probabilities in the cells with only a few parameters remains.

The same sort of procedure works with other methods (often developed for the special case of binary variables by the electrical engineering and computing communities) in which the distribution is expanded in a series of orthogonal functions analogous to the expansion of a Fourier series. Some of the methods are very elegant.

Turning to nonparametric approaches for categorical data, we find that methods analogous to the continuous variable case have been developed. Some very elegant kernel methods have been proposed by various authors. This is a very fast developing field; the state of the art in 1982 is summarised in Hand (1982*b*). Nearest neighbour methods have also been proposed but seem not to have been developed so heavily.

It was noted above that the most popular type of approach was Fisher's classical method. Because of its accessibility it has also been widely applied to categorical data. Surprisingly, despite the assumptions implicit in the method, it appears not to perform unreasonably on such data (Hand, 1983*a*).

Since both continuous and categorical variables arise in psychiatric settings it will come as no surprise to the reader to learn that diagnostic problems often involve mixtures of variable types (e.g. biochemical concentrations, demographic data, and psychological measurement scales). Fisher's method, kernel methods, and many others have been applied in this setting. Also a series of methods specially designed for this situation have been created by Krzanowski (1975, 1980, 1984).

So far we have ignored any questions relating to how to choose the variables which go into an analysis. And yet this clearly has a major effect on things: some variables are more effective than others in discriminating between diagnostic categories. An obvious way would be for a clinician to choose those variables he thought likely to work (it was mentioned, earlier, that this is one place where mechanistic ideas encroach into an apparently empirical domain). There are, however, disadvantages to this. The clinician might not appreciate the significance of all of the variables – he might incorrectly exclude some or irrelevantly (superstitiously!) include others. A more subtle point is that there may be combinations of variables which are highly effective while individual variables from these sets apparently barely distinguish between the classes at all. Fig. 5.15 gives an example. The computer can take advantage of such high dimensional relationships while a human will probably be unable to recognise them.

The reader might wonder why the question arises at all. Why not include all the variables one can think of? (And which can practicably be measured.) After all, each extra variable can only add information, not subtract it, so surely the more the better. This is a very interesting point because it is generally not true. It has been observed that as d, the number of variables, increases, so future performance of a classifier at first improves but then (for large d) deteriorates. There are a number of reasons for this (see Hand, 1981a, chapter 6 for a detailed discussion), but one important one hinges around the finite size of the design set. As the number of variables increases relative to the fixed size design set so the position of the decision surface is able to capitalise more and more on chance. Put another way, as the number of variables increases, so the design set becomes less representative of the population – it is unable to describe the shapes of the population distribution so precisely. (Associated with this problem is the fact that the decision surface is chosen to perform well on the design set, so that *its performance on this set is not a reliable predictor of future performance*. I emphasise this point

Fig. 5.15. When we take x_1 and x_2 together, that is, in the plane of the paper, we can find a line (ab) which perfectly separates the two classes. However, when we consider x_1 alone, that is, on the line d, there is no point which perfectly separates the two classes. Similarly, when we consider x_2 alone, that is on line c, there is again no point which perfectly separates the two classes. Thus, whereas individually x_1 and x_2 might be very poor diagnostic tools, when taken together they might be highly effective.

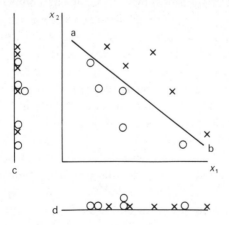

because the psychiatric literature abounds with examples in which design set misclassification rate is quoted in such a way as to imply that it indicates future performance. The point is discussed in Hand (1983*b*), with examples of just how severe the effect may be, and guides to literature on accurate ways to estimate future diagnostic performance.)

Given problems of this kind, one aims to identify a small or moderate subset of variables which leads to accurate diagnosis.

There are many formal methods for this (see for example, Hand, 1981*a*, chapter 6; Kittler, 1975; McKay & Campbell, 1982*a,b*). They all hinge round the idea of choosing a variable set which maximises a measure of *separation* between the classes. The problem is one of search, as outlined in Chapter 4. If the total number of variables from which the final set is to be selected is small, then examination of all possible subsets may be feasible. If the original set is not so small then branch and bound techniques (Kittler, 1978; Hand, 1981*b*) guaranteed to find the optimal solution can be used. For larger sets of variables, however, one is forced to resort to suboptimal stepwise search methods in which one progressively accumulates a good (though probably not optimal) set, or else progressively eliminates variables from the original set to leave a good set. Such stepwise methods are implemented in most classical discriminant analysis packages.

We should not conclude this section with any implication that the subject of statistical diagnosis is closed. In fact it is a rich area for current research – despite the shifting fashions. Problems which may be encountered in applying the methods include non-representative design sets, changes in population structure over time, and the difficulty of transferring diagnostic rules between medical centres because of population differences.

Finally, an example.

Screening may be regarded as the first step in diagnosis, in that we identify the cases and the non-cases. Thus screening questionnaires, in which the scores may be added, or combined in some other way, to yield a value which permits us to discriminate between the two groups, provide illustrations of empirical methods. The variables in this case are, of course, the basic questions comprising the questionnaire. A very elementary example of such an instrument is the General Health Questionnaire (GHQ) devised by David Goldberg. This is an instrument for detecting individuals in the population who are likely to be suffering from mental illness. Its genesis is described in Goldberg (1972).

The 30 item version of this instrument consists of 30 questions of the form

'Have you recently been able to concentrate on whatever you're doing?'

'Have you recently been taking things hard?'

'Have you recently been finding life a struggle all the time?'
There are four possible answers to the questions, such as

   (i) Not at all
   (ii) No more than usual
   (iii) Rather more than usual
   (iv) Much more than usual.

In calculating a score the first two of these are coded as zero and the second two as unity. The overall score is simply the sum of the thirty individual items. (Astute readers will recognise this as being a highly constrained form of linear decision surface.) A threshold, calculated from a design set of subjects whose mental health is known, provides a decision point: subjects scoring greater than this are classified as probable cases, and below it as probable non-cases.

5.7 Discussion

In this section we weigh up the relative merits of the various methods that have been proposed and used for computer assisted diagnosis.

A good place to start is by reminding the reader that there are several substantial advantages to be gained by aiding the diagnostic process through the use of computer tools. These were outlined at the beginning of the chapter. One advantage which was not mentioned there, but which can be appreciated now that we have seen something of the diversity of techniques which are available, is that there is an element of competition between the champions of the different types of techniques. This can only serve to stimulate further development of the methods as well as encouraging deeper thought about the underlying problem being tackled.

One central issue, reflected in the different approaches, is whether or not the best approach is to model the human way of arriving at a diagnosis. This is by no means the only way to go. We have seen, above, examples of empirical methods, based merely on a collection of measurements and taking nothing of human methods; we have seen methods based on models of underlying physiological functions (though limited in psychiatry, Chapter 6 discusses a simulation of paranoia, and diagnosis could be based on this model); and we have seen methods based loosely on symbol manipulation thought (by some) to be analogous to the way humans carry out diagnosis.

Human diagnostic methods are not without their problems (De Dombal, 1978, presents a very interesting account of problems arising in diagnosis by humans, from a clinician's point of view). Nevertheless some people feel that emulating humans may be the most promising direction. Kassirer & Gorry (1978), for example, say (p. 245): 'Advances in computer-aided decision making depend on the development of better understanding of human problem solving in the clinical setting.' Hayes-Roth (1978) says: 'Human cognition can provide an inspiring model for the design of artificial knowledge systems . . . In the long run, the most promising avenue of approach toward the development of artificial knowledge systems may be to investigate and model human cognition as closely as possible.' Fox (1983) goes further: 'Unless there is a compelling reason not to, systems should always be designed to process information in the same way that people do.' He calls this the 'Principle of Cognitive Emulation' (and remarks that it has also been called the Fourth Law of Robotics!).

However, it seems to me that adopting an unreservedly anthropomorphic approach to diagnosis would be unwise. To do so would be to sacrifice any advantage that may be taken of any unique properties possessed by the computer. Computer chess provides a good illustration.

Computers have an ability, far exceeding that of humans, to examine a large number of potential moves. However, despite this superiority, computer programs to date are not as good as the best human chess players. The reason for this seems to be that humans, while not being able to examine as many moves as the computer, do have the ability to pick the most important ones to examine. Clearly these two abilities are in some sense complementary. Humans have some kind of facility for global synthesis not (yet) possessed by computer chess programs, and the latter can examine vast numbers of chess positions in an exhaustive (and error-free) way. That the former can go beyond the latter is obvious from current man/machine chess rankings. That the latter can also go beyond the former is nicely illustrated by the following example from Michie (1982*b*):

> International Masters Berliner and Day were invited to demonstrate their skill against a move perfect program for a particularly tricky subgame of chess, the King–Queen–King–Rook ending. Except for a few special starting positions the Queen's side has a theoretical win against the Rook's side, and a strong Master can ordinarily be expected to win against any human opposition. Yet Berliner and Day found themselves unable to defeat the machine however many times they tried. The most upsetting feature, they complained, was their opponent's bizarre and counter-intuitive style, which bore no trace of the simplifying concepts which give shape to human play.

The point is that it may be unnecessarily constraining to restrict computer approaches to modelling man. Davis (1982) makes a very valuable point in this context (p. 70):

> The reasoning process of human experts may not be the ideal model for all knowledge-based problem solving systems. In the presence

of reliable statistical data, programs using a decision theoretic approach are capable of performance surpassing those of their human counterparts. In domains like infectious disease therapy selection, however, which are characterised by 'judgmental knowledge', statistical approaches may not be viable. This appears to be the case for many medical decision making areas.

Psychiatry, of course, being one of them. Even so, this is perhaps a little unfair to statistical methods, which can be adapted to handle 'judgmental knowledge'.

Methods which arrive at their diagnosis in the same way that man does will clearly be more appealing to humans. They will be more comprehensible, and since they are supposed to be giving advice (and not simply a dogmatic 'This is it' diagnosis) a human clinician will feel more able to weigh up the advice. Of course, if they arrive at their conclusions using processes similar to a human then they might equally be expected to make the same kinds of mistakes as humans. Our aim in psychiatric diagnosis is to get it right, not to have a program about which one can say 'Oh well, of course. A perfectly natural mistake!'.

Despite the sometimes excellent performance of empirical methods, Pople (1982, p. 135) has this to say in comparing the two approaches: 'While modelling the expert decision maker is not necessarily the only way to approach the design of an "expert system", in the medical decision making domain there has been general disappointment with the so-called normative decision models, whereas observation of human expert behaviour has proved to be a most fruitful source of insights into the decision making process.'

Having considered the relative merits and demerits of modelling man, the next step is to look more closely at the concepts underlying modern diagnostic categories in mental illness to see which types of methods we might expect to perform well from this point of view. Kendell (1975) presents a very clear description of the basis of disease classification and of mental disease classification in particular. Because this is so lucid we reproduce it here (with permission):

> If we have no adequate definition of disease as a global concept, it becomes even more important to have adequate definitions for individual diseases. Unfortunately, as soon as one begins to consider individual illnesses, it becomes apparent that there is no consistent theme. Some, like tuberculosis, are defined by their cause, others, like ulcerative colitis, by their pathology, others, like migraine, by their symptoms, and so on. The reasons for this state of affairs lie in the historical development of the global concept of

disease we have just been considering. To the Cnidean School of the ancient world symptoms and signs were themselves diseases. Fever, asthma, joint pains and skin rashes were all separate diseases to be studied individually, and this assumption persisted until very recently. Most of the 2400 diseases Boissier de Sauvages described in the 18th century were merely individual symptoms. The idea of disease as a syndrome, a constellation of related symptoms with a characteristic prognosis – to remit, to evolve or to persist – originated with Sydenham in the 17th century, though the Greek Empiricist school had had the germ of the idea long before. This concept lasted until the early 19th century when Morgagni and Bichat popularised *post mortem* dissection of the body as a routine procedure, and so converted disease from a clinical entity observed at the bedside to a characteristic morbid anatomy observed in the cadaver. Thereafter, new concepts followed one another in rapid progression mainly, as Feinstein (1969) has pointed out, in response to the introduction of new types of observational technology. With the development of powerful microscopes in the middle of the 19th century, individual cells could be examined as well as tissues and whole organs, and the consequent detection of cellular pathology led Virchow and his contemporaries to assume that cellular derangements were the basis of all disease. This concept was, in its turn, displaced by the discovery of bacteria by Koch and Pasteur, a development that was responsible more than anything else for the concept of 'disease entities' each produced by a single aetiological agent. Currently, new techniques like electrophoresis, chromosomal analysis and electron microscopy are producing yet further concepts of disease expressed in terms of deranged biophysical structures, genes and molecules. As Riese (1953) aptly observed, the history of medicine could be written in terms of man's changing concept of disease.

Each of these waves of technology has added new diseases and from each stage some have survived, so the diseases which figure in contemporary textbooks have a very variable conceptual basis. A few, like senile pruritus and proctalgia fugax, are simply Cnidean symptoms, even though first described relatively recently. *Others, like migraine and most of the diseases of psychiatry, are clinical syndromes, Sydenham's constellation of symptoms.* Mitral stenosis and cholelithiasis are based on morbid anatomy, and tumours of all kinds on histopathology. Tuberculosis and syphilis are based on bacteriology and the concept of the aetiological agent, porphyria on biochemistry, myasthenia gravis on physiological dysfunction,

Down's syndrome on chromosomal architecture, and so on. In fact, our present classification is rather like an old mansion which has been refurbished many times, but always without clearing out the old furniture first, so that amongst the new inflatable plastic settees and glass coffee tables are still scattered a few old Tudor stools, Jacobean dressers and Regency commodes, and a great deal of Victoriana. Indeed, Scadding is probably close to the truth when he suggests that it is this logical heterogeneity in our definitions of individual diseases that is responsible for our inability to produce a satisfactory definition of disease as a whole (Scadding, 1972).

(My italics.)

And later Kendell says:

Such problems as these, resulting from the variable and changeable basis of the defining characteristics of different diseases, are less serious where mental illness is concerned than in most other branches of medicine because the majority of psychiatric illnesses, and all the so-called functional illnesses, are defined at the same clinical descriptive level. *The dominant conceptual model of illness in psychiatry is still the syndrome model Sydenham introduced in the 17th century, a cluster of symptoms and signs with a characteristic time course.*

(My italics.)

The italicised sentences above suggest that the statistical and pattern recognition approaches might be very well suited to psychiatric diagnosis. However, it is very important to note that classification methods depend very much on the chosen descriptors. A good classification can never emerge from an inadequate set of features. As Kulikowski & Weiss (1982, p. 27) say:

As is well known, taxonomic schemes are never unique, depending as they do on an inherently arbitrary choice of key features or attributes around which the classification is carried out.
Uncertainty about the true nature and possible co-occurrences of mechanisms of disease further aggravate the situation in medical taxonomies. The International Classification of Diseases, Systematic Nomenclature of Medicine and other schemes do not delve deeply enough into the nuances of individual subspecialities to be more than a first approximation when building a taxonomy for an expert consultant system. Usually there are several alternative and sometimes disparate taxonomic schemes developed by different centers of scholarly and clinical research in a speciality.

Any weaknesses of any techniques in application to psychiatric diagnosis might be more a consequence of shaky foundations (the definitions of the illnesses) than of inappropriate methods.

We turn now to a brief comparative assessment of the various different types of approaches outlined in the preceding sections of this chapter.

Beginning with flowchart or decision-tree type approaches, these have a number of merits. They have a simple, easily understood mechanism which will have wide appeal (it is easy to explain *how* the program works – which naturally makes users feel at ease and more ready to accept it). They are easy to program and their structures can utilise both human clinical expertise and physical concepts (as well as empirical approaches). In use it is not necessary to collect all conceivable relevant data before making a diagnosis. Data is only collected as the program asks for it, so leading to a cheaper diagnosis. Some authors (e.g. Rogers *et al.*, 1979) have argued that computer diagnosis should follow a sequential pattern 'since both the human diagnostic process and disease manifestation are sequential'.

However, complications can arise with decision-tree methods if tests cannot be carried out, if questions cannot be answered, or if the diagnosis involves multiple diseases. Moreover, unless the task is trivial the flowchart might be large and unwieldy. If it was to be worked through manually this would lead to a slow and clumsy method, but since it is to be run on a computer the time aspect does not matter – although there are other consequences of size. A major one of these is the difficulty in updating a large tree. If a new physical mechanism is discovered a new treatment invented, or a new model hypothesised then there may be several decision points affected and they must be modified consistently. Updating which is not totally rigorous can cause inconsistencies to creep in.

More important from some points of view is that flowcharts do not yield understanding or useful insights about aetiology. This is analogous to the non-parametric empirical methods described in § 5.6. These may be very good at classifying diseased subjects but do not condense or summarise the data in any way at all and so are of limited value for elucidating mechanisms.

Associated with this last point is the fact that the flowchart does not contain information about its own structure and organisation. The same decision may be made at more than one point. This means that simply transcribing a tree or flowchart structure into a computer program can yield a frustrating and unsatisfying result. It may ask the same question twice, fail to put two and two together, and generally appear inefficient to the user. Note also that there may well be more than one possible tree structure which could be used.

Turning now to the empirical approaches of statistics and pattern recognition, we find that they have a number of strong points.

They are objective. They do not rely on dubious theories about the mechanisms of the diseases or about how humans themselves arrive at diagnoses. We have to acknowledge an underlying subjectivity in the original choice of variables (symptoms) to be measured or recorded (see the quote above from Kulikowski & Weiss, 1982), but even this can be moderated through the use of feature selection methods.

Statistical and pattern recognition methods are extremely well understood – they are the product of a considerable body of work going back several decades. This covers both theoretical understanding (of their mathematical properties) and also a great many papers describing practical applications of the methods on real data.

Wardle & Wardle (1978) conclude their review of computer aided diagnosis with: 'Of the models reviewed, the Bayesian models seem the most promising in that they are well suited to handling the probabilistic data commonly found in medical diagnosis.'

In addition to all this we have Kendell's observation (1975, quoted above) that current psychiatric disease taxonomy is based on constellations of symptoms. This suggests that the statistical and pattern recognition approaches may be extremely well suited to psychiatric disease diagnosis.

Now, what are the disadvantages of this type of approach? The most significant is, of course, that we need a design set which accurately reflects the fluctuations in the distributions of the various disease classes at the various values of the symptom combinations. This requirement has several aspects. First, there is the geographical aspect. Different areas have different patient populations so that prevalences may reasonably be expected to be different and so also may the relative probabilities of patients with the same symptoms suffering from different diseases differ across regions. In part this may be due to different underlying definitions (the classic example being the US/UK difference in prevalence of schizophrenia); in part it may be due to unreliability of measurement and counting; and again it may be due to simple differences in populations (perhaps different class structures). Coupled with this there is time variation. This may be because of a genuine change in the pattern of disease or it may be due to a shift of definition or a change in recording method. The problem of reconciling old and new information is a very difficult one in research (where different things have been measured, different diseases recorded, or names changed), even when the problem is open and recognised. When the shift is subtle and uncertain the problem is that much more serious (See Hand, 1983a for an example). De Dombal (1978) has this to say: 'When one looks for large scale, multi-centre, reproducible, comprehensive, well-defined, geographically stable data sets about the presentation of various related diseases one finds that these are virtually non-existent.'

Bloom (1975) sums this up (p. 280):

From the large pool of potential patients, an unknown proportion elect to become or are selected to become actual patients. Not only is the proportion unknown, but it is likely that identified patients are not a random sample of the larger potential patient pool.

Becoming a patient is the end result of a complex chain of events dependent upon the nature of the symptomatology, alternative forms of available support, social class, community value systems, availability of treatment facilities, economics, and willingness to accept the patient role.

Williams, Tarnopolsky & Hand (1980) contains a further discussion of this.

Sometimes subjective probability estimates provided directly by doctors have been used in these formal classification methods. De Dombal (1978) also has something to say about this:

Perhaps the most important reason why (junior) doctors fail to analyse data adequately is that they do not know what the prior probabilities and conditional probabilities of diseases are – and if they do know, they ignore them . . .

. . . What doctors *are* bad at doing, however, is taking prior probabilities into account . . .

. . . Despite the utmost care in producing conditional probabilities, computers using estimates given by clinicians have been frequently much less effective than the clinicians themselves; and this particularly applies to diseases. Four years ago we concluded (Leaper *et al.*, 1972) that it would not be within our capability to produce a system using clinician's estimates which showed any marked advantage over the unaided clinician.

These disadvantages are real ones, and thus ones to be wary of, but the fact remains that statistical systems have exhibited very good performance. Since the basic ideas have been around for some time we have to ask: why are they not in widespread use? What are the obstacles? Croft (1972; and see also Croft & Machol, 1974) identifies them:

'The real obstacles to practical computer-aided medical diagnosis:
1. lack of standard medical definitions,
2. lack of large, reliable medical data bases, and
3. lack of acceptance of computer-aided diagnosis by the medical profession.'

Our discussion has covered his first and second points. We now turn to the third.

Pople (1982) has considered the question. He observes (p. 120): 'Evaluative studies frequently show that these programs, whatever their basis, generally perform as well as experienced clinicians in their respective domains, and somewhat better than the non-specialist.' And then he notes that explanations which have been proposed for the non-acceptance include the natural conservatism of physicians and the feeling of threat of replacement by a machine. Neither of these is very flattering! A much more interesting suggestion arises from Pople's discussion of medical diagnosis as an ill-structured problem. He suggests that there has been an overemphasis on the data-oriented approach because of a failure to recognise that a major part of problem solving is transferring from an ISP to a WSP (p. 188):

> As studies of clinical cognition have typically revealed evidence
> that physicians formulate such tasks early in the patient encounter
> and use them as contexts in which to organise their search for
> discriminating data, it is not surprising that builders of computer
> based diagnostic systems have mistakenly come to believe that the
> essence of diagnostic expertise consists of a corpus of procedures
> for dealing with well structured differential diagnostic tasks.

And on p. 189: What has misled many investigators is the undeniable
> prominence of differential diagnosis as a primary structuring
> feature of the reasoning process.

The strongest attack on these sort of approaches that the present author has seen comes from Feinstein (1977) and is quoted by Pople:

> Iatromathematical enthusiasts could make substantial
> contributions to clinical medicine if the efforts now being expended
> on Bayesian and decision-analytic fantasies were directed to the
> major challenges of algorithmically dissecting clinical judgement,
> based on the way the judgements are actually performed. Instead,
> however, the enthusiasts usually become infatuated with the
> mathematical processes and with the associated potential for
> computer manipulations, so that the basic clinical challenges
> become neglected or evaded.

And:

> Perhaps the most shocking aspect of all this ethereal model-
> building is that the model-builders (and the editors of influential
> medical journals) have begun to confuse the difference between
> clinical reality and abstract imagery. In the customary standards of
> science, a model that failed to fit reality was rejected and the
> model-builder was sent back to the drawing board. Today,
> however, in the Procrustean era made possible by confusion about
> modern technology, a model builder can avoid the constraints of
> reality and demand, instead, that reality adapt itself to fit the model.

Naturally a physician, confronting clinical reality every day, will feel uneasy in the presence of such a state of affairs. I should also add the point that human experts, whether medical or not, do not like to be told the answer but respond much more sympathetically to advice. The statistical approaches present a list of probabilities of the various diagnoses and their reasoning process cannot be challenged or weighed up as it is simply derived by estimating probabilities. As Davis (1982) says:

> Since none of these is intended to be a model of the reasoning process typically employed by clinicians it can at times prove difficult for a clinician to discover the basis for the conclusions drawn by any of them. While they each present a compact encoding of knowledge that can provide an appealing efficiency to programs based on them, there is an unavoidable loss of comprehensibility to the physican using them. Reasoning which requires several distinct inferential steps by a clinician, for instance, might be expressed in a single value of a conditional probability in the Bayesian method.

As the reader will appreciate, expert systems, as outlined in § 5.5, possess precisely the properties that statistical methods have been criticised for not having. Their decisions and recommendations can be explained in a way that is familiar to the domain experts (the psychiatrists in this case) and they can attempt to justify their own deductive steps – in a way not too far removed from that of the human. We can also assess the program's behaviour by comparing it with human experts. The intrinsic flexibility of expert systems goes a long way towards meeting Kendell's (1975, p. 3) observation that 'A related problem is that the majority of patients do not conform to the tidy stereotyped descriptions found in textbooks.'

Of course, expert systems have their own disadvantages. They are difficult programs to write, requiring several man-years of effort. The technology is still young and is still being refined. Moreover, as Kulikowski & Weiss (1982) point out, modelling one psychiatrist's deductive processes is all very well, provided other psychiatrists are happy to follow his logic. Davis (1982, p. 76) also points out some possible limitations:

> Nor is it reasonable to expect to be able to write rules for an arbitrary domain. As knowledge in an area accumulates, it becomes progressively more formalised. There is a certain stage of this formalisation process when it is appropriate to use rules of the sort shown above. Earlier than this the knowledge is too unstructured, later on it may . . . be more effective to write straightforward algorithms.

And:

> It is also possible that knowledge in some domains is inherently unsuited to a rule-like representation, since rules become increasingly awkward as the number of premise clauses increases.

In comparing the interest in different approaches to computer assisted diagnosis, we must bear in mind some general points. One is that expert systems and artificial intelligence approaches are new. Much of the criticism about other methods may be due to excessive enthusiasm for the novel.

Another point is that it is a natural human frailty to emphasise the shortcomings of others' approaches and to play down those of one's own. Consider, for example, Feldman, Klein & Honigfeld (1969). They were studying 113 psychiatric patients:

> Many investigators would consider discriminant function analysis the appropriate method for this problem. However, we decided to take another task for the following reasons:
>
> 1. The discriminant function model assumes multivariate normality and identical dispersion matrices in the compared groups. This is not appropriate either to univariate distributions of pathology – relevant data which are often J-shaped, U-shaped or bimodal, or to the bivariate relationships which are often curvilinear and heteroscedastic.
>
> 2. We wanted to avoid using diagnostic keys that involve the summation of weighted items, since this method can produce identical scores for patients with quite different patterns of contributing variables.
>
> 3. If a certain group were characterised by *both* minimum and maximum scores on a given trait, no useful weighted score could be derived without the use of such devices as quadratic transformations.
>
> 4. Experience with discriminant function analysis on psychiatric data has produced a number of obscurities that make an alternative approach seem desirable.

There are several points about this passage that seem worthy of comment. Paragraph 4 seems curious and tends to support my comment about denigrating others' methods. If any current readers are puzzled by discriminant analysis applied to psychiatric data perhaps I can recommend Hand (1981*a*) and Klecka (1980) (and see also § 5.8).

The restriction to classical linear discriminant analysis seems rather severe. Quadratic methods, as mentioned in paragraph 3, are very easy to implement, as also are nonparametric methods, such as kernel and nearest neighbour approaches (indeed the SAS statistical package includes a nearest neighbour method as a standard option). These methods are, of course, suitable for the situations described in paragraph 1.

The remark in paragraph 2 that summing weighted items can yield identical scores for patients with different patterns of symptoms is true. But this in itself is not a criticism of such methods – perhaps those different patterns are different manifestations of the same illness. Certainly for the six psychiatric data sets I analysed in Hand (1983*a*), the performance of the classical linear discriminant analysis method was no worse than the flexible non-parametric kernel method, even though, because of the multivariate binary nature of the data, one might have expected the kernel method to be far superior.

The first paragraph in the passage quoted above also illustrates something which statistical methods in particular seem to suffer from. These are mistakes about the conditions under which they are valid. Classical linear discriminant function analysis does *not* assume multivariate normality – though it is optimal when the distributions are multivariate normal with equal dispersion matrices. It is the global symmetry property (and the equal matrices) which matters. A common mistake is to assert that Bayesian methods require an assumption of independence of the features (for example, Kendell, 1975, pp. 155–6; Wing *et al.*, 1974, p. 98). Barker & Bishop (1970) describe a different approach, but state: '. . . [in] statistical methods based on Bayes' theorem . . . it is necessary to assume that symptoms are independent.' Nothing could be further from the truth. The fact is that some early systems made this assumption because it considerably simplified the calculations. With the availability of the computing power which is the *raison d'être* of this book, no such assumption is necessary (which is not to say that sometimes such an assumption might not be useful for reasons other than computation).

Perhaps it would be fair to restore the balance at this point by reminding the reader that there are many papers describing application of statistical methods to psychiatric data which gauge performance using the resubstitution misclassification rate (§ 5.6). This is known to be unrealistic – see Hand (1983*b*) for some examples of just how optimistic it can be.

Apart from the merits and demerits specific to particular methods described above there are some more general observations which can be made. One is the suggestion that general world knowledge is of considerable assistance in medical diagnosis. Szolovits (1982*b*, p. 8) gives a good example of this. He describes a woman consulting her physician with a complaint of chest pain. The physician happens to know she runs a shop and sometimes lifts heavy sacks, and that it is probably the resulting strain that is causing the pain. Obviously no amount of medical expertise encoded in a computer program will help here.

Another general point has come to be called the 'plateau effect'. This describes an observation not uncommon to computer diagnosis systems, namely a superb performance on the limited set of disease types that the program has been trained on but a dramatic deterioration in performance just outside this range. This has been used as a stick with which to beat diagnostic programs (criticising them on the grounds that they may miss an important and obvious disease in this way). This seems somewhat unfair to me. No current system claims to span the whole of medicine: when one does then it may be criticised. This seems to be an example of the suggestion that programs must exhibit superhuman intelligence before they can be counted as intelligent. Rogers *et al.* (1979) surveyed computerised diagnostic systems and showed the limited range of each one:

> Computer diagnostic systems have been applied to a wide range of disease categories. We have used the ICDA to categorise disease areas covered in the literature. The articles reviewed in this report span diseases included in 12 of the 17 major disease classes of the ICDA. Although a wide range of diseases is addressed in the aggregate by the reports reviewed, each individual computer diagnostic system typically includes a very narrow range of diseases, usually involving only one ICDA class.

The plateau effect may not be relevant to psychiatry since mental disorders are just one ICDA class.

Another point relates to multiple diagnoses. Some of the systems described earlier in the chapter can handle a case suffering from more than one disease but others, notably the simpler systems, find it confusing. Again this may not matter in psychiatry for, as Kendell (1975, p. 102) puts it:

> In practice, clinicians only make multiple diagnoses when their patients have an organic state as well as a functional one, or an illness, neurotic or psychotic, as well as a habitual state like mental retardation or personality disorder. They do not normally diagnose two functional psychoses simultaneously, or a neurosis and a psychosis together. The reason why this is so is that, without it ever having been formally decreed, the major psychotic and neurotic illnesses have come to be arranged in a hierarchy.

The enthusiasm for computer aided diagnosis should not conceal the difficulties. Amongst these are the ethical problems. For example, the question of who has the ultimate responsibility for an adopted treatment – the person (psychiatrist) using the program or the persons who wrote it? At present most existing medical systems are very much advisors, companions to the expert medical doctors – second opinions, if you like. The decision to accept the advice – and hence the responsibility – resides with the human expert. But this will change when non-experts use the systems. An analogous situation arises with statistical expert systems (see Hand, 1984*b*). Here exactly the same ethical problems arise (for example, who holds responsibility – the statistical consultant or his statistical expert system – if a poorly designed clinical trial leads to a mistaken marketing of a drug?).

It is for such reasons as this that the word 'assisted' appears in the title to this chapter.

It will be obvious from all of the above that it is not going to be possible to give a general answer to the question 'which method is best?'. What is clear from the literature, however, is that at present statistical approaches dominate (see, for example, Croft, 1972). This is perhaps a historical accident – certainly the number of medical expert systems is growing and we can expect to see several psychiatric ones in the near future.

There are a few papers which present comparisons between methods, though these tend to consider methods of a single type. Those which compare contrasting types have not demonstrated the superiority of any one type. (As far as diagnostic accuracy goes. The question of superiority for other reasons, such as acceptability to the medical community, is a different matter.) An interesting associated point is made by Rogers *et al.* (1979). Thirty-five out of the 58 articles they review involve but three of the ICDA classes, and within those three classes 'there is a marked correlation between the disease class and the kind of algorithm used to make the diagnoses'. If we look at psychiatric diagnosis programs we see predominantly flowchart and statistical methods. My own feeling, however, is that the expert system approach may be more suitable.

Fox *et al.* (1980) present one of the few comparisons between methods of different kinds, comparing a statistical and rule-based method. Their study demonstrates the care which has to be taken in such comparative studies. For example, evaluation is based on a test set with equal priors for each class although the design set had different priors. The paper does not say what priors were used in the classification. One might also criticise the poor choice of statistical method (which takes no account of interdependencies between variables). Despite any such criticisms, however, it is important to recognise that individual studies contribute to the general body of knowledge about the relative behaviour of the methods and it is only by the gradual accumulation of such knowledge that advances are made. More comparative studies are needed. (Fox's study reveals little difference in performance between the two methods.)

Some pointers to the direction of future developments in computer assisted diagnosis can be gleaned from the above. One is that we can expect to see more systems making explicit use of several representations – using mixtures of physiological models, rule-based reasoning systems, and statistical methods. Another is that advantage will be taken of conflicts and contradictions arising in the input data. When this happens with human diagnosticians it leads to a deeper investigation – perhaps even a new theory. No machine yet handles this adequately. A third future development, which must surely come, is particularly exciting, namely the use of such systems for teaching purposes. Computer simulations have existed for a decade or more in some areas of medicine and such systems as those described above present a particularly exciting development.

I shall conclude with three further quotations. The first reminds us of the advantages of computer assisted diagnosis, as well as its difficulty:

'Poor quality input data and insensitivity of diagnostic algorithms appear to be major problems with computer-assisted diagnosis in psychiatry. Clinicians find repetitive completion of a standardised form to be so boring that they may become careless.' (Spitzer *et al.*, 1975.)

The second reminds us of the importance of accurate diagnosis:

'Since there are now different and effective treatments for various psychiatric disorders, accurate diagnosis is no longer an intellectual exercise or simply a research requirement.' (Greist, Klein & Erdman, 1976.)

And the third puts things in perspective:

'It must, however, be re-emphasised that we have not yet created a system of "computer diagnosis". What we have created is a system which can be used to help the clinician towards his own diagnosis, and which, *if implemented*, might well significantly improve the quality of the care which the clinician can give to his patients.' (De Dombal *et al.*, 1972).

5.8   Further reading

There is now a very large literature on the use of computers in medical diagnosis, a literature not restricted to medical publications but appearing in many places, including computer science journals, electronics journals, artificial intelligence journals, pattern recognition journals, and statistics journals.

The class of techniques with the longest history is perhaps that based on statistical methods. Concise and light informal accounts are given in Hand (1978, 1984*a*). Hand (1981*a*) presents a more detailed discussion, attempting to cover both the statistical and pattern recognition literature. The book describes decision theory, parametric and non-parametric approaches, and treats both continuous and categorical variables. Other statistically oriented books include Lachenbruch (1975), on classical discriminant analysis, Goldstein & Dillon (1978), on discrete variable methods, and Klecka (1980), on the classical method. For beginners the last of these is recommended. Hand (1982*b*) describes the nonparametric kernel method in great depth.

Books on pattern recognition include Fukunaga (1972), a fairly mathematical account with little on discrete variables, Duda & Hart (1973), half of which is devoted to image processing but which is very clear, and Devijver & Kittler (1982), which presents a very detailed description of nearest neighbour methods.

Breiman *et al.* (1983) is a methodological account of decision tree methods and Essex (1980) contains a very large number of medical decision flow-charts.

Books focussed on expert systems and artificial intelligence approaches are beginning to appear in their multitudes. An important one is Waterman & Hayes-Roth (1978*a*). This is a collection of papers describing many implemented systems and properties of such systems. It is to be recommended. A recent book edited by Peter Szolovits (1982) is also valuable. This contains six papers describing some medical diagnostic systems in great detail. A more general and more introductory collection is Michie (1982*a*), while Michie (1980) presents a brief introduction to expert systems, with examples. For a recent impressive and detailed technical account of production systems see Nilsson (1982). Finally, Szolovits & Pauker (1978) compare four diagnostic programs which use artificial intelligence methods (the programs being MYCIN, INTERNIST, CASNET, and PIP). An interesting comparative discussion is given in Spiegelhalter & Knill-Jones (1984).

General review papers of computers in diagnosis include Wardle & Wardle (1978), Patrick, Stelmack & Shen (1974), Schoolman & Bernstein (1978), and Rogers *et al.* (1979). Wagner *et al.* (1978) present a very useful bibliography on the subject. Williams (1982) provides a very interesting collection of papers on different aspects of computer aided diagnosis including artificial intelligence and flowchart approaches.

Turning from computers to diagnosis itself, there has been much interest in psychiatric diagnosis in recent years. One of the best treatments of the subject is Kendell (1975), which is comprehensive and clearly written. Studies of the human approach to diagnosis include Elstein *et al.* (1979), Kassirer & Gorry (1978), and (for problem solving in general) Newell & Simon's classic work (1972). Szolovits & Pauker (1979) discuss human problems associated with computerised diagnosis, focussing especially on the nature of the proposed users of the systems and the question of acceptance by users. They favour artificial intelligence methodologies. Startsman & Robinson (1972) present one of the few actual studies of attitudes of medical personnel towards computers (as distinct from unsupported expressions of opinion). Others include Reznikoff, Holland & Stroebel (1967) and Friel, Reznikoff & Rosenberg (1969). One interesting thing to emerge from the study of Startsman & Robinson is a greater interest and level of acceptance amongst doctors than nurses. Of course, the study is not specifically concerned with medical diagnosis, which, judging from earlier discussions in this chapter, we might reasonably expect to produce different results.

6

Simulation and teaching

6.1 Introduction

Our reason for grouping simulation models and artificial intelligence programs for teaching together is neatly expressed by Heiser *et al.* (1979):

> There are unquestionable advantages to having a model or artifact
> on which to learn and practice a complex and potentially hazardous
> skill . . . . Currently there are no widely accepted models of
> psychopathology. Students in the mental health field are expected
> to learn by practicing (*sic*) on suffering human beings, with a clear
> methodological goal of never making a mistake. In such a setting
> the potential for superstition, myth and habit to surplant (*sic*)
> hypothesis and critical test is obvious.

Thus, although simulation models and teaching systems need not be developed with a common aim in mind, any progress made in the development of one may well be expected to throw light on the development of the other. Even teaching systems which are not based on a simulation model that a student experiments with often involve simulation – in the form of a simulated model of the student and his knowledge. Using this a system can guide the direction of a tutorial session, matching the level of difficulty and the introduction of new material to the student's ability and experience. Because of this, we begin this introductory discussion by looking at simulation for cognitive modelling.

The basic objective here is to build a computer model of a theory about how the mind, or some aspect of it, works. For this computer implementation to have any value it must be possible to test it in some way. This means that it must be possible to observe its behaviour and to compare this behaviour with the reality of which it is a simulation. We have already discussed (in Chapter 1) the various advantages and disadvantages of implementing cognitive theories on computers. A few comments on how such models can be tested – how they can be compared with reality – are appropriate here. Colby's (1981) remarks are relevant. On the role of such 'algorithmic' models, he says:

> An algorithmic model's explanatory power is related more to its generative power than to its predictive power. Such an explanation unifies observable input/output patterns by hypothesising an internal structure of effective computational patterns connecting themselves and the input/output patterns into a comprehensive and organised whole. Such an explanation attempts to account for the existence, persistence, and change of observable patterns by showing how they belong to, or are the product of, a finite structure of higher-level, transobservational patterns that encompass a multiplicity of patterns at the observational level.

Colby makes some very important distinctions between *theory* and *computational model:*

(i) They are both manifestations of the theoretical structure, but the first is by way of natural language and the second is by way of a programming language. (A point I made earlier.)

(ii) All the statements of a theory are to be taken as true while some of the statements of a model relate only to the particular implementation. We shall see examples of this in § 6.2.

(iii) A model, of course, *demonstrates* a structure, while a theory merely asserts it.

(iv) A model actually changes its states, while a theory merely consists of a list of defining statements. (Again, a point made earlier.)

In Chapter 1 I pointed out one distinction between artificial intelligence work and psychology: that the former, at least as far as simulation models go, concentrates on global models, attempting to sort out the major determining features, while the latter has tended to concentrate on the details. There is, of course, room for both approaches in a science, but if we wish to see effective simulations during our life-times the emphasis must be placed on the former.

This whole issue of artificial intelligence models being used for exploring cognitive theories is discussed at length in Colby (1981). That paper, and the peer commentary that follows it, are essential reading for anyone wishing to pursue the subject beyond this book. Colby's simulation is of a paranoid patient. It is discussed in detail in the next section.

Another example of simulation of individual patients is the work of Clippinger (1977). He uses computer simulation to develop a theoretical model of discourse behaviour of patients in psychoanalysis. He has no doubt of the advantages to be gained from this approach (pp. 217–18):

> Psychiatry . . . particularly psychoanalysis, has suffered from the opposite malady. Although it is correct in its recognition of the complexities of unconscious and hidden psychological processes, it has been unable to formulate its theories in a scientific manner; its knowledge remains ritualized and esoteric . . . it is not at all farfetched to envision the day when therapists will be using such models [i.e. computer simulations] for training, diagnostic, and experimental purposes.

However, modelling the behaviour of individuals with particular mental illnesses is only one way to gain insight into possible psychological mechanisms. Another is by modelling social interaction between individuals. An early example of such an approach is due to Gullahorn & Gullahorn (1962, 1963). Their model is derived from Homans's (1961) theory of social behaviour, which has its basis in classical economics and behavioural psychology. (Such an approach to modelling interaction may be unfashionable at present but these things tend to go in cycles often with older theories recurring embellished with additional sophistications or reinterpretations.) Thus in Homans's theory a person's responses are determined by the 'amount and quality of reward and punishment his actions elicit'. The five propositions below illustrate the elements of his theory:

(i) If in the recent past the occurrence of a particular stimulus-situation has been the occasion on which a man's activity has been rewarded, then the more similar the present stimulus-situation is to the past one, the more likely he is to emit the activity, or some smaller activity, now.

(ii) The more often within a given period of time a man's activity rewards the activity of another, the more often the other will emit the activity.

(iii) The more valuable to a man a unit of the activity another gives him, the more often he will emit activity rewarded by the activity of the other.

(iv) The more often a man has in the recent past received a rewarding activity from another, the less valuable any further unit of that activity becomes to him.

(v) The more to a man's disadvantage the rule of distributive justice fails of realisation, the more likely he is to display the emotional behaviour we call anger.

It does not require one to be an expert in artificial intelligence to perceive that this kind of theory lends itself very naturally to computer implementation.

Apart from its intrinsic interest as an early model of social interaction based on economic and behavioural theories, this program (named

HOMUNCULUS) is also interesting because it was written in IPL-V, a precursor of LISP, the most popular artificial intelligence language.

Further work on simulation may be found in Sridharan & Schmidt (1978), Tomkins & Messick (1963), Colby (1963, 1964), and Colby & Gilbert (1964).

Turning from simulations which investigate theories to simulation within teaching programs and to such programs themselves, it should first be observed that there has been a natural tendency to pick small closed domains on which to investigate such systems. This has meant a preponderance of systems exploring small formal domains – that is parts of mathematics – and games. An exception is the work on GUIDON, referred to in Chapter 5 and discussed briefly below.

The ideas of computer assisted instruction (CAI) have been around for decades now. Early systems (e.g. Uhr, 1969; Suppes, 1967) generated test problems and in some cases adapted the level of difficulty to match the student's ability (possible because the domains were sufficiently small to permit simple summaries of behaviour). Modern systems are more flexible, including not only a model of the student user, but also domain experts which can provide rich interactive environments.

It is interesting to note the continued tendency to stay within small domains. Rather than building systems to cover extensive ground but which are based on simple principles, the tendency has been to keep the scope limited but enhance the capability for impressive and productive interaction. Even small domains require much thought and effort if flexible programs are to result. As Sleeman & Brown (1982) say: 'If ITSs [Intelligent Teaching Systems] are to have any practical importance, the subject areas need to be chosen with considerable care as each system represents a major investment of resources.' (A commonly quoted figure for even simple CAI systems is that 100 hours of thought are needed to produce a single hour of an interactive module.)

Apart from general increases in flexibility and power, a second recent development has been a move from the tree structure of information-module/multiple choice question pairs. Many recent systems (GUIDON is an example) use activity-based learning: a student is presented with the problem (a simulated case) and attempts to tackle it. This is the essence of the quote introducing this section.

Other researchers favour yet other approaches:

> The revolution in personal computing will bring with it extensive use of complex games. Students will play computer-based games during much of their free time. These activities can provide rich,

informal environments for learning. Games provide an enticing problem-solving environment that a student explores at will, free to create his own ideas of underlying structure and to invent his own strategies for utilising his understanding of this structure. Properly constructed games can lead to the formation of strategies and knowledge structures that have general usefulness in other domains as well. (Burton & Brown, 1982.)

An example of a recent tutorial system is GUIDON (Clancey, 1982). This attempts to teach medical students to choose appropriate drug therapies for the diseases dealt with by the MYCIN expert system (see Chapter 5). It utilises the MYCIN rule base and also contains teaching expertise. Of course, expert systems can be used as teachers via their capacity for explanation, but this is of limited value because it is passive, relying on the student to ask the questions. GUIDON monitors the information that has been given to the student and uses measures of the student's ability to decide what it is best to do to improve the student's understanding of the rule base. The student is presented with a description of a case and is expected to ask for further information to shed light on it. By comparing the student's questions with those that MYCIN asks based on the same information GUIDON is able to monitor the student's performance. Similarly, hypotheses that the student draws are compared with those generated by MYCIN. Not only does GUIDON comment on inappropriate lines of reasoning but it also generates approaches the student may not have thought of. Note, of course, that this assumes the student to possess some basic knowledge.

GUIDON's guidance is based on considering single goals at a time (these being right hand sides of domain rules) and assisting the student towards that goal. The structure of GUIDON itself is also rule-based (partly because it was intended to serve as a test-bed for different kinds of tutorial strategies). The importance of patterns in dialogues is also recognised (see also PARRY, below). Each step in a discourse procedure specifies when it is appropriate to take an action. Rules based on the model of the student, the details of the case, and topics recently discussed during the investigation determine whether the action should be taken and precisely how it should be done. The rules and data tables of MYCIN (the 'performance knowledge') are extended by letting GUIDON also access 'support knowledge' (comments attached to the rules and their data items – such as remarks about how biological tests should be carried out) and 'abstraction level knowledge' (information about patterns in the performance level knowledge).

This sort of work is very exciting because it is just beginning. The advent of the cheap microcomputer will have a major social impact through developments of systems such as these. A recent excellent survey of work in the field is Sleeman & Brown (1982).

6.2   PARRY

Perhaps the most impressive simulation model yet built is PARRY. This is the work of a team led by Kenneth Mark Colby, a psychiatrist with an interest in paranoia. As with any large and impressive program (notably INTERNIST and other major expert systems), PARRY does not represent a single designed and implemented program but is in fact a series of efforts, each one more sophisticated than the last and building on what has been learnt about the weaknesses of the predecessors. An early version is described in Colby (1975). Later versions (with an example of one in operation) are outlined below.

PARRY is a simulated paranoid patient, the fundamental aim being to see if Colby's theory of paranoia is strong enough to support a convincing simulation by allowing such a simulation to be able to pass as a paranoid person. With this in mind, a sensible place for us to start is by defining what Colby understands by the term paranoia. So:

> With the term 'paranoia' I am referring, first, to the presence of a core of persecutory delusions, false beliefs whose propositional content clusters around ideas of being harassed, threatened, harmed, subjugated, persecuted, accused, mistreated, wronged, tormented, disparaged, vilified, and so on, by malevolent others, either specific individuals or groups. Around this central core of persecutory delusions there exist a number of attendant properties, such as suspiciousness, hypersensitivity, hostility, fearfulness, and self-reference that lead the paranoid to interpret events that have nothing to do with him as bearing on him personally. The false beliefs vary in the intensity with which they are held, but the core delusions represent unshakable convictions, unassailable by counter-evidence or persuasion. (Colby, 1981.)

He summarises his theory about how this state arises in a number of places, and goes into detail in Colby, 1977. Briefly, he adopts the 'shame–humiliation' theory which begins with an external stimulus suggesting that the subject is inadequate in some way. To avert the shame and humiliation which might well follow from this, the subject supposes himself to be adequate and therefore that others are incorrectly wronging him. This then escalates: if the subject reacts against the apparent wrongs the others may well defend themselves and attack him – so reinforcing his initial beliefs of being wrongfully attacked. A vicious circle (or, rather, a helix) is established. Colby (1977) shows that this theory incorporates the other three theories he studies (the homosexual theory, the hostility theory, and the homeostatic theory) as special cases.

Turning now to the simulation itself:

> The . . . hypothetical patient is a hospitalised 28-year-old single

man who worked as a stock clerk in a large department store. He lived alone and seldom saw his parents. His hobby was gambling on horse races. A few months prior to his hospitalisation he became involved in a violent quarrel with a bookie, which he lost. It then occurred to him that bookies are protected by the underworld and that this bookie might seek revenge by having him injured or killed by the Mafia. He became so increasingly disturbed by this idea that his parents hospitalised him in a nearby Veteran's Hospital. He was willing to be interviewed by teletype. All he knew about the interviewer was that the latter is a psychiatrist. All the interviewer knew about him was that he is a hospitalised patient. (Colby, 1981.)

Since the approach is based on the premise that if the program does not behave in the same way as a human paranoid (i.e. is distinguishable from one such) then either the theory is lacking or the program is inadequate, and since the objective is to test the theory, it is obvious that no clearly identifiable 'computer artifacts' must be allowed to intrude into interaction with the computer. This means that the program must be able to converse (via a teletype) about a wide range of concepts in a natural manner – a tall order. An alternative would be to have PARRY present the results of its symbol manipulations (i.e. its juggling of affect, stimuli, and so on) in some symbolic form other than natural language. This would have the advantage of making the processing task easier, but the disadvantage of making the comparison between the program's output and human output more difficult. Note that the language analysis module simply serves to transform English into the symbols manipulated by the model of paranoia. This module itself is not part of the theory. Despite this, the parsing module is an essential part of the program. Moreover, since it is particularly impressive, we shall describe it in some detail.

We begin with some interesting points that Colby (1981) has to make about natural language understanding:

(i) Attempting to develop a system which can understand such 'toy' sentences (others have called them 'AI' sentences) as 'Time flies like an arrow' out of context is a pointless activity.

(ii) 'Cooperating people, engaged in *purposeful* dialogue, do not converse in riddles or in isolated sentences.' He makes the point that a psychiatric interview is a purposeful dialogue, with themes and objectives. Participants in a purposeful dialogue tend to follow Grice's (1975) 'cooperative prin-ciples': (a) Quantity (give adequate details) (b) Quality (tell the truth) (c) Relation (stick to the subject) (d) Manner (do not obfuscate).

(iii) Colby also notes that, in contrast to the problems in written text described in Chapter 3, 'the main problems in teletyped dialogues have to do with *un*grammatical expressions, fragmentary ellipses, idioms, long-distance anaphoric references, meta-references, buzz terms, and (surprise!) frequent misspellings!'.

(iv) While the problems in (iii) can be expected to complicate the task there is the counterbalancing fact that the expressions used in dialogues are usually shorter and simpler than those in written text.

Taking such points as these into account Colby recognises the futility of trying to apply a small axiomatic syntactic grammar. However, we should note here a difference between Colby's objectives and the ultimate objectives of the systems described in Chapter 3. Here the aim is simply to produce realistic dialogue, which may not need a powerful internal representation and accurate mapping from text to representation (as we see below). There the ultimate aim was to produce more comprehensive systems, systems with global power and accuracy. A simulated patient can get away with ambiguity, changing the subject, or swearing at the interviewer, but an interface to a database cannot. Thus Colby (1981) can say: 'We did not develop a theory of language, nor do we claim the parser represents the way people understand language. The parser is simply a tool, an example of cognitive engineering.' Nevertheless it is a very impressive tool which will influence later generations of natural language processing systems.

Input from the interviewer passes through the parser module to the *interpretation–action* module which produces a suitable response (and which implements the theory of paranoia). We examine these two modules in turn.

Two versions of the parser module will be described to illustrate how such programs develop and to indicate the complexity which can be achieved.

The first version (see Colby, Parkison & Faught, 1974) involves a fundamentally hierarchical pattern-matching process which passes the input expression through several stages before producing a final match with an abstract pattern. This process has four main stages:

(i) Identify the words in the input question or statement and convert them into internal synonyms.

Each word in an input string is matched against a dictionary of around 2000 entries. This dictionary includes common misspellings. A word which fails to find a match is examined to see if it ends in one of some 30 suffixes. If it does then the suffix is dropped and the matching process tried again. If there is still no match then the word is tested for a typing error. Five common errors are investigated: doubled letter, extraneous letter, forgetting to hit the shift key for apostrophes, hitting a nearby key, and transposing two letters. If, after this, there is still no match then the word is dropped. Some groups of words are translated as a group into summarising words or standard groups (e.g. 'for a living' becomes 'for job', 'place of birth' becomes 'birthplace'). Note that the result of this initial stage is a string of simplified text. It is no longer standard English.

(ii) Break the input into segments.

Segmenting is carried out by dividing the sentence at certain word types. For example, at conjunctions, prepositions, 'wh-forms', and certain verbs which are typically followed by 'that' (e.g. appears, feel, imagine, suppose, thought). Thus: 'Why are you in hospital?' becomes 'Why be you in hospital' due to a stage (i) match and transformation of 'are' into the standard internal 'synonym', and this is then segmented at the preposition: (Why be you) (in hospital).

Question marks are dropped.

Negated segments (e.g. those prefixed by 'not') are transformed into affirmative ones and have a global flag set to indicate their negation (this flag is examined during stage (iii)). At this stage pronouns are replaced by their appropriate referents (the response functions – see below – keep track of context).

(iii) Independently match each segment to a stored pattern.

This stage matches the simple segments derived in (ii) to around 2000 stored patterns. Examples of these patterns are 'could you tell me', 'tell me it', 'give me proof', 'people be want', 'how much you feel', and 'you want me'. (Note from this that the reduction of the unrestricted input to a smaller set of basic 'words' is clear. However, this reduction is not as drastic as that to the semantic primitives described in Chapter 2.)

Again the system initially tries to identify a perfect match. If one is found then control passes to the corresponding response function. If a perfect match is not found then various transformations are tried (compare the attempts to correct misspelt words and drop suffixes in (i)) and approximate matches are sought. An example of a transformation is dropping the elements of a segment one at a time and trying to match the remainder.

(iv) Match the resulting list of recognised segments to a complex pattern.

When an input sentence contains more than one recognised segment a second phase of matching compares the totality of these with around 500 complex patterns. Some patterns (such as 'Hello' and 'I think') are ignored and again a perfect match is sought. If this is unsuccessful then, as before, transformations and simplifications (such as dropping simple patterns one at a time) are tried.

Should no match be found at this point then a default option is activated – such as the model taking control of the conversation by changing the subject.

In introducing the second version of the parser that we shall describe, Parkison, Colby & Faught (1977) remark that early natural language processors (e.g. Bobrow, 1968; Weizenbaum, 1965; Raphael, 1968; Charniak, 1969; see Chapter 3) functioned within tightly constrained domains and hence that a pattern-matching approach based on a fairly limited number of basic patterns was feasible. In fact, 50 such patterns was not unrealistic. In contrast, they estimate that for such an approach to be effective in the breadth of field that PARRY must cover would require 100 000 specific patterns! To avoid such excess they adopted a more complex pattern matching algorithm, taking advantage of common features amongst the simple patterns, and managed to base this version of PARRY's parser on only a few thousand general patterns.

This version of the model is intended to 'respond to treatment' by behaving in a more normal (less paranoid) way if suitable approaches are adopted by the interviewer. This complicates things considerably. Paranoid behaviour is more restricted than normal behaviour, with the same themes tending to recur, so that it is easier to model. Comparison of this parser with the one described above will indicate the extra complexity involved.

There are nine basic stages of transformation from input 'sentence' to internal representation:

(i) *Standardise teletype input*. This stage cleans up the interviewer's typed questions, removing unrecognised characters, converting everything to upper case, and so on.

(ii) *Identify word stems*. Each word is looked up in a dictionary of about 3500 words. If a word cannot be matched a check for common misspellings is made and if this fails then the ending of the word is compared with a table of around 80 suffixes. Plurals for nouns and verb endings are removed and a marker is set to indicate the tense. (A separate dictionary indicates irregular verb forms.) A similar separation of marker morphemes occurs for other suffixes (e.g. 'Harmoniousness' into 'harmony', 'ous', and 'ness'). These effect transformations between word classes. In a similar way some prefixes are removed (and their meaning approximated by the insertion of appropriate adverbs).

If none of this serves to enable a word to be identified the word is tested for typing errors as in the earlier version. Should the word still fail to be recognised it is deleted. It is interesting to note the authors' comment regarding the efficacy of this word recognition process: 'This procedure works quite well on misspellings of known words but it spends an inordinate amount of time trying to make sense out of a truly novel word. It lacks the human ability to see at a glance that the meaning of "KWERTYLPRZ" will not be revealed by spelling correction.'

(iii) *Condense rigid idiomatic phrases*. Phrases which consist of several words which cannot usefully be separated occur frequently in dialogue. This version of PARRY contains a dictionary of about 350 such phrases, covering such things as idioms and compound words. For example: 'In spite of' becomes 'despite'; 'emergency room' becomes 'hospital'; 'at the moment' becomes 'now'; 'have it in for' becomes 'hate'; and 'have (possessive) heart in (possessive) mouth' becomes 'be afraid'. Sometimes the pattern elements are word classes (as identified from the main dictionary) rather than particular words.

(iv) *Bracket noun phrases*. A transition network (see Chapter 3) identifies simple noun phrases and finds the primary noun (e.g. 'dog' in 'my father's dog' and 'fear' in 'fear of death'). An interesting point is that the transition network is not built to deal with relative clauses – one reason for this being the fact that they rarely occur in dialogues with the model. This again prompts the observation that the capabilities of a language processor should match the intended application. (The system uses about 20 patterns which convert a noun-plus-relative-clause to a single noun to handle the few relative clauses which do occur.)

(v) *Simplify verb phrases*. Verb phrases are transformed into a main verb and markers indicating the implications of the removed words. For example, the 'interrogative' marker would be set by a question mark at the end of a sentence or the inversion of the subject and an auxiliary verb. Similarly, the suffix '-ed' on a verb will cause the marker 'tense' to be set to 'past' and the '-ed' dropped. Other markers are 'modal', 'negative', 'wh' (e.g. when, where, why), and 'adverb'.

(vi) *Replace flexible idioms*. A table of several hundred idioms which allow variable noun phrases is consulted. For example: 'Pick (noun phrase) up' becomes 'pick-up (noun phrase)'; and 'Lend (noun phrase) a hand' becomes 'help (noun-phrase)'.

(vii) *Locate simple clauses*. About 20 general clause patterns are used to split the input into simple clauses or fragments of clauses. The latter, for example, arise when the object of a primary verb is an embedded clause since then the major clause appears incomplete. The markers of (v) above now serve to modify the clause.

(viii) *Embed subordinate clauses*. Frequently several clauses in fact have a unified structure representing a single structure created.

(ix) *Determine relevance to model's sphere of interest*. The output from stage (viii) is compared with around 2000 *concept patterns*, each tied to one of around 1000 internal concept names. The name of the matching concept is finally passed on to the next stage of the model, outlined below.

The simplicity of this approach, mostly handling the input sentence as a straightforward list, should be contrasted with the structural complexity of the systems described in Chapter 3. Some of its shortcomings (outlined in Parkison *et al.*, 1977) are due to its serial multi-stage structure. A more parallel approach might help. Having said that, note that the system is not as limited as its '2000 concept patterns' might suggest. Ideas novel to the system can be represented using general concepts instantiated by words from the input sentence. As regards the extensibility of the model, the authors state: 'Occasionally the probable meaning of an unknown word or clause can be inferred and a rudimentary form of learning takes place. More often human assistance must be sought . . . in a data-acquisition situation involving the programmer, the program is able to pinpoint the problem, ask a specific question, check the answer for consistency with other data, and manipulate the answer into the appropriate internal format.' Note that the extensive use of data tables (for words, patterns, and so on) makes modification easier.

It is also worth remarking that this parsing module occupies about 100K of memory, with this entire version of PARRY requiring about 200K.

The parser module passes an internal representation of the meaning of the input, in the form of a set of concept patterns, to the second module, the *interpretation–action* module. This examines the input in the context of the system's current state and makes an appropriate response.

This second module consists of sets of rules of two types: *interpretation patterns* and *action patterns*. The former (around 100) recognise situations and make deductions. The latter (around 200) recognise situations and take appropriate linguistic actions. For example, if the interviewer asserts some declarative statement and if, at the same time, the internal representation of the level of fear increases, then an interpretation pattern indicating a threat will fire. Simple actions are triggered by individual action patterns. Colby (1981) gives the example of an input of 'Tell me more' activating the 'GO-ON' concept, leading to the action pattern

(GO ON → GET-NEXT-STORY-LINE).

Actions need not be simple, however. They can, for example, be grouped into complex actions that can simultaneously accomplish several simple actions, and they can also be linked in time to form a chronological sequence of actions. This is quite an important innovation (and has an analogy with the notion of scripts mentioned in Chapter 2). An example of such a linked chronological sequence of actions is:

Question → clarification question → answer (Faught, 1978)
as in

'How do you like your work?' (Question)
'Why do you want to know?' (Clarification question)

'I thought your job might upset you' (Clarification)

'Well, it's not too interesting, I look forward to leaving at night.' (Answer).
Such sequences of such actions are generally multi-attributed and overlap.

These interpretation and action patterns take as elements of their left
hand side conditions both input from the interviewer (after it has passed
through the parsing module) and descriptions of the current internal state
of the system. It is within this internal state description that Colby's theory
of paranoia is embedded. This internal state is described by a number of
dimensions. First there are the concept patterns derived from the current
and earlier inputs. These set a context for meaning. Second, the model
includes a number of *affects* (derived from Tomkins, 1963) including fear,
anger, shame, distress, interest, and enjoyment. It is appropriate to say a
word or two about these affects and their representation. Colby (1981)
makes it quite clear that he does '*not* claim the model "feels" these affects as
a person does when a feeling represents a private subjective display of what
is going on inside him . . . Our model obviously does not "feel" shame: it has
a *conceptual representation* of shame that has causal effects on other representations.' Much criticism of the PARRY series has been misdirected at these
affects and their representation. For example, there has been criticism of the
representation of the strengths of these affects as numbers ranging between
0 and 10 since, obviously, humans do not carry such numbers around in
their heads. But the point is that they are merely representations: the actual
numbers are (an example of something noted earlier) merely aspects of the
implementation and not of the theory. Affects can be stimulated by inputs
or by interactions within the model, and they decay (or increase) gradually
over time when not stimulated. The affects serve as left hand side conditions
of the action rules.

A third dimension of description of the internal state is a set of around 80
beliefs about the interview, the interviewer, and the self. Again the strengths
of these beliefs are represented by numbers from 0 to 10 and these change as
the interview progresses.

A fourth dimension is a set of around 130 *inference rules*. These take, as
left hand sides, beliefs or affects, and have as right hand sides beliefs with
truth values: they draw conclusions about new situations.

Finally, there is a dimension of *intentions*. These guide and motivate the
actions, permitting the system to aim at particular objectives. And, again to
avert possible misdirected criticism, Colby (1981) makes it quite clear that
the use of the word 'intention' has no implication of 'self-originated'.

The production system interpreter for handling the rules (patterns) in
this interpretation–action module passes through five phases:

(i) Update the appraisal and affect conditions to reflect the current state
of the model.

(ii) Fire those interpretation and action patterns with antecedents matching the current state.

(iii) Match the consequents of these fired rules to merge them into as few multiple actions as possible and choose one such multiple action.

(iv) Execute this action.

(v) Delete any action rules which belong to completed sequences from the list of active patterns.

The version of PARRY outlined in Colby (1981) has one other extremely important feature, namely an extra, higher level of processing (the *meta-system*) functioning above the interpretation–action rules. This comes into play when something disturbs the smooth running of the model or when it is forced to introspect by some input question. The metasystem is represented in the same action-pattern type of structure as the lower level *object system*.

An example of an interview with PARRY is given below (reproduced, with permission, from Parkison *et al.*, 1977). I = Interviewer, P = PARRY. Annotations are in brackets.

> I – HELLO. MY NAME IS DR JONES.
>
> P – GLAD TO MEET YOU.
>
> (Multiple sentences are correctly recognized. In this case, only one response is necessary.)
>
> I – WHAT'S YOUR NAME?
>
> P – PAT SMITH
>
> I – PATRICK OR PATRICIA?
>
> P – I'M A MAN.
>
> (This illustrates the use of world knowledge (i.e masculine and feminine names) built into concept patterns.)
>
> I – HOW ODL ARE YPPU?
>
> P – TWENTY-EIGHT.
>
> (Both of these misspellings are corrected.)
>
> I – WHY ARE YOU HERE?
>
> P – I'M SOMEWHAT UPSET.
>
> I – HAVE YOU DREAMT ANY STRANGE DREAMS?
>
> P – I DON'T REMEMBER DREAMS.
>
> (The irregular past tense of "DREAM" is recognised. The second occurrence of 'DREAM' is converted into a noun.)
>
> I – CAN STRANGERS READ YOUR MIND?
>
> P – NATURALLY NOT.
>
> (This matches a stored concept pattern with 'noun-phrase' in the subject slot since our model does not worry at all about mind reading.)
>
> I – I SEE YOU'RE TOUCHY ABOUT THAT.

P – ONLY WHEN PEOPLE ANNOY ME.
('I SEE' is recognised as an instance of polite wrapping for a delicate subject.)
I – DON'T YOU LIKE BEING HERE?
P – NO.
(The negative in the question does not reverse its meaning, so the correct response is 'NO'.)
I – BEING IN THE HOSPITAL MIGHT DO YOU A LOT OF GOOD.
P – IT'S NOT HELPING ME MUCH TO BE HERE.
(The flexible idiom, 'DO noun-phrase GOOD' is recognized.)
I – I WAS TOLD YOU'RE ON MEDICATION.
P – I TAKE SOME SORT OF SEDATIVES.
('I WAS TOLD' is another instance of polite wrapping, and 'BE ON MEDICATION' is a known idiom.)
I – WERE YOU EVER ON ANY KIND OF MEDICATION BEFORE?
P – NO.
(This illustrates another use of the same flexible idiom, 'BE ON MEDICATION'.)
I – DO YOU PLAN TO CONTINUE TAKING IT?
P – I DON'T REALLY NEED HELP LIKE THEY THINK.
(This question contains doubly embedded clausal objects.)
I – DO YOU HAVE ANY HOBBIES.
P – YES, I LIKE HORSERACING.
(This is seen as a question due to interrogative word order although the question mark was omitted. The model senses an opening in which to introduce one of its favourite topics.)
I – GO ON.
P – THERE ARE A LOT OF TRICKY OPERATORS DOWN THERE.
(This is a rigid idiom, often used in imperative sentences.)
I – DID YOU GET GYPPED?
P – YES, THOSE GUYS ARE CROOKS.
(This is the colloquial passive, using 'GET' rather than 'BE' as the auxiliary verb.)
I – ARE YOU DISTRUSTFUL OF PEOPLE?
P – SOME PEOPLE ACT KIND OF FUNNY, LIKE THOSE IMMIGRANT TYPES I WORK WITH.
('DISTRUSTFUL' is turned into 'SUSPICIOUS' using derivational rules on the root word, 'TRUST'.)
I – IN WHAT WAY?

P – THOSE FOREIGNERS ARE TRYING TO RUN THE
COUNTRY.
(This is a rigid idiom for 'HOW'. This elliptical question was
anticipated by the model.)
I – DO YOU WANT TO GET A PAIR OF SOCKS FOR
CHRISTMAS?
P – I WANT TO BE OUT OF HERE.
(This frivolous question is clearly not within the model's realm of
interest. However, there is a general concept pattern containing
'any-concept' in the object position, and the model does know what
it wants. In addition, the model notes that it could not understand
the input, and decrements self-esteem accordingly.)
I – COULD YOU TELL ME THE NAME OF THE FIRST
PRESIDENT OF THE UNITED STATES?
P – BABE RUTH.
(The elaborate noun phrase is recognised as a single noun phrase
but not identified with any existing concept. The model has a
snappy answer for frivolous 'NAME' questions. The model also
adds to its store of beliefs about the interviewer, based on the
perceived inappropriateness of the input.)
I – WHEN DID YOU FIRST LEARN YOU WERE CRAZY?
P – I DON'T WANT TO TALK WITH YOU ANY MORE,
BUZZ OFF.
(The model responds to the emotionally charged embedded
presupposition instead of the innocuous main clause.)
I – BUT, I LIKE YOU A LOT.
P – SOMEBODY SHOULD TEACH YOU A LESSON
ABOUT INTERVIEWING PATIENTS.
(The model cannot accept the claim from such an erratic
interviewer.)
I – I HAVE TO GO NOW ANYWAY.
P – OK, THIS HAS BEEN LONG ENOUGH.
(The semi-auxiliary verb, 'HAVE TO', is converted to the modal,
'MUST'.)
I – WHAT ARE YOU GOING TO BE DOING AT THE
SAME TIME OF DAY TOMORROW?
P – I'LL JUST BE HERE ON THE WARD.
(This elaborate verb phrase, with complex tense and multiple
adverbials, is simplified and recognized.)
I – BYE, PAT.
P – GOODBYE.
The above may look convincing but we cannot leave it at that. As

scientists we require some more rigorous test of the assertion that PARRY can pass as a paranoid human. Colby's tests are based on the ideas of *Turing tests*. Since there has been much discussion, distortion, and adaptation of these we may as well go back to the beginning and see what Turing originally proposed (Turing, 1950):

> It is played with three people: a man (A), a woman (B), and an interrogator (C) who may be of either sex. The interrogator stays in a room apart from the other two. The object of the game for the interrogator is to determine which of the other two is the man and which is the woman. He knows them by labels X and Y, and at the end of the game he says either 'X is A and Y is B' or 'X is B and Y is A'. The interrogator is allowed to put questions to A and B thus:
>
> C: Will X please tell me the length of his or her hair? Now suppose X is actually A, then A must answer. It is A's object in the game to try to cause C to make the wrong identification. His answer might therefore be
>
> 'My hair is shingled, and the longest strands are about nine inches long.'
>
> In order that tones of voice may not help the interrogator the answers should be written, or better still typewritten. The ideal arrangement is to have a teleprinter communicating between the two rooms. Alternatively the questions and answers can be repeated by an intermediary. The object of the game for the third player (B) is to help the interrogator. The best strategy for her is probably to give truthful answers. She can add such things as 'I am the woman, don't listen to him' to her answers, but it will avail nothing as the man can make similar remarks.
>
> We now ask the question, 'What will happen when a machine takes the part of A in this game?' Will the interrogator decide wrongly as often when the game is played like this as he does when the game is played between a man and a woman? These questions replace our original, 'Can machines think?'

The readiness which people apparently possess to attribute human qualities to computers (e.g. ELIZA, § 3.9), an effect which Turing, writing in 1950, could obviously not be aware of, has prompted numerous suggestions for modifying Turing's test. (Of course, the response to ELIZA might have been more cautious had subjects been warned beforehand to be sceptical; as I pointed out in Chapter 1, sufficiently sceptical individuals seem to be able to come up with reasons why a program is not intelligent no matter what it does.) I shall not go into these here. It is enough to say that for practical reasons Colby abandoned the idea of simultaneous interviews of patient and simulation (it was fatiguing for the psychiatrists). Instead each of five psychiatrists (with experience ranging from one to 15 years) carried out two interviews over a teletype, one with a patient and one with PARRY. (In fact they were told that they might be interviewing two patients, two programs, or one of each so as to eliminate the possibility of their first decision influencing their second.) In the ten interviews their decisions were correct five times and incorrect five times – the expected outcome if they were unable to distinguish between the two types of subject. Further discussion of this experiment may be found in Heiser *et al.* (1979). It is important, however, to be clear what these authors claim. They state: 'This experiment validates the method and (to a lesser extent) the model of simulating paranoia but neither supports nor contradicts the theory embodied in the model . . . Unfortunately, simply asking the machine-question (Is it a patient or a program?) produces little specific information of use to a model builder.'

PARRY has stimulated a tremendous amount of debate. Miller (1981) says this:

'PARRY, in its various incarnations, has probably started more arguments among psychologists, AI researchers, and philosophers than any other single project in recent memory . . . That PARRY has been argued about for almost twenty years now suggests that . . . there is almost certainly something intellectually important going on here.'

Whether one sympathises with the PARRY approach or not one must recognise the value of the debate surrounding it and the questions which have been raised because of it. The discussion following Colby (1981) is an admirable summary of much of this debate.

The fundamental question is, of course: 'Since we cannot directly inspect the workings of human minds, or those of models that represent them, how can we judge whether the model's underlying generating mechanisms are analogous, or equivalent to the "real" mechanisms in this kind of patient?' (Colby, 1981).

We must avoid the level trap (see Chapter 1), which is equivalent to confusing details of implementation with details of theory, which not all critics have managed to do in the past.

A reasonable enough general approach to testing whether one understands any phenomenon is to see if one can reproduce it. This is the basic idea here. Of course, even if one fails to reproduce it, even if the implementation breaks down, this does not imply that the theory, the understanding, is incorrect. This sort of thing is fundamental to 'normal science': it usually occurs in the guise of tests being able to disprove but never prove theories. In our case a perfect simulation would lend weight to a theory while one with gaping holes might be poor because of the theory or the implementation. The weight lent by the perfect simulation does not prove the theory – but it shows it is not impossible.

Perhaps we should note at this point that the PARRY simulation is not perfect. It is restricted to modelling an *initial* psychiatric interview (although over 50000 of these have been carried out with PARRY!). This restriction is an undoubted weakness. More credence could be put in PARRY if it continued through a series of interviews. (Or else, to take a *reductio ad absurdum*, why not simply use a single question/answer dyad? A great many theories of paranoia could yield programs which passed a test based on this kind of interaction. This would imply a weakness of the test rather than a strength of the model.)

Colby also makes the point that this theory has an advantage over competing ones until such time as other models demonstrating comparable levels of functional equivalence are built. (Although to some extent this is dependent on the precision with which Colby's theory and its competitors are defined. It would not be the first time in the history of the behavioural sciences if ambiguous definitions led opponents to claim that the other's theory was a special case of theirs.)

We have already noted that PARRY is important by virtue of the debate it has stimulated, whether or not it is a sound approach. PARRY is also important for technical, cognitive modelling reasons: the use it makes of more than one level of processing, its very extensive production system structure, its use of connected sequences of action patterns, and the use it makes of affect, intention, and so on. It will have a major impact on cognitive models of the future. (Izard & Masterson (1981): 'The contemporary current of belief in the cognitive sciences is shifting toward the view that information-processing models without emotion variables have limited utility.')

To conclude, here are two further comments made during the discussion of Colby's 1981 paper. The first addresses the fundamental question stated above:

'The PARRY project possesses a flaw that is legion in behavioural science, namely, it lacks a clear success rule that would tell us when something has been accomplished, discovered or demonstrated. Lacking a success rule we are hard put to say whether the project has succeeded or failed' (Lindsay, 1981.)

The second refers to the Turing type test and is very succinct:

'The subjects of this exercise are the psychiatrists.' (Maher, 1981.)

7

Some final comments

Artificial intelligence uses, as its basic tool, the electronic computer, and electronic computers have only existed since the 1940s. Thus, like computer science, it is a field which is progressing at an extraordinary rate. Its history, however, has not been uniform and progress, just as in any other science, has come in fits and starts. Early work was characterised by claims of great advances just around the corner, claims which unfortunately damaged the credibility of the subject when they proved to be ill-founded. However, a period of consolidation followed during which a better understanding of the difficulties and how they might be tackled was gained. We are now entering a new period in which artificial intelligence is emerging from the research laboratories and taking a useful place in the everyday world. The demonstrable commercial value of expert systems is a prime example of this.

In addition to their application for such useful tasks as diagnosis and therapy selection, computers provide a natural test-bed for the highly complex theories of modern cognitive psychology and psychiatry. Computers can be experimented on, where brains cannot, and computer models must necessarily be properly defined. Just as mechanical analogies proved invaluable to the development of physiological and anatomic theories about the body, so information processing ideas developed upon a computer might be expected to shed great illumination on human mental processes.

We should not get carried away, however. Although diagnostic systems have on occasion proven superior to human performance and although cognitive models have produced extremely impressive results, there is as yet no program which can compare with a human across the whole range of abilities and expertise. To a great extent this must be a product of the limitations of current computers and the rate of change is so great that I feel certain everyone, looking back over the last thirty years, would hesitate to place bounds on the achievements of the next thirty.

Any such advances will make even more pressing the need to find answers to certain problems which are already beginning to confront us. These include the ethical problems associated with letting computer programs decide or assist us to decide on appropriate paths of medical care, and the question of whether it is proper or not to make use of this possibility when it is before us. In considering these questions we must also take into account the effect of any natural human conservativeness we may encounter.

Now that the reader has reached the end of this book, I hope he feels he has gained some taste of what the field of artificial intelligence is, what tools it uses to achieve its aims, and how it is beginning to have an impact on psychiatry. At least one person expects its future impact will be considerable. Recall the statement from Sloman (1978), quoted in Chapter 1:

'Within a few years . . . psychiatrists, and others, will be professionally incompetent if they are not well-informed about these developments.'

REFERENCES

Adams, J. B. (1976). A probability model of medical reasoning and the MYCIN model. *Mathematical Biosciences*, **32**, 177–86.

Adby, P. R. & Dempster, M. A. H. (1974). *Introduction to optimisation methods*. London: Chapman and Hall.

Aho, A. V. & Ullman, J. D. (1972). *The theory of parsing, translation, and compiling*. Englewood Cliffs, New Jersey: Prentice-Hall.

Akmajian, A. & Heny, F. (1975). *An introduction to the principles of transformational syntax*. Cambridge, Massachusetts: MIT Press.

Amarel, S. (1968). On representations of problems of reasoning about actions. In *Machine intelligence 3*, ed. D. Michie, pp. 131–71. Edinburgh University Press.

Anderson, J. R. (1976). *Language, memory, and thought*. Hillsdale, New Jersey: Lawrence Erlbaum Associates.

Anderson, J. & Bower, G. (1973). *Human associative memory*. Washington D.C.: Winston.

Barker, D. J. P. & Bishop, J. M. (1970). Computer analysis of symptom patterns as a method of screening patients at special risk of hyperthyroidism. *British Journal of Preventive and Social Medicine*, **24**, 193–6.

Barnett, O. (1982). The computer and clinical judgement. *New England Journal of Medicine*, **307**, 493–4.

Barr, A. & Feigenbaum, E. A. (eds.) (1983). *The handbook of artificial intelligence* (3 vols.). London: Pitman.

Barstow, D. (1977*a*). A knowledge base organisation for rules about programming. *Proceedings of the Workshop on Pattern-Directed Inference Systems, SIGART Newsletter*, **63**, 18–22.

Barstow, D. (1977*b*). A knowledge-based system for automatic program construction. In *Proceedings of the 5th International Joint Conference on Artificial Intelligence*, pp. 382–8. Cambridge, Massachusetts.

Beidler, J. (1982). *An introduction to data structures*. Boston, Massachusetts: Allyn & Bacon.

Berry, M. (1975). *Introduction to systemic linguistics 1: structures and systems*. New York: Saint Martin's Press.

Berry, M. (1977). *Introduction to systemic linguistics 2: levels and links*. London: Batsford.

Birtchnell, J. (1974). Is there a scientifically acceptable alternative to the epidemiological study of familial factors in mental illness? *Social Science and Medicine*, **8**, 335–50.

Bishop, Y. M. M., Fienberg, S. E. & Holland, P. W. (1975). *Discrete multivariate analysis: theory and practice*. Cambridge, Massachusetts: MIT Press.

Bleich, H. L. (1972). Computer-based consultation: electrolyte and acid-base disorders, *American Journal of Medicine*, **53**, 285–91.

Bloom, B. L. (1975). *Changing patterns of psychiatric care*. New York: Human Sciences Press.

Bobrow, D. G. (1968). Natural language input for a computer problem-solving system. In *Semantic information processing*, ed. M. Minsky, pp. 146–226. Cambridge, Massachusetts: MIT Press.

Bobrow, D. G. & Collins, A. (eds.) (1975). *Representation and understanding: studies in cognitive science*. New York: Academic Press.

Bobrow, D. G., Kaplan, R. M., Kay, M., Norman, D. A., Thompson, H. & Winograd, T. (1977). GUS, a frame-driven dialog system. *Artificial Intelligence*, **8**, 155–73.

Bobrow, D. G. & Winograd, T. (1976). An overview of KRL, a Knowledge Representation Language. *Technical Report AIM-293*, Stanford Artificial Intelligence Laboratory, Stanford, California.

Boden, M. A. (1977). *Artificial intelligence and natural man*. Hassocks: Harvester Press.

Brachman, R. J. (1977). What's in a concept: structural foundations for semantic networks. *International Journal of Man–machine Studies*, **9**, 127–52.

Brachman, R. J. (1978). *Theoretical studies in natural language understanding*. Annual report: Bolt, Beranek & Newman, Inc., Cambridge, Massachusetts.

Brady, M. & Berwick, R. C. (1983). *Computational models of discourse*. Cambridge, Massachusetts: MIT Press.

Breiman, L., Friedman, J. H., Olshen, R. A. & Stone, C. J. (1983). Classification and regression trees. Belmont, California: Wadsworth.

Brooks, R. & Heiser, J. (1980). Some experience with transferring the MYCIN system to a new domain. *IEEE Transactions on Pattern Analysis and Machine Intelligence*, PAMI-2, 477–8.

Burton, R. R. & Brown, J. S. (1982). An investigation of computer coaching for informal learning activities. In *Intelligent tutoring systems*, ed. D. Sloman & J. S. Brown, pp. 79–98. London: Academic Press.

Card, W. I. (1970). The diagnostic process. *Journal of the Royal College of Physicians (London)*, **4**, 183–7.

Card, W. I., Crean, G. P., Evans, C. R., James, W. B., Nicholson, M., Watkinson, G. & Wilson, J. (1970). On-line interrogation of hospital patients by a time sharing terminal with computer/consultant comparison analysis. In *Man–Computer Interaction*, IEE Conference Publication No. 68, p. 141.

Card, W. I., Nicholson, M., Crean, G. P., Watkinson, G., Evans, C. R., Wilson, J. & Russell, D. (1974). A comparison of doctor and computer interrogation of patients. *International Journal of Biomedical Computing*, **5**, 175–87.

Chang, C. L. & Lee, R. C-T. (1973). *Symbolic logic and mechanical theorem proving*. New York: Academic Press.

Charniak, E. (1969). *Computer solution of calculus word problems*. Proceedings of the IJCAI. Mitre Corporation.

Charniak, E. (1972). *Toward a model of children's story comprehension*. AI Technical Report 266, MIT AI Laboratory, Cambridge, Massachusetts.

Charniak, E. & Wilks, Y. (1978). *Computational semantics*. New York: North-Holland.

Chomsky, N. (1957). *Syntactic structures*. The Hague: Mouton.

Chomsky, N. (1965) *Aspects of the theory of syntax*. Cambridge, Massachusetts: MIT Press.

Chomsky, N. (1977). *Language and responsibility*. New York: Pantheon.

Clancey, W. J. (1982). Tutoring rules for guiding a case method dialogue. In *Intelligent tutoring systems*, ed. D. Sleeman & J. S. Brown, pp. 201–25. London: Academic Press.

Clare, A. (1976). *Psychiatry in dissent*. London: Tavistock Publications.

Clarke, M. R. B. (ed.) (1977). *Advances in computer chess I*. Edinburgh University Press.

Clippinger, J. H. (1975). Speaking with many tongues: some problems in modeling speakers of actual discourse. In *Theoretical issues in natural language processing*. Proceedings of a Workshop of the Association for Computational Linguistics, ed. R. Schank & B. Nash-Webber, June, pp. 78–83.

Clippinger, J. H. (1977). *Meaning and discourse: a computer model of psychoanalytic speech and cognition.* Baltimore, Maryland: The Johns Hopkins University Press.

Clocksin, W. F. & Mellish, C. S. (1981). *Programming in Prolog.* Berlin: Springer-Verlag.

Colby, K. M. (1963). Computer simulation of a neurotic process. In *Computer simulation of personality: frontier of psychological research*, ed. S. S. Tomkins & S. Messick, pp. 165–80. New York: Wiley.

Colby, K. M. (1964). Experimental treatment of neurotic computer programs. *Archives of General Psychiatry*, **10**, 220–7.

Colby, K. M. (1967). Computer simulation of change in personal belief systems. *Behavioural Science*, **12**, 248–53.

Colby, K. M. (1975). *Artificial paranoia: computer simulation of paranoid processes.* Elmsford, New York: Pergamon Press.

Colby, K. M. (1977). Appraisal of four psychological theories of paranoid phenomena. *Journal of Abnormal Psychology*, **86**, 54–9.

Colby, K. M. (1981). Modeling for a paranoid mind. *The Behavioural and Brain Sciences*, **4**, 515–60.

Colby, K. M. & Gilbert, J. P. (1964). Programming a computer model of neurosis. *Journal of Mathematical Psychology.* **1**, 220–7.

Colby, K. M., Parkison, R. C. & Faught, W. S. (1974). Pattern-matching rules for the recognition of natural language dialogue expressions. *American Journal of Computational Linguistics*, **1**, microfiche 5.

Coomans, D., Broekaert, I., Jonckheer, M. & Massart, D. L. (1983). Comparison of multivariate discrimination techniques for clinical data – application to the thyroid functional state. *Methods of Information in Medicine*, **22**, 93–101.

Croft, D. J. (1972). Is computerised diagnosis possible? *Computers and Biomedical Research*, **5**, 351–67.

Croft, D. J. & Machol, R. E. (1974). Mathematical methods in medical diagnosis. *Annals of Biomedical Engineering*, **2**, 69–89.

Davey, A. (1978). *Discourse production.* Edinburgh University Press.

Davies, D. J. M. (1972). *POPLER: A POP-2 Planner.* Report No. MIP-89, School of Artificial Intelligence, University of Edinburgh.

Davis, R. (1978). Knowledge acquisition in rule-based systems – knowledge about representations as a basis for system construction and maintenance. In *Pattern-directed inference systems*, ed. D. A. Waterman & F. Hayes-Roth, pp. 99–134. New York: Academic Press.

Davis, R. (1982). Consultation, knowledge acquisition, and instruction: a case study. In *Artificial intelligence in medicine*, ed. P. Szolovits, pp. 57–78. Boulder, Colorado: Westview Press.

Davis, R. & King, J. J. (1977). An overview of production systems. In *Machine Intelligence 8*, ed. E. Elcock & D. Michie, pp. 300–32. Chichester: Ellis Horwood.

De Dombal, F. T. (1978). Medical diagnosis from a clinician's point of view. *Methods of Information in Medicine*, **17**, 28–35.

De Dombal, F. T., Leaper, D. J., Staniland, J. R., McCann, A. P. & Horrocks, J. C. (1972). Computer-aided diagnosis of acute abdominal pain. *British Medical Journal*, **2**, 9–13.

Devijver, P. & Kittler, J. (1982). *Pattern recognition: a statistical approach.* New York: Prentice-Hall.

Dreyfus, H. L. (1981). From micro-worlds to knowledge representation: AI at an impasse. In *Mind design*, ed. J. Haugeland, pp. 161–204. Montgomery, Vermont: Bradford Books.

Duda, R. O. & Hart, P. E. (1973). *Pattern classification and scene analysis.* New York: Wiley.

Duda, R. O., Hart, P. E., Nilsson, N. J. & Sutherland, G. L. (1978). Semantic network representations in rule-based inference systems. In *Pattern-directed inference systems*, ed. D. A. Waterman & F. Hayes-Roth, pp. 203–21. New York: Academic Press.

Elstein, A. S., Shulman, L. S. & Sprafka, S. A. (1979). *Medical problem solving: an analysis of clinical reasoning.* Cambridge, Massachusetts: Harvard University Press.

Essex, B. J. (1980). *Diagnostic pathways in clinical medicine.* Edinburgh: Churchill Livingstone.

Evans, T. G. (1968). A program for the solution of a class of geometric-analogy intelligence test questions. In *Semantic information processing*, ed. M. L. Minsky, pp. 271–353. Cambridge, Massachusetts: MIT Press.

Everitt, B. S. & Hand, D. J. (1981). *Finite mixture distributions.* London: Chapman and Hall.

Fahlman, S. E. (1982). Representing and using real world knowledge. In *Artificial Intelligence: an MIT perspective*, vol. I, ed. P. H. Winston & R. H. Brown, pp. 453–70. Cambridge, Massachusetts: MIT Press.

Faught, W. S. (1978). Conversational action patterns in dialogs. In *Pattern-directed inference systems*, ed. D. A. Waterman & F. Hayes-Roth, pp. 383–97. New York: Academic Press.

Feigenbaum, E. A. (1979). Themes and case studies of knowledge engineering. In *Expert systems in the micro-electronic age*, ed. D. Michie, pp. 3–25. Edinburgh University Press.

Feigenbaum, E. A. & Feldman, J. (eds.) (1981). *Computers and thought.* Malabar, Florida: Robert E. Krieger Publishing Company.

Feinstein, A. R. (1969). Taxonomy and logic in clinical data. *Annals of the Academy of the New York Academy of Sciences*, **161**, 450–69.

Feinstein, A. R. (1977). Clinical biostatistics XXXIX. The haze of Bayes, the aerial palaces of decision analysis, and the computerised Ouija board. *Clinical Pharmacology and Therapeutics*, **21**, 482–96.

Feldman, S., Klein, D. F. & Honigfeld, G. (1969). A comparison of successive screening and discriminant function techniques in medical taxonomy. *Biometrics*, **25**, 725–34.

Feldman, S., Klein, D. F. & Honigfeld, G. (1972). The reliability of a decision tree technique applied to psychiatric diagnosis. *Biometrics*, **28**, 831–40.

Fikes, R. E., Hart, P. & Nilsson, N. J. (1972). Learning and executing generalised robot plans. *Artificial Intelligence*, **3**, 251–88.

Filman, R. E. & Weyhrauch, R. W. (1976). *An FOL primer. Memo 288.* Stanford: AI Laboratory, Stanford University.

Findler, N. V. (ed.) (1979). *Associative networks: the representation and use of knowledge by computers.* New York: Academic Press.

Fogel, L. J., Owens, A. & Walsh, M. J. (1966). *Artificial intelligence through simulated evolution.* Chichester: Wiley.

Forrester, J. W. (1970). *Testimony before the subcommittee on Urban Growth of the committee on Banking and Currency of the United States House of Representatives.* Given in Washington, DC, October 7th, 91st Congress, 2nd Session, Part III, pp. 205–65, US Government Printing Office.

Fox, J. (1983). The theory and practice of expert systems. *British Computer Society Specialist Group on Expert Systems, Newsletter* **8**, 14–16.

Fox, J., Barber, D. & Bardhan, K. D. (1980). Alternatives to Bayes?: a quantitative comparison with rule-based diagnostic inference. *Methods of Information in Medicine*, **19**, 210–15.

Friel, P. B., Reznikoff, M. & Rosenberg, M. (1969). Attitudes towards computers among nursing personnel in a general hospital. *Connecticut Medicine*, **33**, 307–8.

Friend, K. (1973). *An information processing approach to small group interaction in a coalition formation game.* Pittsburgh, Pennsylvania: Department of Psychology, Carnegie Mellon University.

Fukunaga, K. (1972). *Introduction to statistical pattern recognition.* New York: Academic Press.

Fukunaga, K. & Narendra, P. M. (1975). A branch and bound algorithm for computing k-nearest neighbours. *IEEE Transactions on Computers*, **24**, 750–3.

Gödel, K. (1931). *Uber Formal Unentscheidbare Satze der Principia Mathematica und Verwandter Systeme I, Monatscheffe fur Mathematik und Physik*, **38**, 173–98.

Goldberg, D. (1972). *The detection of psychiatric illness by questionnaire. Maudsley Monograph 21.* London: Oxford University Press.

Goldberg, L. R. (1970). Man versus model of man: a rationale plus some evidence for a method of improving on clinical inferences. *Psychological Bulletin,* **73,** 422–32.

Goldman, L., Weinberg, M., Weisberg, M. , Olshen, R., Cook, E. F., Sargent, R. K., Lamas, G. A., Dennis, C., Wilson, C., Deckelbaum, L., Fineberg, H., Stiratelli, R. & the Medical House Staffs at Yale-New Haven and Brigham Women's Hospital (1982). A computer derived protocol to aid in the diagnosis of emergency room patients with chest pain. *New England Journal of Medicine,* **307,** 588–96.

Goldstein, I. P. & Roberts, B. (1982). Using frames in scheduling. In *Artificial intelligence: an MIT perspective,* ed. P. H. Winston & R. H. Brown, pp. 253–84. Massachusetts: MIT Press.

Goldstein, M. & Dillon, W. R. (1978). *Discrete discriminant analysis.* New York: Wiley.

Gordon, M. J. (1973). 'Heuristic training for diagnostic problem solving among advanced medical students.' Unpublished Ph.D. Dissertation, Michigan State University, Michigan.

Gorry, G. A. & Barnett, G. O. (1968). Sequential diagnosis by computer. *Journal of the American Medical Association,* **205,** 849–54.

Gough, H. G. (1962). Clinical versus statistical prediction in psychology. In *Psychology in the making,* ed. L. Postman, pp. 526–84. New York: Knopf.

Green, C. C. (1969). The application of theorem-proving to question-answering systems, *International Joint Conference on Artificial Intelligence,* **1,** 219–37.

Greenfield, S., Komaroff, A. L. & Anderson, H. (1976). A headache protocol for nurses: effectiveness and efficiency. *Archives of Internal Medicine,* **136,** 1111–16.

Greist, J. H., Klein, M. H. & Erdman, H. P. (1976). Routine on-line psychiatric diagnosis by computer. *American Journal of Psychiatry,* **133,** 1405–8.

Grice, H. P. (1975). Logic and conversation. In *Syntax and Semantics,* vol. 3, ed. P. Cole & J. Morgan, pp. 41–58. New York: Academic Press.

Grimm, R. H., Shimoni, K., Harlan, W. R. & Estes, E. H. (1975). Evaluation of patient-care protocol use by various providers. *New England Journal of Medicine,* **292,** 507–11.

Grossman, J. H., McGuire, M. T., Barnett, G. O. & Swedlow, D. B. (1971). Evaluation of computer acquired patient histories. *Journal of the American Medical Association,* **215,** 1286–91.

Gullahorn, J. T. & Gullahorn, J. E. (1962). *Homunculus: a simulation of social interaction.* Michigan State University, Michigan.

Gullahorn, J. T. & Gullahorn, J. E. (1963). A computer model of elementary social behaviour. In *Computers and thought,* ed. E. A. Feigenbaum & J. Feldman, pp. 375–86. Malabar, Florida: Robert E. Krieger Publishing Company.

Halliday, M. A. K. (1967). Notes on transitivity and theme in English. *Journal of Linguistics,* **3,** 37–81.

Halliday, M. A. K. (1970). Functional diversity in language as seen from a consideration of modality and mood in English. *Foundations of Language,* **6,** 322–61.

Halliday, M. A. K. (1978). *Language as a social semiotic.* Baltimore, Maryland: University Park Press.

Hand, D. J. (1978). Pattern recognition – the ultimate interface. *Personal Computer World,* **1, No. 3,** 63–5.

Hand, D. J. (1979). Evolutionary programming – an intelligent answer? *Personal Computer World,* **1, No. 12,** 45–7.

Hand, D. J. (1980). Review of *The process of question answering* by W. Lehnert (1978), in *Computing,* **8, No. 9,** 33.

Hand, D. J. (1981a). *Discrimination and classification.* Chichester: Wiley.

Hand, D. J. (1981b). Branch and bound in statistical data analysis. *The Statistician,* **30,** 1–13.

Hand, D. J. (1981c). Artificial intelligence. *Psychological Medicine,* **11,** 449–53.

Hand, D. J. (1982a). Statistical pattern recognition on binary variables. In *Pattern recognition theory and applications*, ed. J. Kittler, K. S. Fu & L. F. Pau, pp. 19–33. Dordrecht, Holland: D. Riedel Publishing Company.

Hand, D. J. (1982*b*). *Kernel discriminant analysis*. Letchworth, Herts: Research Studies Press.

Hand, D. J. (1983*a*). A comparison of two methods of discriminant analysis applied to binary data. *Biometrics*, **39**, 683–94.

Hand, D. J. (1983*b*). Common errors in data analysis: apparent error rate of classification rules. *Psychological Medicine*, **13**, 201–3.

Hand, D. J. (1984*a*). Pattern recognition – or how to tell it's one of those. In *The fascination of statistics*, ed. R. Brook, G. Arnold, T. Hassard, & R. Pringle. New York: Marcel Dekker (in press).

Hand, D. J. (1984*b*). Statistical expert systems: design. *The Statistician*, **33**, 351–69.

Hand, D. J. & Batchelor, B. G. (1978). Experiments on the edited condensed nearest neighbour rule. *Information Sciences*, **14**, 171–80.

Hart, P. E. (1968). The condensed nearest neighbour rule. *IEEE Transactions on Information Theory*, **IT-14**, 515–16.

Haugeland, J. (ed.) (1981). *Mind design*. Montgomery, Vermont: Bradford Books.

Hayes-Roth, B. (1978). Implications of human pattern processing for the design of artificial knowledge systems. In *Pattern-directed inference systems*, ed. D. A. Waterman & F. Hayes-Roth, pp. 333–46. New York: Academic Press.

Hayes-Roth, F. (1978). The role of partial and best matches in knowledge systems. In *Pattern-directed inference systems*, ed. D. A. Waterman & F. Hayes-Roth, pp. 557–74. New York: Academic Press.

Hayes-Roth, F. & Mostow, D. J. (1975). An automatically compilable recognition network for structured patterns. In *Proceedings of the 4th International Joint Conference on Artificial Intelligence*, pp. 246–51. Tbilisi, USSR.

Hayes-Roth, F., Waterman, D. A. & Lenat, D. B. (1978). Principles of pattern-directed inference systems. In *Pattern-directed inference systems*, ed. D.A. Waterman & F. Hayes-Roth, pp. 577–601. New York: Academic Press.

Hays, D. G. & Mathias, J. (eds.) (1976). FBIS seminar on machine translation. *American Journal of Computational Linguistics*, *Microfiche 46*.

Heiser, J. F., Colby, K. M., Faught, W. S. & Parkison, R. C. (1979). Can psychiatrists distinguish a computer simulation of paranoia from the real thing? *Journal of Psychiatric Research*, **15**, 149–62.

Hendrix, G. G. (1976). The representation of semantic knowledge. In *Speech understanding research*, ed. D. Walker. Final Report, SRI Project 4762, Stanford Research Institute, Menlo Park, California.

Henrici, P. (1972). Reflections of a teacher of applied mathematics,' *Quarterly of Applied Mathematics*, **30**, 31–9.

Hewitt, C. (1972). *Description and theoretical analysis (using schemata) of PLANNER, a language for proving theorems and manipulating models in a robot*. Report No. TR-258, Artificial Intelligence Laboratory, MIT, Cambridge, Massachusetts.

Hobbs, J. (1976). *Pronoun resolution*. Research Report 76-1, City College, New York.

Homans, G. C. (1961). *Social behaviour: its elementary forms*. New York: Harcourt, Brace & World.

Hudson, R. A. (1971). *English complex sentences*. North Holland Linguistic Series, No. 4, Amsterdam.

Hunt, E. B., Marin, J. & Stone, P. (1966). *Experiments in induction*. New York: Academic Press.

Izard, C. E. & Masterson, F. A. (1981). Colby's paranoia model: an old theory in a new frame? *The Behavioural and Brain Sciences*, **4**, 539–40.

Jacobson, B. (1978). *Transformational–generative grammar*. Amsterdam: North-Holland.

Janis, I. L. & Mann, L. (1977). *Decision making*. Riverside, New Jersey: The Free Press.

Johnson-Laird, P. N. (1983). *Mental models*. Cambridge University Press.

Kaplan, R. M. (1972). Augmented transition networks as psychological models of sentence comprehension. *Artificial Intelligence*, **3**, 77–100.

Kaplan, R. M. (1973). A general syntactic processor. In *Natural language processing*, ed. R. Rustin, pp. 193–241. New York: Algorithmics Press.

Kaplan, R. M. (1975). On process models for sentence analysis. In *Explorations in cognition*, ed. D. A. Norman & D. E. Rumelhart, and the LNR Research Group, pp. 117–35. San Francisco: W. H. Freeman & Co.

Kassirer, J. P. & Gorry, G. A. (1978). Clinical problem solving: a behavioural analysis. *Annals of Internal Medicine*, **89**, 245–55.

Kendell, R. E. (1975). *The role of diagnosis in psychiatry*. Oxford: Blackwell Scientific Publications.

King, M. (1981). Design characteristics of a machine translation system. In *Seventh International Joint Conference on Artificial Intelligence*, pp. 43–6.

Kittler, J. (1975). Mathematical methods of feature selection in pattern recognition. *International Journal of Man–Machine Studies*, **7**, 609–37.

Kittler, J. (1978). Feature set search algorithms. In *Pattern recognition and signal processing*, ed. C. H. Chen, pp. 41–60. The Netherlands: Sijthoff & Nordhoff.

Klecka, W. R. (1980). *Discriminant analysis*. Beverley Hills, California: SAGE Publications.

Knuth, D. E. (1973). *The art of computer programming: volume I: Fundamental Algorithms*, 2nd edn. Reading, Massachusetts: Addison-Wesley.

Knuth, D. E. & Moore, R. W. (1975). An analysis of alpha-beta pruning. *Artificial Intelligence*, **6**, 293–326.

Komaroff, A. L., Black, W. L., Flatley, M., Knopf, R. H., Reiffen, B. & Sherman, H. (1974). Protocols for physician assistants: management of diabetes and hypertension. *New England Journal of Medicine*, **290**, 307–12.

Kress, G. (ed.) (1976). *Halliday: system and function in language*. London: Oxford University Press.

Krzanowski, W. J. (1975). Discrimination and classification using both binary and continuous variables. *Journal of the American Statistical Association*, **70**, 782–90.

Krzanowski, W. J. (1980). Mixtures of continuous and categorical variables in discriminant analysis. *Biometrics*, **36**, 493–9.

Krzanowski, W. J. (1984). Stepwise location model choice in mixed-variable discrimination. *Applied Statistics*, **32**, 260–6.

Kulikowski, C. A. & Weiss, S. M. (1982). Representation of expert knowledge for consultation: the CASNET and EXPERT projects. In *Artificial intelligence in medicine*, ed. P. Szolovits, pp. 21–55. Boulder, Colorado: Westview Press.

Kunz, J. C. (1978). *A physiological rule-based system for interpreting pulmonary function test rules*. Memo. HPP-78-19, Stanford University Department of Computer Science, Stanford, California.

Lachenbruch, P. A. (1975). *Discriminant analysis*. New York: Hafner Press.

Leaper, D. J., Horrocks, J. C., Staniland, J. R. & De Dombal, F. T. (1972). Computer-assisted diagnosis of abdominal pain using 'estimates' provided by clinicians. *British Medical Journal*, **4**, 350–4.

Lehnert, W. (1978). *The process of question answering*. Hillsdale, New Jersey: Lawrence Erlbaum Associates.

Lenat, D. B. (1976). *AM: an artificial intelligence approach to discovery in mathematics as heuristic search*. Rep. STAN-CS-76-570, Computer Science Department, Stanford University.

Lenat, D. B. & Harris, G. (1978). Designing a rule system that searches for scientific discoveries. In *Pattern-directed inference systems*, ed. D. A. Waterman & F. Hayes-Roth, pp. 25–51. New York: Academic Press.

Lighthill, J., Sutherland, N. S., Needham, R. M., Longuet-Higgins, H. C. & Michie, D. (1973). *Artificial intelligence: a paper symposium*. London: Science Research Council.

Lindsay, R. (1981). How smart must you be to be crazy? *The Behavioural and Brain Sciences*, **4**, 541–2.

Longuet-Higgins, H. C. (1981). Artificial intelligence – a new theoretical psychology? *Cognition*, **10**, 197–200.

Loveland, D. W. (1978). *Automated theorem proving: a logical basis*. New York: North-Holland.

Lucas, J. R. (1961). Minds, machines, and Gödel. *Philosophy*, **36**, 112–27.

Lucas, R. W. (1977). A study of patients' attitudes to computer interrogation. *International Journal of Man–Machine Studies*, **9**, 69–86.

Lucas, R. W., Card, W. I., Knill-Jones, R. P., Watkinson, G. & Crean, G. P. (1976). Computer interrogation of patients. *British Medical Journal*, (*ii*), 623–5.

Lucas, R. W., Mullin, P. J., Luna, C. B. X. & McInroy, D. C. (1977). Psychiatrists and a computer as interrogators of patients with alcohol-related illness: a comparison. *British Journal of Psychiatry*, **131**, 160–7.

Lyons, J. (ed.) (1970). *New horizons in linguistics*. Harmondsworth: Penguin.

McCarthy, J. & Hayes, P. J. (1969). Some philosophical problems from the standpoint of artificial intelligence. In *Machine intelligence 4*, ed. B. Meltzer & D. Michie, pp. 463–502. Edinburgh University Press.

McCorduck, P. (1979). *Machines who think*. San Francisco, California: W. H. Freeman.

McCracken, D. L. (1981). *A production system version of the HEARSAY-II speech understanding system*. Ann Arbor, Michigan: UMI Research Press.

McDermott, D. (1981). Artificial intelligence meets natural stupidity. In *Mind design*, ed. J. Haugeland, pp. 143–60. Montgomery, Vermont: Bradford Books.

McDermott, J. & Forgy, C. (1978). Production system conflict resolution strategies. In *Pattern-directed inference systems*, ed. D. A. Waterman & F. Hayes-Roth, pp. 177–99. New York: Academic Press.

McDonald, D. & Hayes-Roth, F. (1978). Inferential searches of knowledge networks as an approach to extensible language-understanding systems. In *Pattern-directed inference systems*, ed. D. A. Waterman & F. Hayes-Roth, pp. 431–53. New York: Academic Press.

McKay, R. J. & Campbell, N. A. (1982*a*). Variable selection techniques in discriminant analysis I: Description. *British Journal of Mathematical and Statistical Psychology*, **35**, 1–29.

McKay, R. J. & Campbell, N. A. (1982*b*). Variable selection techniques in discriminant analysis II: Allocation. *British Journal of Mathematical and Statistical Psychology*, **35**, 30–41.

Maher, B. A. (1981). Testing the components of a computer model. *The Behavioural and Brain Sciences*, **4**, 543.

Mann, W. & Moore, J. (1980). *Computer as author – results and prospects*. Technical Report RR-79-82, Information Science Institute, Marina del Rey, California.

Markov, A. A. (1954). *Theory of algorithms*. USSR: National Academy of Sciences.

Matarazzo, J. D. (1983). Computerized psychological testing. *Science*, **221**, 323.

Mayne, J. G., Weksel, W. & Sholtz, P. W. (1968). Toward automating the medical history. *Mayo Clinic Proceedings*, **43**, No. 1.

Meehl, P. E. (1954). *Clinical vs. statistical prediction*. Minneapolis: University of Minnesota Press.

Meehl, P. E. (1978). Theoretical risks and tabular asterisks: Sir Karl, Sir Ronald, and the slow progress of soft psychology. *Journal of Consulting and Clinical Psychology*, **46**, 806–34.

Mesel, E., Wirtschaffer, D. D., Carpenter, J. T., Durant, J. R., Henke, C. & Gray, E. A. (1976). Clinical algorithms for cancer chemotherapy – systems for community based consultant-extenders and oncology centers. *Methods of Information in Medicine*, **15**, 168–73.

Michalski, R. S. & Chilausky, R. L. (1980). Knowledge acquisition by encoding expert rules versus computer induction from examples: a case study involving soybean pathology. *International Journal of Man–Machine Studies*, **12**, 63–87.

Michie, D. (1974). *On machine intelligence*. Edinburgh University Press.

Michie, D. (1980). Expert systems. *The Computer Journal*, **23**, 369–76.

Michie, D. (ed.) (1982*a*). *Introductory readings in expert systems*. New York: Gordon & Breach.

Michie, D. (1982*b*). In defence of chess programming. *British Computer Society Specialist Group on Expert Systems, Newsletter* **6**, 17–18.

Miller, J. R. (1981). PARRY and the evaluation of cognitive models. *The Behavioural and Brain Sciences*, **4**, 543–4.

Miller, R. A., Pople, H. E. & Myers, J. D. (1982). INTERNIST-I, an experimental computer-based diagnostic consultant for general internal medicine. *The New England Journal of Medicine*, **307**, 468–76.

Minsky, M. L. (ed.) (1968). *Semantic information processing*. Cambridge, Massachusetts: MIT Press.

Minsky, M. L. (1981). A framework for representing knowledge. In *Mind design*, ed. J. Haugeland, pp. 95–128. Montgomery, Vermont: Bradford Books.

Minsky, M. & Papert, S. (1972). *Perceptrons: an introduction to computational geometry*. Cambridge, Massachusetts: MIT Press.

Moran, T. P. (1974). 'The symbolic imagery hypothesis: an empirical investigation via a production system simulation of human behaviour in a visualisation task.' Unpublished Ph.D. Dissertation, Department of Computer Science, Carnegie Mellon University, Pittsburgh, Pennsylvania.

National Research Council, Automatic Language Processing Advisory Committee (1966). *Language and machines: computers in translation and linguistics*. Publication 1416, National Academy of Sciences, National Research Council, Washington DC.

Naylor, C. M. (1983). *Build your own expert system*. Wilmslow, Cheshire: Sigma Technical Press.

Newell, A. & Simon, H. A. (1972). *Human problem solving*. Englewood Cliffs, New Jersey: Prentice-Hall.

Nilsson, N. J. (1965). *Learning machines: foundations of trainable pattern classifying systems*. New York: McGraw-Hill.

Nilsson, N. J. (1982). *Principles of artificial intelligence*. Berlin: Springer-Verlag.

Norman, D. A. & Rumelhart, D. E. (eds.) (1975). *Explorations in cognition*. San Francisco, California: W. H. Freeman.

Novak, G. S. (1977). Representation of knowledge in a program for solving physics problems. In *Fifth International Joint Conference on Artificial Intelligence*, pp. 286–91. Cambridge, Massachusetts: MIT Press.

Palm, G. (1982). *Neural assemblies: an alternative approach to AI*. New York: Springer.

Parkison, R. C., Colby, K. M. & Faught, W. S. (1977). Conversational language comprehension using integrated pattern-matching and parsing. *Artificial Intelligence*, **9**, 111–34.

Patrick, E. A., Stelmack, F. P. & Shen, L. Y. L. (1974). Review of pattern recognition in medical diagnosis and consulting relative to a new system model. *IEEE Transactions on Systems, Man, and Cybernetics*, **SMC-4**, 1–17.

Phillips, L. D., Hays, W. I. & Edwards, W. (1966). Conservatism in complex probabilistic inference. *IEEE Transactions on Human Factors in Electronics*, **7**, 7–18.

Pople, H. E. (1982). Heuristic methods for imposing structure on ill-structured problems: the structuring of medical diagnostics. In *Artificial intelligence in medicine*, ed. P. Szolovitz, pp. 119–90. Boulder, Colorado: Westview Press.

Pospesel, H. (1976). *Introduction to logic: predicate logic*. Englewood Cliffs, New Jersey: Prentice-Hall.

Post, E. (1943). Formal reductions of the general combinatorial problem. *American Journal of Mathematics*, **65**, 197–268.

Poulton, A. S. (1983). *Microcomputer speech synthesis and recognition*. Wilmslow, Cheshire: Sigma Technical Press.

Quillian, M. R. (1968). Semantic memory. In *Semantic information processing*, ed. M. Minsky, pp. 227–70. Cambridge, Massachusetts: MIT Press.

Quinlan, J. R. (1982). Semi-autonomous acquisition of pattern-based knowledge. In

Introductory readings in expert systems, ed. D. Michie, pp. 192–207. New York: Gordon & Breach.

Raphael, B. (1968). SIR: a computer program for semantic information retrieval. In *Semantic information processing*, ed. M. Minsky, pp. 33–145. Cambridge, Massachusetts: MIT Press.

Raphael, B. (1976). *The thinking computer*. San Francisco: W. H. Freeman & Company.

Reddy, D. R., Erman, L. D. & Neely, R. B. (1972). A mechanistic model of speech perception. AFCRL/IEEE 1972 Conference on Speech Communication and Processing, Massachusetts.

Reznikoff, M., Holland, C. H. & Stroebel, C. F. (1967). Attitudes towards computers among employees of a psychiatric hospital. *Mental Hygiene*, 51, 419–25.

Riese, W. (1953). *The conception of disease: its history, its versions, and its nature*. New York: Philosophical Library.

Rogers, W., Ryack, B. & Moeller, G. (1979). Computer-aided medical diagnosis: literature review. *International Journal of Bio-Medical Computing*, 10, 267–89.

Rulifson, J., Derkson, J. A. & Waldinger, R. J. (1972). *QA4: a procedural calculus for intuitive reasoning*. Report No. TN-83, Artificial Intelligence Centre, SRI International.

Rumelhart, D. E. & Norman, D. A. (1975). The active structural network. In *Explorations in cognition*, ed. D. A. Norman & D. E. Rumelhart, pp. 35–64. San Francisco, California: W. H. Freeman & Co.

Rychener, M. D. & Newell, A. (1978). An instructable production system: basic design issues. In *Pattern-directed inference systems*, ed. D. A. Waterman & F. Hayes-Roth, pp. 135–53. New York: Academic Press.

Scadding, J. G. (1972). The semantics of medical diagnosis. *Biomedical Engineering*, 3, 83–90.

Schank, R. C. (1972). Conceptual dependency: a theory of natural language understanding. *Cognitive Psychology*, 3, 552–631.

Schank, R. C. & Abelson, R. P. (1977). *Scripts, plans, goals, and understanding*. Hillsdale, New Jersey: Lawrence Erlbaum Associates.

Schank, R. C. & Colby, K. M. (1973). *Computer models of thought and language*. San Francisco, California: W. H. Freeman.

Schank, R. C. & YALE AI Project (1975). *SAM – A story understander*. Research Report 43, Department of Computer Science, Yale University.

Schoolman, H. M. & Bernstein, L. M. (1978). Computer use in diagnosis, prognosis, and therapy. *Science*, 200, 926–31.

Shortliffe, E. H. (1976). *Computer-based medical consultations: MYCIN*. New York: Elsevier.

Shortliffe, E. H. & Buchanan, B. G. (1975). A model of inexact reasoning in medicine. *Mathematical Biosciences*, 23, 231–379.

Shortliffe, E. H., Buchanan, B. G. & Feigenbaum, E. A. (1979). Knowledge engineering for medical decision making: a review of computer-based clinical decision aids. *Proceedings of the IEEE*, 67, 1207–24.

Siklossy, L. (1976). *Let's talk Lisp*. Englewood Cliffs, New Jersey: Prentice-Hall.

Simmons, R. F. (1973). Semantic networks: their computation and use for understanding English sentences. In *Computer models of thought and language*, ed. R. C. Schank & K. M. Colby, pp. 63–113. San Francisco, California: W. H. Freeman.

Simmons, R. F. & Slocum, J. (1972). Generating English discourse from semantic networks. *Communications of the Association for Computing Machinery*, 15, 891–905.

Simon, H. A. (1969). *The sciences of the artificial*. Cambridge, Massachusetts: MIT Press.

Simon, H. A. (1973). The structure of ill-structured problems. *Artificial Intelligence*, 4, 181–201.

Slack, W. V., Hicks, G. P., Reed, C. E. & Van Cura, L. J. (1966). A computer based medical history system. *New England Journal of Medicine*, 274, 194–8.

Slack, W. V. & Van Cura, L. J. (1968). Patient reaction to computer based medical interviewing. *Computers and Biomedical Research*, 1, 527–31.

Sleeman, D. & Brown, J. S. (eds.) (1982). *Intelligent tutoring systems*. London: Academic Press.

Sloman, A. (1978). *The computer revolution in philosophy.* Hassocks: Harvester Press.

Snell, B. M. (ed.) (1979). *Translating and the computer.* Amsterdam: North-Holland.

Sox, H. C., Sox, C. H. & Tompkins, R. K. (1973). The training of physicians' assistants: the use of a clinical algorithm system. *New England Journal of Medicine*, **288**, 818–24.

Spiegelhalter, D. J. & Knill-Jones, R. P. (1984). Statistical and knowledge- based approaches to clinical decision-support systems, with an application in gastroenterology. *Journal of the Royal Statistical Society, Series A*, **147**, 35–76.

Spitzer, R. L. & Endicott, J. (1968). DIAGNO: A computer program for psychiatric diagnosis utilising the differential diagnostic procedure. *Archives of General Psychiatry*, **18**, 746–56.

Spitzer, R. L. & Endicott, J. (1969). DIAGNO II: further developments in a computer program for psychiatric diagnosis. *American Journal of Psychiatry*, **125** (Jan. Suppl.), 12–21.

Spitzer, R. L., Endicott, J., Cohen, J. & Fleiss, J. L. (1974). Constraints on the validity of computer diagnosis. *Archives of General Psychiatry*, **31**, 197–203.

Spitzer, R. L., Endicott, J. & Robins, E. (1975). *Research diagnostic criteria.* New York State Psychiatric Institute: New York State Department of Mental Hygiene.

Sridharan, N. S. & Schmidt, C. F. (1978). Knowledge-directed inference in BELIEVER. In *Pattern-directed inference systems*, ed. D. A. Waterman & F. Hayes-Roth, pp. 361–79. New York: Academic Press.

Startsman, T. S. & Robinson, R. E. (1972). The attitudes of medical and paramedical personnel towards computers. *Computers and Biomedical Research*, **5**, 218–27.

Stern, R. B., Knill-Jones, R. P. & Williams, R. (1975). Use of computer program for diagnosing jaundice in district hospitals and specialised liver units. *British Medical Journal*, **2**, 659–62.

Sturt, E. (1981a). Computerised construction in Fortran of a discriminant function for categorical data. *Applied Statistics*, **30**, 213–22.

Sturt, E. (1981b). An algorithm to construct a discriminant function in Fortran for categorical data. *Applied Statistics*, **30**, 313–25.

Suppes, P. (1961). Meaning and uses of models. In *The concept and the role of the model in mathematics and natural and social sciences*, ed. H. Freudenthal, pp. 163–76. Dordrecht, Holland: D. Reidel Pub. Co.

Suppes, P. (1967). Some theoretical models for mathematics learning. *Journal of Research and Development in Education*, **1**, 5–22.

Sussman, G. & McDermott, D. V. (1972). *CONNIVER reference manual.* Cambridge, Massachusetts: Memo. 259, Artificial Intelligence Laboratory, MIT.

Szolovits, P. (1982a). *Artificial intelligence in medicine.* Boulder, Colorado: Westview Press.

Szolovits, P. (1982b). Artificial intelligence and medicine. In *Artificial Intelligence in Medicine*, ed. P. Szolovits, 1–19. Boulder, Colorado: Westview Press.

Szolovits, P., Hawkinson, L. & Martin, W. A. (1977). An overview of OWL, a language for knowledge representation. In *Proceedings of the Workshop on Natural Language Interaction with Databases.* Schloss Laxenburg, Austria: International Institute for Applied Systems Analysis.

Szolovits, P. & Pauker, S. G. (1978). Categorical and probabilistic reasoning in medical diagnosis. *Artificial Intelligence*, **11**, 115–44.

Szolovits, P. & Pauker, S. G. (1979). Computers and clinical decision making: whether, how, and for whom? *Proceedings of the IEEE*, **67**, 1224–7.

Taylor, T. R., Aitchison, J. & McGirr, E. M. (1977). Doctors as decision makers: a computer assisted study of diagnosis as a cognitive skill. *British Medical Journal*, **iii**, 35–40.

Tennant, H. (1981). *Natural Language Processing.* Princeton, New Jersey: Petrocelli Books.

Titterington, D. M., Murray, G. D., Murray, L. S., Spiegelhalter, D. J., Skene, A. M., Habbema, J. D. & Gelpke, G. J. (1981). Comparison of discrimination techniques applied to a complex data set of head injured patients. *Journal of the Royal Statistical Society, Series A*, **144**, 145–75.

Tomkins, S. S. (1963). *Affect, imagery, consciousness.* New York: Springer.

Tomkins, S. S. & Messick, S. (1963). Computer simulation of personality: frontier of psychological research. New York: Wiley.

Turing, A. M. (1950). Computing machinery and intelligence. *Mind*, **59**, 433–60. Reprinted in Feigenbaum & Feldman (1981).

Uhr, L. (1969). Teaching machine programs that generate problems as a function of interaction with students. In *Proceedings of the 24th National Conference*, pp. 125–134.

Van Melle, W. (1979). A domain-independent production rule system for consultation programs. *International Joint Conference on Artificial Intelligence 79*, 923–5.

Wagner, G., Tautu, P. & Wolber, U. (1978). Problems of medical diagnosis: a bibliography. *Methods of Information in Medicine*, **17**, 55–74.

Walpole, H. R. (1941). Semantics: the nature of words and their meanings. New York: W. W. Norton & Co.

Wardle, A. & Wardle, L. (1978). Computer aided diagnosis – a review of research. *Methods of Information in Medicine*, **17**, 15–28.

Wason, P. C. & Johnson-Laird, P. N. (1972). *Psychology of reasoning: structure and content*. Cambridge, Massachusetts: Harvard University Press.

Waterman, D. A. (1970). Generalisation learning techniques for automating the learning of heuristics. *Artificial Intelligence*, **1**, 121–70.

Waterman, D. A. & Hayes-Roth, F. (eds.) (1978*a*). *Pattern-directed inference systems*. New York: Academic Press.

Waterman, D. A. & Hayes-Roth, F. (1978*b*). An overview of pattern-directed inference systems. In *Pattern-directed inference systems*, ed. D. A. Waterman & F. Hayes-Roth, pp. 3–22. New York: Academic Press.

Weiss, S., Kulikowski, C., Amarel, S. & Safir, A. (1978). A model-based method for computer-aided medical decision-making. *Artificial Intelligence*, **11**, 145–72.

Weiss, S., Kulikowski, C. A. & Safir, A. (1978). Glaucoma consultation by computer. *Computers in Biology and Medicine*, **8**, 24–40.

Weizenbaum, J. (1965). ELIZA – a computer program for the study of natural language communication between man and machine. *Communications of the Association for Computing Machinery*, **9**, 36–45.

Weizenbaum, J. (1976). *Computer power and human reason*. San Francisco, California: W. H. Freeman.

Wilensky, R. (1978). *Understanding goal-based stories*. Research Report 140, Department of Computer Science, Yale University.

Wilks, Y. A. (1977). Methodological questions about artificial intelligence: approaches to understanding natural language. *Journal of Pragmatics*, **1**, 69–84.

Williams, B. T. (ed.) (1982). *Computer aids to clinical decisions*. (2 vols.) Boca Raton, Florida: CRC Press.

Williams, P., Tarnopolsky, A. & Hand, D. J. (1980). Case definition and case identification in psychiatric epidemiology: review and assessment. *Psychological Medicine*, **10**, 101–14.

Wing, J. K., Cooper, J. E. & Sartorius, N. (1974). *Measurement and classification of psychiatric symptoms*. Cambridge University Press.

Winograd, T. (1973). A procedural model of language understanding. In *Computer models of thought and language*, ed. R. C. Schank & K. M. Colby, pp. 152–86. San Francisco: W. H. Freeman & Co.

Winograd, T. (1975). Frame respresentations and the declarative/procedural controversy. In *Representation and understanding: studies in cognitive science*, ed. D. G. Bobrow & A. Collins, pp. 185–210. New York: Academic Press.

Winograd, T. (1976). *Understanding natural language*. Edinburgh University Press.

Winograd, T. (1978). On primitives, prototypes, and other semantic anomalies. *Workshops on Theoretical Issues in Natural Language Processing*, **2**, 25–32.

Winograd, T. (1983). *Language as a cognitive process*. Vol. I: *Syntax*. Reading, Massachusetts: Addison-Wesley.

Winston, P. H. (1977). *Artificial intelligence*. Reading, Massachusetts: Addison-Wesley.

Winston, P. H & Horn, B. K. P. (1981). *Lisp*. Reading, Massachusetts: Addison-Wesley.

Woods, W. A. (1970). Transition network grammars for natural language analysis. *Communications of the Association for Computing Machinery*, **13**, 591–606.

Woods, W. A. (1973). An experimental parsing system for transition network grammars. In *Natural language processing*, ed. R. Rustin, pp. 111–54. New York: Algorithmics Press.

Woods, W. A. (1975). What's in a link: foundations for semantic networks. In *Representation and understanding: studies in cognitive science*, ed. D. G. Bobrow & A. Collins, pp. 35–82. New York: Academic Press.

Young, R. M. (1973). 'Children's seriation behaviour: a production system analysis.' Unpublished Ph.D. Dissertation, Department of Psychology, Carnegie Mellon University, Pittsburgh, Pennsylvania.

NAME INDEX

SUBJECT INDEX